Global Issues Series

General Editor: **Jim Whitman**

This exciting new series encompasses three principal themes: the interaction of human and natural systems; cooperation and conflict; and the enactment of values. The series as a whole places an emphasis on the examination of complex systems and causal relations in political decision-making; problems of knowledge; authority, control and accountability in issues of scale; and the reconciliation of conflicting values and competing claims. Throughout the series the concentration is on an integration of existing disciplines towards the clarification of political possibility as well as impending crises.

Titles Include:

Malcolm Dando
PREVENTING BIOLOGICAL WARFARE
The Failure of American Leadership

Brendan Gleeson and Nicholas Low (*editors*)
GOVERNING FOR THE ENVIRONMENT
Global Problems, Ethics and Democracy

Roger Jeffery and Bhaskar Vira (*editors*)
CONFLICT AND COOPERATION IN PARTICIPATORY NATURAL RESOURCE MANAGEMENT

Ho-Won Jeong (*editor*)
GLOBAL ENVIRONMENTAL POLICIES
Institutions and Procedures

W. Andy Knight
A CHANGING UNITED NATIONS
Multilateral Evolution and the Quest for Global Governance

W. Andy Knight (*editor*)
ADAPTING THE UNITED NATIONS TO A POSTMODERN ERA
Lessons Learned

Graham S. Pearson
THE UNSCOM SAGA
Chemical and Biological Weapons Non-Proliferation

Andrew T. Price-Smith (*editor*)
PLAGUES AND POLITICS
Infectious Disease and International Policy

Michael Pugh (*editor*)
REGENERATION OF WAR-TORN SOCIETIES

Bhaskar Vira and Roger Jeffery (*editors*)
ANALYTICAL ISSUES IN PARTICIPATORY NATURAL RESOURCES MANAGEMENT

Simon M. Whitby
BIOLOGICAL WARFARE AGAINST CROPS

Global Issues Series
Series Standing Order ISBN 0-333-79483-4
(*Outside North America only*)

You can receive future titles in this series as they are published by placing a standing order.
Please contact your bookseller or, in case of difficulty, write to us at the address below with
your name and address, the title of the series and the ISBN quoted above.

Customer Services Department, Macmillan Distribution Ltd, Houndmills, Basingstoke,
Hampshire RG21 6XS, England

Preventing Biological Warfare

The Failure of American Leadership

Malcolm R. Dando
Professor of International Security
Department of Peace Studies
University of Bradford

palgrave

First published 2002 by
PALGRAVE
Houndmills, Basingstoke, Hampshire RG21 6XS and
175 Fifth Avenue, New York, N.Y. 10010
Companies and representatives throughout the world

PALGRAVE is the new global academic imprint of
St. Martin's Press LLC Scholarly and Reference Division and
Palgrave Publishers Ltd (formerly Macmillan Press Ltd).

ISBN 0–333–79309–9

This book is printed on paper suitable for recycling and made from fully managed and sustained forest sources.

A catalogue record for this book is available from the British Library.

Library of Congress Cataloging-in-Publication Data
Dando, Malcolm.
    Preventing biological warfare : the failure of American leadership / Malcom R. Dando.
      p. cm. – (Global issues)
    Includes bibliographical references and index.
    ISBN 0–333–79309–9 (cloth)
    1. Convention on the Prohibition of the Development, Production, and Stockpiling of Bacteriological (Biological) and Toxin Weapons and on Their Destruction (1972) 2. Biological arms control – United States. 3. Bioterrorism – Prevention. I. Title. II. Global issues series (Palgrave (Firm))
    KZ5825.3 .D36 2002
    341.7'35–dc21   2001057534

10   9   8   7   6   5   4   3   2   1
11   10   09   08   07   06   05   04   03   02

Printed and bound in Great Britain by
Antony Rowe Ltd, Chippenham, Wiltshire

Contents

List of Tables   vii

Preface   x

Introduction   xii

1 The Problem of Biological Warfare   1

Developments in arms control before the BTWC   2
Negotiation of the BTWC   5
Verification possibilities   15
Civil production   19

2 The Chemical Weapons Convention and the Worldwide Chemical Industry   23

The protracted negotiations   26
Chemical weapons   27
Production of chemical weapons agents   29
The civil chemical industry   32
Verification of the CWC   33
The initial stages of implementation of the CWC   40

3 Developing the BTWC, 1975–1995   41

Enhanced consultation   42
Confidence-Building Measures (CBMs)   44
VEREX   47
The objective of verification   54

4 Genomics and the New Biotechnology   62

The 'old' biotechnology   63
Understanding the 'new' biotechnology   65
The pharmaceutical industry   67
The US pharmaceutical industry   69
What is of concern?   72

5	**The Negotiation of the BTWC Protocol**	**75**
	The structure of the negotiation process	78
	The strong conceptual differences	94
6	**Compliance Measures: Declarations and Visits**	**99**
	The structure of Article III	102
	The associated annexes and appendices	104
	Follow-up after submission of declarations	106
	Summary	112
7	**The Debate on Visits**	**113**
	The Ad Hoc Group beginnings	116
	Practical investigations	121
	Practice visits	123
	The process of erosion	128
8	**The Role of US Industry**	**132**
	Alternative US viewpoints	133
	The pharmaceutical/biotechnology industry	133
9	**The Chairman's Text**	**140**
	The composite Protocol text	140
	An assessment of the composite Protocol text	163
10	**The United States and the BTWC Protocol**	**166**
	Fashioning US policy?	167
	The reception of the Chairman's text	170
	Renewed debate in the United States	172
	The 24th Session of the Ad Hoc Group in July 2001	174
	Futures?	179
11	**Epilogue**	**181**
	Appendix 1 The 1972 Biological and Toxin Weapons Convention	185
	Appendix 2 Statement by the United States to the Ad Hoc Group	189
	References	198
	Index	218

List of Tables

1.1	The 1925 Geneva Protocol	3
1.2	The BTWC negotiations	7
1.3	The Biological and Toxin Weapons Convention	7
1.4	Extract from the Yugoslav control proposal	11
1.5	Amount of toxin required for lethality in various attack scenarios	16
1.6	Stages in acquiring a militarily significant offensive biological weapons capability	18
1.7	Stages in acquiring a militarily significant offensive biological weapons capability: Process Flow	19
1.8	Some examples of Biopreparat facilities	21
2.1	The functions of verification	24
2.2	Technical challenges in nerve gas production	30
2.3	Chemical production processes	31
2.4	US trade in chemicals in 1998	32
2.5	The Chemical Weapons Convention	34
2.6	Mechanisms for building confidence in the CWC	35
2.7	Chemicals controlled by the OPCW	38
2.8	The chemical control regimes under the CWC	39
3.1	Summary of the confidence-building measures agreed in 1986	45
3.2	Characteristics of particularly important outbreaks	46
3.3	Summary of the confidence-building measures agreed in 1991	47
3.4	Main criteria used for the evaluation of potential verification measures in VEREX	49
3.5	Potential verification measures identified in VEREX I	51
3.6	Examples of combinations of measures producing synergistic effects	52
3.7	Summary of the essential elements of the Protocol to be considered by the Ad Hoc Group	53
3.8	Derivation of the trillion dose criterion	55
3.9	Initial State Party VEREX working papers	58
3.10	The US position at the 1994 Special Conference	61
4.1	The historical development of biotechnology	64

4.2   Major products and worldwide market value in   64
       US$ millions in 1981 before commercial application
       of genetic engineering
4.3   Examples of human proteins cloned in   65
       E. coli (bacteria)
4.4   The new operational matrix in the biotech century   66
4.5   Industrial categories of potential relevance to   69
       the BTWC
4.6   Development of 152 global drugs by country   70
       of origin, 1975–1994
4.7   Categories of sites chosen for monitoring in Iraq   73
5.1   Participation of States Parties in the early meetings 76
       of the Ad Hoc Group
5.2   Working Papers produced by various States   76
       Parties in early meetings of the AHG
5.3   Numbers of delegates representing States Parties   77
       at the AHG in the 12th (XII) session
5.4A   Friends of the Chair at the 21st session   79
5.4B   Facilitators at the 21st session   79
5.5   Formal meetings of the AHG on mandate topics   81
       during sessions I–VI
5.6   Number of pages of text on the FOC's topics in   81
       Annex I of procedural reports for sessions I–VI
5.7   Number of working papers produced by States   82
       Parties and Friends of the Chair on the topics under
       discussion in AHG sessions I–VI
5.8   Structure of the verification Protocol   85
5.9   Number of pages of text on the articles,   86
       annexes and appendices of the six versions of the
       rolling text of the verification Protocol, 1997–98
5.10   Friends of the Chair papers, October 1998   88
5.11   Later versions of the rolling text   89
5.12   Articles, annexes and appendices of the rolling   95
       text in BWC/AD HOC GROUP/54
6.1   Major issues in the BTWC Protocol   99
6.2   The stated position of the EU in March 2000   101
6.3   Article III compliance measures   103
6.4   Article III D declarations: I. submission of   103
       declarations: initial declarations
6.5   Article III D declarations: I. submission of   104
       declarations: annual declarations

6.6 Article III D declarations: II. follow-up after submission of declarations ... 104
6.7 Examples from the list of human and zoonotic pathogens ... 106
7.1 The potential benefits of visits ... 118
7.2 Practice non-challenge visits ... 124
7.3 Reasons why CPI control works ... 126
7.4 Elements of US views on transparency visits ... 131
8.1 PhRMA's views on appropriate restrictions ... 135
8.2 PhRMA's objections to visits ... 135
9.1 Comparison of the composite Protocol text and the final version of the rolling text ... 141
9.2 Declaration triggers in the final version of the rolling text ... 146
9.3 Declaration triggers in the composite Protocol text ... 147
9.4 Appendices on declarations required by Article 4 of the composite Protocol text ... 149
9.5 Annual declarations of biodefence facilities ... 151
9.6 Some relevant definitions from Article 2 ... 154
9.7 Sections of Article 9 investigations ... 161

Preface

On 25 July 2001 the United States announced that it could not accept a Protocol to the Biological and Toxin Weapons Convention which had been some ten years in the making. This essentially brought the negotiations to an end as some other major countries were unlikely to accept a Protocol that the US would not join. Though the US was clearly not solely responsible for the failure of the negotiations, it is probable that agreement could have been reached had the world's only superpower taken a strong, consistent, leadership role throughout. This book, which began as a study of the negotiations, is therefore necessarily also concerned with the deeply ambiguous role of the United States and its responsibility for the failure to seize this opportunity to help prevent biological warfare.

The book is dedicated to David Yates. David took his BA in the Department of Peace Studies at the University of Bradford in the early 1990s and was the joint recipient of the Edward Lynn Memorial Prize for the best BA final year student in the Department in 1993. He then moved to the University of Lancaster and in 1995 completed an MA in Defence and Security Studies which included a dissertation on 'Verification of the Biological Weapons Convention: Learning from the Chemical Weapons Convention'. Following work on security issues for the International Security Information Service (a London-based non-governmental organization), David returned to Bradford and was awarded a University Scholarship for his PhD studies. He was studying the negotiation of the Protocol to the Biological and Toxin Weapons Convention at the time of his sudden death in July 1997. This was a grievous loss to all of us who knew him personally and, further, to the scholarly community more generally because he seemed destined for an outstanding academic career. It is fitting that our annual MA prize in the Department of Peace Studies is named after him.

This book originated from my discussions with David in the first year of his PhD We had no idea in 1996/97 that the negotiations he was intent on studying would drag on until mid-2001 (and may still not be at an end). We were convinced, however, of the need for a sophisticated view of verification to be applied to this complex area of arms control. I hope that some of those discussions and some of David's drafts are reflected in this manuscript. After David's death my own work became more focused on the continuing negotiations, as our departmental Project on Strengthening the Biological and Toxin Weapons gathered pace.* I would not have been able to undertake the writing of this book without the award of a grant from the Airey Neave Trust. I am most grateful to the Trust for their support and for their sympathetic responses to my having to delay finishing the book until now. I am also grateful to Palgrave, and their series editor Dr. Jim Whitman, for their patience with these delays. Though we do not know what the final outcome of the Protocol negotiations will be, the presentation of a composite text by the Chairman earlier this year and its subsequent rejection as a basis for further negotiation by the United States in July, gave me a clear point at which I could draw my analysis to a conclusion.

The book is based on primary and secondary written sources. I have not sought to supplement these sources with interviews as I prefer to work from published documentation. I would, however, like to acknowledge the many friends and colleagues who have, in oral presentations or in conversation, at various seminars, Pugwash workshops, NATO ARWs and ASIs, and in Geneva, given me further food for thought about the problem of strengthening the BTWC. A special word of thanks is due to my associates in our project at Bradford – Graham Pearson, Paul Rogers and Simon Whitby – for all their help and encouragement.

Finally, it is a pleasure to thank my wife Janet both for typing this manuscript and for her tireless efforts to make my English intelligible. Any errors that remain are my responsibility.

MALCOLM DANDO

---

*Official documentation and commentary on the negotiations used in this book can be found through our website at <http://www.brad.ac.uk/acad/sbtwc>.

Introduction

In August 1972 President Nixon wrote to the United States Senate transmitting – for advice and consent to ratification – the Convention on the Prohibition of the Development, Production and Stockpiling of Bacteriological (Biological) and Toxin Weapons and on their Destruction, that is, the Biological and Toxin Weapons Convention or BTWC. In his letter President Nixon wrote:

> It was about two years ago that this Government renounced, unilaterally and unconditionally, the use of all biological and toxin weapons and affirmed that we would destroy our existing stocks and confine our programs to strictly defined defensive purposes...
>
> ... We accompanied our renunciation of these weapons with support for the principles and objectives of the United Kingdom's 1969 draft convention in this field. On December 6, 1971, the Convention transmitted herewith, which would provide a binding international prohibition on the weapons we have renounced, was overwhelmingly commended by the General Assembly of the United Nations.[1]

The President continued, '[T]his Convention is the first international agreement since World War II to provide for the actual elimination of an entire class of weapons from the arsenal of nations'. Hopes seemed high for, according to the President's letter, the Pine Bluff biological warfare (production) facility was to be turned into a national centre for the study of chemical contamination of the environment, while the Fort Detrick military biological research facility was to become a centre for cancer research. The Convention entered into force in 1975.

In 1996, however, the director of the United States Arms Control and Disarmament Agency (ACDA) stated the belief that: 'twice as many countries now have or are actively pursuing offensive biological weapons programs as when the Convention... went into force in 1975'.[2] This ominous doubling, in a little over two decades, of the number of countries thought to be involved in offensive biological weapons programmes included the startling example of the former Soviet Union which, along with the United States and the United Kingdom, was one of the three Depositary States for the BTWC![3,4] Moreover, this was no minor violation on the USSR's part. According to the 1993 ACDA report to Congress:

> The United States has determined that the Russian offensive BW program, inherited from the Soviet Union, violated the Biological Weapons Convention through at least March 1992. *The Soviet offensive BW program was massive and included production, weaponisation and stockpiling...*[2] (emphasis added)

As has become increasingly well understood, one of the main factors which allowed this disastrous state of affairs to develop was that the BTWC contained no effective means of verifying that States Parties were in fact living up to their obligations.[5]

This book begins by considering how this original omission came about and how attempts were made to rectify it by the addition of Confidence-Building Measures (CBMs) – annual data exchanges – at the second and third Review Conferences of the Convention in 1986 and 1991. These CBMs failed, and with the fears in 1991 that Coalition forces in the Gulf could have been attacked with biological weapons by Iraq, attention turned again to the question of whether it was possible to find better ways of assuring compliance with the Convention. It is this process, which began with the VEREX meetings of 1992 and 1993 and led on to the 1994 Special Conference and then to the work of the current Ad Hoc Group since 1995, which is the focus of this book. As will be seen, the mandate given to the Ad Hoc Group by the Special Conference of States Parties in 1994 had a number of requirements, but what is of prime concern here is whether the measures almost agreed to ensure compliance – some 25 years after the Convention entered into force – could be adequate to help stem the proliferation of offensive biological weapons as the modern biotechnology/genomics revolution spreads around the world, opening up many more potential routes to misuse of the new technology.[6]

This book is necessarily, therefore, mostly about the vexed question of verification. In order to avoid confusion it is essential to have a clear understanding of the meaning of the word 'verification' when it is used here. The meaning I ascribe to the word was clearly set out in Congressional Hearings on the negotiations of the Protocol to the BTWC in the United States in July 2001. This viewpoint suggests that:

> Verification is the process of determining whether the behavior of other parties is consistent with the arms control treaty. *Verification*

serves three essential functions. First, it provides *early warnings of violations* to civilian and military policymakers who must protect national security. Second, verification *deters violators* of treaties with the threat of detection. Finally, verification *builds confidence* in the arms control process.[7] (emphases added)

So to my mind verification is not just about detecting cheating, it is a much more complex function. Furthermore, in order to avoid another potential source of confusion, it is necessary to be aware that in the United States there has been a long-running debate about how to judge whether the verification in an agreement suffices. A specific terminology is used in that debate:

There are two standards, adequate verification and effective verification. *Adequate verification is the ability to identify evasion on a large enough scale to pose a significant risk* and can be done in time to mount a sufficient response. *Effective verification means having the ability to detect a violation, regardless of its significance.* (emphases added)

Particularly when the terms are used by US officials, it is important to grasp precisely what is and what is not being said.

1
The Problem of Biological Warfare

Developments in biology and medicine a hundred years ago were to have a dramatic impact on human society. As Roy Porter has argued: 'the latter part of the nineteenth century brought one of medicine's few true revolutions: *bacteriology*. Seemingly resolving age-old controversies over pathogenesis, a new and immensely powerful aetiological doctrine rapidly established itself...'.[1] The work of scientists of the calibre of Koch in Germany and Pasteur in France demonstrated that specific micro-organisms caused specific diseases in humans, animals and plants. The knowledge gained in this 'Golden Age of Bacteriology' was quickly applied to medical practice. The British Royal Army Medical Corps training manual of 1908, for example, graphically reads:

> diseases like enteric fever, cholera, dysentery, small-pox, plague, malaria and a number of others, all of which are caused by the entering into the body from without of the cause, which is a living thing or germ. *It is quite clear that, from the nature of their causation, the various diseases... are more or less preventable...* [2] (emphasis added)

Despite setbacks like the unexpected growth of antibiotic resistance in dangerous bacteria in recent decades, progress in the understanding and potential control of infectious diseases has continued: the 'Golden Age' of virology in the 1950s, for example, led to a proper description of viruses, while advances in genetic engineering and genomics in recent years hold out the promise of major improvements in our capabilities for controlling infectious diseases.[3]

What is far less well known is that the very same knowledge has been applied in a series of offensive biological weapons programmes in major states over the past century.[4] During the First World War, for example, both sides were attempting to use disease agents such as anthrax and glanders to damage the valuable draft animal stocks of the opposition. That war was followed by major programmes in a number of countries, France for example, and a huge programme was run by Japan both before and during the Second World War. The United Kingdom produced what is believed to have been the first effective biological weapon during the Second World War and passed the details on to the United States during the war. The massive American programme, which led to the weaponization of a number of anti-personnel and anti-plant agents,[5] was terminated only in the late 1960s/early 1970s, just before agreement of the Biological and Toxin Weapons Convention (BTWC). The even larger, modern, Soviet programme ran from that time through at least until the early 1990s, and the existence of at least two other recent programmes – in Iraq and South Africa – have been officially admitted. Furthermore, it is widely believed that these are far from the only other programmes in existence in recent years.[6]

Developments in arms control before the BTWC

As we shall see, international legal restrictions on biological weapons are inextricably linked to restrictions on chemical weapons. This linkage makes good sense today because the non-living chemical toxins produced by living micro-organisms – such as botulinal toxins – can be used as warfare agents and it is therefore important to ensure that there is no gap between the regulation of the two types of weaponry. In the past, prohibitions on both types of weapons were generated by a general abhorrence of the use of poison. This abhorrence is of long standing, having become customary by the end of the classical Greek and Roman periods, but it was gradually subjected to better definition in the seventeenth and eighteenth centuries in Europe and began to be codified in the nineteenth century.[7]

Writing on 'CBW and Laws of War', in Volume III of the major study by the Stockholm International Peace Research Institute (SIPRI) in the early 1970s, Anders Boserup argued that: 'The records of the Brussels Conference show that in 1874 the reference to poison and poison weapons was meant to include the spreading of disease on enemy territory...'.[8] Whilst the 1874 Declaration of Brussels, made by 14 European nations, was not ratified, Boserup notes that it fed directly into the Hague Conferences of 1899 and 1907 and:

> In line with this, the US Army manual from 1914 (as well as the manual from 1940) stated that the prohibition of poison expressed in Article 23(a) of the Hague Regulations applied 'to the use of means calculated to spread contagious diseases'...

Unfortunately, these restrictions on chemical and biological warfare did not survive the desperate fighting of the First World War.

Following the large-scale use of chemical weapons during that war, it was perhaps not surprising that there was a widespread desire to achieve some measure of control of these weapons for the future. Eventually, at the Conference for the Supervision of the International Trade in Arms and Ammunition and in Implements of War in Geneva in 1925, an agreement to ban the *use* of these weapons was reached. However, the Polish delegate drew attention to the omission of bacteriological warfare. He pointed out that such agents could be produced more easily and cheaply than chemicals and could have major long-term effects. He also noted that both chemical and bacteriological weapons had been the subject of discussion at the conference and thus should both be included in the ban. This argument was accepted and the 1925 Geneva Protocol was agreed (Table 1.1).[9] Boserup noted that it constitutes an extremely wide ban:

> the use of *biological* agents against plants and animals is undoubtedly prohibited by the Protocol. This results, first, from the extreme generality of the expression 'bacteriological *methods of warfare*', which, as regards the target of attack, does not leave room for any restrictive interpretation...

'Bacteriological' agents are now understood to cover all possible biological agents, including viruses, and despite the many initial reservations

Table 1.1   The 1925 Geneva Protocol*

Protocol for the Prohibition of the Use in War of Asphyxiating, Poisonous or other Gases, and of Bacteriological Methods of Warfare. Signed at Geneva on 19th June 1925

The Undersigned Plenipotentiaries in the name of their respective Governments,

Whereas the use in war of asphyxiating, poisonous or other gases, and of all analogous liquids, materials or devices, has been justly condemned by the general opinion of the civilized world; and

Whereas the prohibition of such use has been declared in Treaties to which the majority of the Powers of the world are Parties; and

To the end that this prohibition shall be universally accepted as a part of International Law, binding alike the conscience and the practice of nations;

Declare:

That the High Contracting Parties, so far as they are not already Parties to Treaties prohibiting such use, accept this prohibition, agree to extend this prohibition to the use of bacteriological methods of warfare and agree to be bound as between themselves according to the terms of this declaration...

Note: *From Chapter 1, reference 8.

which rendered the protocol only a 'no-first-use' agreement amongst parties, now – 75 years later – the Geneva Protocol is seen as a universally applicable ban in customary international law.

Though now not widely known, considerable efforts were made within the League of Nations system to move beyond a ban on use of these weapons. Before the rise of Hitler put an end to discussions, the United Kingdom put forward a draft convention in 1933 which summarized the progress that had been made to that date. Section II of this draft convention was entitled 'Prohibition of preparations for chemical, incendiary and bacterial warfare' and it had a first article (number 51 of the convention) which stated, 'All preparations for chemical, incendiary or bacterial warfare shall be prohibited in time of peace as in time of war'. Unfortunately, as Joseph Goldblat has commented, 'The proposals put forward were to a great extent declaratory in character, no effective means having been provided to secure their implementation ... '.[10] Despite this failure, and the undoubted attempts by the Japanese to use biological weapons in China before and during the Second World War, the prohibition on the use of chemical and biological weapons fortunately remained largely intact during the Second World War.

After that war, as after the First World War, measures were taken to ensure that Germany did not again develop chemical or biological weapons. In the mid-1950s, in the run-up to the formation of the Western European Union (WEU) and the rearmament of West Germany, the 1948 Brussels Treaty was revised and here, as Perry Robinson – writing in 1971 – noted, 'the FRG agreed never to manufacture CB or nuclear weapons on it own territory'.[11] However, the biological controls proved to be much more difficult for the WEU to implement than for chemicals. The reason, according to Perry Robinson, was that: 'The problem that has continually faced the Agency is that of commercial secrecy ... the council [of the WEU] has considered it impossible to enforce full controls at private factories ... '. This, of course, has strong echoes in current discussions on how the BTWC might be strengthened.

Within the United Nations system the Commission for Conventional Armaments in 1947 held a majority opinion that the best way to define conventional armaments was to begin with a definition of *weapons of mass destruction* (i.e. those which were not conventional). Thus the United States submitted a draft resolution: 'by which weapons of mass destruction would be defined as including "atomic explosives, radioactive material, lethal chemical and biological weapons, and any weapons developed in the future which have characteristics comparable in destructive effect" ... '.[10] This designation of chemical and biological weapons as weapons of mass destruction has remained intact since that time. However, until the late 1960s, very little effort was made to find means of bringing them under better international legal control. Indeed, as one detailed and careful US legal study concluded at that time:

> the most optimistic conclusion that can be reached is that in the past twenty-five years only minimal and irresolute actions have been taken toward bringing into effect international multilateral conventional limitations on resort to or production and possession of chemical and biological weapons.[12]

This, then, was the background to negotiation of the original BTWC in the early 1970s.

Negotiation of the BTWC

At the time of the negotiation of the BTWC, arms control and disarmament had long been at an impasse. In her justly famous book, *The Game of Disarmament: How the United States and Russia Run the Arms Race*, Alva Myrdal suggested that on the surface the problem was centred on the issue of verification (or 'control', as she wished to define verification).

> Without any doubt, the request for tight control, on the one hand [US], and the stubborn unwillingness to accept verification by direct means of inspection [USSR], on the other hand, have been stumbling-blocks in the disarmament negotiations up till now...[13]

However, in Myrdal's opinion: 'Behind their outwardly often fierce disagreements, however, there has always been a secret and undeclared collusion between the superpowers. Neither of them has wanted to be restrained by effective disarmament measures...'. What probably led to the negotiation of the BTWC was a political decision in the United States.

The war in Vietnam was extremely unpopular and the widespread use of chemical tear gas and herbicides was widely deplored.[14] In their recent book, *Plague Wars*, Tom Mangold and Jeff Goldberg have argued that the then US Defense Secretary, Melvin Laird, has not received sufficient credit for closing down the US offensive biological weapons programme:

> Laird...was persuaded that a ban on BW made good sense for political reasons. He felt that the Vietnam anti-war protesters, who were plaguing Nixon, could be deflected if the US ended the use of herbicides and tear gas in Southeast Asia (he had ordered a halt) and if the US moved on BW arms control.[15]

A more cogent military reason may well have been that the United States had become convinced about how devastating the use of biological weapons could be. Thus:

> it was realized that our biological weapons program was pioneering a technology that, although by no means easy to create, could be duplicated with relative ease, making it possible for a large number of states to acquire the ability to threaten or carry out destruction on a level that could otherwise be matched by only a few major powers ... [16]

Continuing the programme was therefore counterproductive for the United States. Stopping the programme, suggesting that these weapons were problematic,[17] and moving towards a ban was a better policy option. Reaching an agreement on this issue could also have been seen as a way to open up routes to agreements with the Soviet Union on nuclear issues.

Myrdal, who was the Swedish representative to the negotiations, described them as having a 'meandering course'. The main points can be picked out from a review of the negotiations prepared for the first five-year Review Conference of the BTWC in 1980.[18] These are set out in Table 1.2. A great deal of time was obviously taken up by the differences between East and West over whether the new convention should cover both chemical and biological weapons or only biological weapons. There were also debates over whether research (as originally proposed in the UK's 1968 paper) should be included in the prohibition or excluded (as in subsequent UK drafts and the eventual BTWC). The United Kingdom had also originally argued that, because of weaknesses in the 1925 Geneva Protocol, the new convention should also ban *use* of biological weapons, but it was unable to achieve the agreement of other States on this point.[19] A summary of the main articles of the BTWC is given in Table 1.3 and the whole text in Appendix 1.

The heart of the BTWC is Article I, which sets out the scope of the Convention:

> Each State Party to this Convention undertakes never in any circumstances to develop, produce, stockpile or otherwise acquire or retain:
>
> 1. Microbial or other biological agents, or toxins whatever their origin or method of production, *of types and in quantities that have no justification for prophylactic, protective or other peaceful purposes;*
> 2. Weapons, equipment or means of delivery designed to use such agents or toxins for hostile purposes or in armed conflict. (emphasis added).

Table 1.2 The BTWC negotiations*

Date	Event
1968	Eighteen-Nation Committee envisages consideration of chemical and biological warfare under 'non-nuclear measures' of its provisional agenda.
1968 (6 August)	UK paper on microbiological warfare suggests supplement to 1925 Geneva Protocol needed and best to separate dealing with chemical and biological weapons
1968 (20 December)	General Assembly resolution requests the Secretary-General to prepare an expert's report on the effects of the possible use of chemical and biological warfare. This report submitted in 1969.
1969 (10 July)	UK draft convention deals with biological weapons only.[a]
1969 (19 September)	Socialist countries draft convention deals with both chemical and biological weapons.
1969 (25 November)	Unilateral renunciation of first use of lethal or incapacitating chemical agents and unconditional renunciation of all biological methods of warfare by United States.
1970 (14 February)	US ban extended to cover toxins.
1971 (30 March)	New draft convention by Socialist countries deals only with biological weapons.
1971 (5 August)	Identical texts of new draft convention submitted by United States and Socialist countries.
1971 (16 December)	General Assembly resolution 2826 (XXVI) commends the Convention.
1972 (10 April)	Convention opened for signature.
1975 (26 March)	Entry-into-force upon deposit of 22nd instrument of ratification.

Note: *From Chapter 1, reference 18.
[a]The UK draft was revised and re-presented on 26 August 1969 and 18 August 1970.

Table 1.3 The biological and toxin weapons convention

Summary of article titles
 1. Not to develop, produce, stockpile or acquire agents, weapons, etc.
 2. To destroy stocks.
 3. Not to transfer or assist others.
 4. To take national measures.
 5. To consult and co-operate in solving problems.
 6. May lodge complaints with the security council.
 7. To provide assistance in the event of a violation.
 8. No detraction from the Geneva Protocol.
 9. Obliged to continue negotiations on chemical weapons.
10. Co-operate for peaceful purposes.
11. Amendment.
12. Review.
13,14,15. Duration, Signature, Ratification, Deposition, Languages.

The part of this article which is emphasized has become known as the General Purpose Criterion. Clearly, this allows for peaceful uses of biological agents but bans all other *purposes*. The prohibition does not just apply to agents and activities known at the time of the Convention's agreement, but to any prohibited purpose to which such agents might be put in the future. As Sims has noted, two activities are not mentioned – research and use – so the prohibition applies to five activities[20] – development, production, stockpiling, acquisition and retention. Article VIII, of course, ensures that there is no limitation or detraction from the Geneva Protocol of 1925 which does indeed prohibit the *use* of such agents.

What provisions there are for assuring that States Parties live up to their obligations are set out in Article IV, in regard to national measures, and particularly in Articles V and VI in regard to international measures. Article V states:

> The States Parties to this Convention undertake to consult one another and to cooperate in solving any problems which may arise in relation to the objectives of, or in the application of the provisions of, the Convention. Consultation and cooperation pursuant to this article may also be undertaken through appropriate international procedures within the framework of the United Nations and in accordance with its Charter.

Article VI states:

> (1) Any State Party to this Convention which finds that any other State Party is acting in breach of obligations deriving from the provisions of the Convention may lodge a complaint with the Security Council of the United Nations. Such a complaint should include all possible evidence confirming its validity, as well as a request for its consideration by the Security Council.

> (2) Each State Party to this Convention undertakes to cooperate in carrying out any investigation which the Security Council may initiate, in accordance with the provisions of the Charter of the United Nations, on the basis of the complaint received by the Council. The Security Council shall inform the States Parties to the Convention of the results of the investigation.

The review of the negotiations produced for the first five-year Review Conference of the BTWC noted:[18] 'The provisions on compliance did not give rise to any particular difficulty...' and that:

> The question of a breach of the obligations to be assumed under the proposed convention was dealt with in close conjunction with the problem of compliance. It was of particular importance in view of the fact that *it was understood from the very beginning that the convention would be based on national rather than on international means of verification*... (emphasis added)

It would therefore appear that there was little or no debate during the negotiation of the BTWC on the total lack of effective international means of assuring compliance with the agreement.

Such a viewpoint might also be derived from the British representative's statement, on 10 July 1969, to the effect that:

> As I have pointed out before to the Committee, verification, in the sense in which that term is normally used in disarmament negotiations, is simply not possible in the field of biological warfare. The agents which might be used for hostile purposes are generally indistinguishable from those which are needed for peaceful medical purposes...[21]

Again, at the end of the negotiations, the US representative told the First Committee of the General Assembly in November 1971 that:

> Articles V and VI of the draft convention represent the result of intensive consultations during the negotiations of this measure. The present formulation represents a carefully worked out compromise among a variety of proposals and, in our view, the strongest possible provision regarding consultation and complaints that could be achieved.[22]

This statement, surely, conveys the impression of a gentlemanly process with few strong objections.

A hint of something rather different is given by Barend ter Haar, in his 1991 consideration of *The Future of Biological Weapons*.[23] A diplomat from the Netherlands with considerable experience of biological and chemical arms control, ter Haar noted that the 10 July 1969 draft convention introduced by the UK was mainly along the lines of the UK's 1968 working paper, 'but the proposed verification measures were different'. He elaborated in this way: 'instead of establishing a body of experts to investigate allegations about noncompliance, a distinction is now made between allegations of use of biological weapons and other allegations...'. These were to be treated differently in the new draft convention:

> If a party believed that biological weapons had been used against it, it could request the secretary general to investigate its complaint; in all other cases (for example, if it...suspected the production of biological weapons) the party would have to ask the Security Council to consider its complaint.

This, naturally, would leave any such consideration subject to the veto power of permanent members of the Security Council.

In fact, ter Haar states that a great deal of time was spent by the negotiators on the subject of verification during 1970. A Canadian working paper of 6 August noted that a number of countries had put forward proposals for dealing with the problem of verification, particularly in regard to chemical weapons, but these often included discussion of biological weapons.[24] These countries included: the UK; the USSR; Hungary, Mongolia and Poland; Sweden; Yugoslavia; Japan; Italy; and Morocco. The Yugoslavian proposals were quite detailed. They included national legislation, measures of international control and procedure in case of suspicion of violation.[25] A partial extract of these proposals is set out in Table 1.4. It will be noted that under this proposal States Parties would have been required to provide relevant data regularly to an international body. There would have been a co-operative means of resolving suspicions of non-compliance, backed up with possible reference to the Security Council if a violation was still suspected after attempts had been made to resolve concerns. The idea of 'verification by challenge' had been put forward by Sweden and was designed as a mainly voluntary system which 'relies on the interest of the party under suspicion'[13] to free itself of suspicion by supplying more information, a process that does not exclude an invited inspection by an outside body.

According to Myrdal, the general idea that the non-aligned delegations were fighting for was:

> to follow a verification procedure of gradually increasing strictures, to begin with requests for information, and to continue, if need be, with preliminary inquiries by an objective body prior to lodging an accusation with the UN body which has the right to take punitive action.[13]

Myrdal's judgement on the verification provisions of the BTWC was quite scathing. In her opinion, 'Requirements for verification and control had

Table 1.4 Extract from the Yugoslav control proposal*

1. NATIONAL LEGISLATIVE MEASURES OF RENUNCIATION AND
   SELF-CONTROL BY EACH COUNTRY
   (a) The enactment of a law prohibiting research for weapons purposes and
       of the development, production or stockpiling of agents for chemical
       and biological weapons.
   (b) The enactment of a law for the compulsory publication of certain data
       from this sphere, which would facilitate international control, as for
       instance, the names of institutions and facilities engaged in or which,
       by their nature, could engage in the activities prohibited...
       Certain data concerning production of such materials or agents...
       would be regularly submitted to an international organ...
2. MEASURES OF INTERNATIONAL CONTROL
   (a) The collection of certain data which States would publish and report in
       line with their internal legislation (Item 1(b) from the first group of
       measures), and other relevant information...
       The collection, receipt of reports and analysis of these data woud be car-
       ried out by an international organ... which might also discharge other
       [control] functions...
   (b) Governments should, of their own initiative, and within the
       framework of consultations and co-operation in good faith, if the need
       arises, make it possible through an appropriately regulated
       procedure, in accordance with the concept of verification by
       challenge, to ascertain that there is no activity on their territory
       prohibited by the treaty.
   (c) The complaints procedure to the Security Council.

Note: *From Chapter 1, reference 25.

been abandoned'. She thought that the BTWC had danger signals for
the future, pointing out that:

> *As no control measures were prescribed, there is in essence no assurance*
> *that it will be implemented.* There might at least have been a require-
> ment to report measures taken to comply... it might also have been
> desirable to have had an accounting of the types and quantities of
> agents and equipment available... (emphasis added)

Moreover, she continued: 'There is no intermediate ground for preliminary work, no assembling of data that might help to allay or confirm suspicions... Even the decision to initiate an investigation on the basis of a
complaint is made dependent on unanimity by the permanent Members
of the Security Council.' Sweden was not alone in its concerns.

Really trenchant criticism came from the French, the guardians of the
1925 Geneva Protocol. A series of stinging criticisms were, for example,

made of the final draft convention in late 1971. In September, Foreign Minister Schumann told the General Assembly in no uncertain terms that:

> France, in so far as disarmament is concerned, neither can nor will be content with words or appearances. Disarmament must consist in eliminating, *under effective international control*, existing arms and in forbidding any new manufacture of them ... [26] (emphasis added)

A series of statements had been made by the French spokesman in regard to the draft of the BTWC. On 9 November 1970, for example:

> My country, which considers that the ban on the use of these weapons was satisfactorily and definitively dealt with by the 1925 Geneva Protocol ... was one of the first to suggest that the manufacture of the weapons in question should likewise be prohibited. ... We should, nevertheless, like to state here and now that any ban on manufacture should be the subject of strict international control ... [27]

and on 29 November 1971:

> International control as a principle is the indispensable corollary to any disarmament measure of a contractual nature, albeit partial. If this element is ignored, the draft convention on the prohibition of the manufacture of biological weapons is an extremely dangerous precedent ... A state cannot merely have faith in the goodwill of other Powers in a field where its security is at stake.[28]

Though enacting the necessary national legislation to carry out the provisions of the BTWC in France, it pointedly refused to go along with adherence to the draft convention.

In short, it does less than justice to a number of countries to maintain that the provisions on compliance did not give rise to any particular difficulty. Indeed, one might argue, on the contrary, that many of the issues being discussed in regard to the BTWC Protocol today – data declarations, data checking, challenge investigations, dealing with non-compliance – were raised by delegations 30 years ago. Moreover, despite the technical difficulties, some delegations, such as Japan,[29] considered that an international study of these problems would be worthwhile. Presumably they, like the French,[27,28] believed that a proper study would allow the development of an effective verification system for the BTWC.

The reasons why the Soviet Union did not wish to have an effective system are relatively easily understood; they objected generally to any idea of inspection of their territory, in *any* arms control agreement. Additionally, they were probably already moving towards the vast expansion of their offensive biological weapons programme – based on the view that these were very effective weapons – and would therefore have had quite specific objections to a system which would have detected such a deviation from the obligations they had undertaken.

A more interesting question is why the United States was willing – in this specific agreement – to give up its traditional demand for tough verification measures. One factor must have been the long-held view that verification was not possible. An American study in 1961, *Arms Control of CBR Weapons*, noted, for example, that:

> To apply a control measure to an existing BW production facility, it would be essential to find and determine the nature of each laboratory or industrial unit that would be capable of BW production. If control measures were applied to all visible or acknowledged units but they were not applied, through ignorance or deliberate deception to important production units, it would be possible for an enemy nation to continue production in spite of a control agreement ... [30]

The document goes on to suggest that some 8,000–15,000 people would be required just to monitor the Soviet Union and Eastern European countries for possible violations of a BW arms control agreement.

This view, of the impossibility of verification, persisted in the United States into the early 1990s. A US study in 1994, *Biological Weapons Proliferation*, noted: 'In the debate surrounding the strengthening of the B[T]WC, *the United States government's position is that the Convention cannot be made verifiable ...*' (emphasis added).[31] It continued:

> This conclusion is based on the large number of facilities that must be included under a verification regime, the ease with which illicit activity can be concealed, and the intensity of investigation that is required to gather information adequate to allow for discrimination between misleading ('false positive') data and genuine evidence of non-compliance ...

At the time of the negotiations Myrdal was particularly struck by what she took to be this wrong-headed American approach.

In Myrdal's opinion, the purpose of a verification system is indeed to provide assurance that disarmament agreements will not be broken secretly. However, she saw two distinct approaches to this problem:

> the practical question is how to construct verification methods which can be applied from the outset so clearly, openly, and as far as possible automatically that they serve as a constant warning to would-be violators that clandestine adventures will not succeed ... [13]

She called this the *ex ante* approach. On the other hand:

> In the *ex post*, or after-the-event approach, the main emphasis has been on police and prosecutor functions to keep parties accountable. Evidence would have to be so strong that it would hold up before a judiciary authority. Thus the accused party preferably should be caught red-handed...

This reasoning, in her opinion, further suggests that: 'only a guaranteed foolproof system for after-the-event verification would allow enough trust to be engendered for an agreement to be concluded. *This is still the position of the United States in regard to some important treaties...*' (emphasis added). Myrdal argued strongly that, on the contrary, the main function of verification was to deter violators, not to be able to track them down after the event. In this view, one might say that in the original negotiation of the BTWC 'the baby was thrown out with the bathwater'. Because a fool-proof *ex post* system of verification was not considered obtainable (technically or politically), the possibility of agreeing an *effective ex ante* system of deterring violations was not properly pursued.

Whilst it was not possible for the Japanese suggestion of a further expert study of verification to be agreed, an interesting experiment was carried out by the Stockholm International Peace Research Institute (SIPRI) at this time.[32] Fourteen research laboratories and production establishments in both Western and Eastern Europe were visited by an inspection team of (usually) two experts plus a secretary for (usually) one to two days. Twenty-five scientists were directly involved in the inspection visits. The aim of the project was: 'to establish, by practical investigation, whether or not it was technically possible to discover if production of BW agents on a militarily significant scale could be carried out in non-secret microbiological research or industrial establishments'. At the end of the experiment: 'the average opinion of those involved in the experiment was that this kind of inspection had about a one in two chance of being successful.... This is important because the amount of material being looked for – 10 kilogrammes of microbial paste or spores – was considered to be less than that needed for one substantial aerosol attack, and it was considered that a medium-sized country would need to produce enough for 100 such attacks in a year (or less) to possess a full military capability.

Thus SIPRI's overall conclusion was that:

> The experiment together with our assessment of the required scale of military capability and the very special safety measures required to produce it, weighs against the view that verification is technically impossible regardless of the political circumstances...

Certainly, it would appear that the graduated system of verification put forward by Yugoslavia and Sweden – ending up with a 50 per cent chance of illicit production being detected during a short visit – might have formed a serious deterrent to violation of the original BTWC. That, however, was not to be. The question of the inadequate verification system agreed in the original BTWC and the efforts that were made in the succeeding five-year Review Conferences of the Convention to agree some means of strengthening it will be considered further in Chapter 3. It is perhaps sufficient comment at this stage to note that not until 1997 were the procedures under Article V tested, when Cuba brought an inconclusive case against the United States.[33] Moreover, the net result of the formal consultative process was a letter from the chairman of the meeting which ended by stating that it was agreed: 'that the experience of conducting this process of consultation had shown the importance of establishing as soon as possible an effective Protocol to strengthen the Convention'.[34] Before moving on to consider the later efforts to strengthen the Convention we need to examine more closely how a violation might come about.

Verification possibilities

Naturally, the amount of biological agent required will depend on the particular military task to be undertaken. That amount will be discussed shortly in some detail. It is essential first to make a very clear distinction between biological weapons and chemical weapons. Biological weapons can have a lethality equivalent to or exceeding that of nuclear weapons. The effects of chemical weapons are of a much lower order. The well-known scenario used by the US Congress Office of Technology Assessment in 1993,[6] for example, suggested that a line source attack with 1000 kilogrammes of sarin nerve agent (chemical) in ideal attack conditions might contaminate 7.8 km^2 of a city and kill 3000–8000 people, whereas just 100 kilogrammes of anthrax spores (biological) in the same conditions could cover 300 km^2 and kill 1–3 million people.

It can, of course, be argued that this difference is in good part due to the fact that biological agents multiply in the victim and do not therefore have to be delivered in such heavy doses as inert chemicals. However, a similar difference can also be seen between even the most toxic (chemical) nerve agents and the most toxic bacterial toxins (even though the latter are also non-living chemicals). This was well understood at the time the BTWC was negotiated, a US working paper prepared in 1970 for the Conference of the Committee on Disarmament noting: '15 tons of nerve agent would cause 50 per cent deaths over an area of up to 60 square kilometers ... about one and one-half kilograms of botulinum toxin could *theoretically* produce the same effect'.[35] Another US working paper, this time for the VEREX meetings (see Chapter 3) in 1992, elaborated on such a toxin attack.[36] In this paper it was assumed that the toxin would be dispersed in air, with a 100-metre boundary ceiling, and that people in the region of attack would have a ventilation rate of 12 litres per minute. It was also assumed that a military base would occupy an area of 10 square kilometres and a city or battlefield larger areas of 1000 and 3000 square kilometres respectively. The amounts of toxin required for various attacks under different assumptions about the toxicity of the agent and the efficiency of its dispersal are shown in Table 1.5. The paper concluded: 'Even with conservative assumptions of low toxicity (100 ng per individual) and extremely poor distribution efficiency (1%), a few tens of kilograms of a toxin can contaminate a large battlefield.' This is the kind of calculation that leads to the view that a small amount only of a biological or toxin agent would be required to mount an attack.

Nevertheless, a little further thought suggests that a few kilogrammes of a biological or toxin agent does not amount to what the military

Table 1.5 Amount of toxin required for lethality in various attack scenarios*

Assumptions	Base	City	Battlefield
LD$_{50}$=10 ng,[a] eff=1%	1 g	1 kg	3 kg
LD$_{50}$=10 ng, eff=50%	0.02 g	20 g	60 kg
LD$_{50}$=100 ng, eff=1%	10 g	10 kg	30 kg

Notes: *From Chapter 1, reference 14.
[a] 1 ng is 1×10^{-9} g or 0.001 µg.

would regard as a significant capability. There would, first of all, have to be sufficient production for weapons testing and field trials (see below), and any cautious military, knowing of the mishaps that occur in war, would surely want more than one weapon set even if only one attack was anticipated – which, in itself, is unlikely. The view taken by the authors of the SIPRI study in 1973, therefore, seems to be correct – that a quantity much larger than a few tens of kilogrammes of agent would be necessary for a really significant military capability.

This is not to argue that much smaller amounts could not be used for some kinds of sabotage missions, or that terrorists would necessarily require such large amounts. Yet the historical record shows that criminals or terrorists have largely confined themselves to inefficient food/water contamination attacks rather than efficient aerosol attacks with biological agents.[37] This suggests that whilst small-scale production may not be difficult for a trained individual, effective weaponization is far from straightforward.[6,38] Indeed, it may be that the greatest danger of biological terrorism would come from leakage from a State-level offensive programme. So deterring such State-level programmes is an effective means of helping to prevent terrorism. Apart from that, the implementation of tough internal legislation nationally, as recently introduced in the United States, could be required in the BTWC Protocol. This would help greatly in limiting the opportunities for internally-generated terrorism by qualified people.

Discussions of the process whereby a State might obtain an offensive biological weapons capability of military significance all note the complexity of the numerous operations involved.[6,30,31,40,41] The detailed study carried out by the US Office of Technology Assessment in 1993, *Technologies Underlying Weapons of Mass Destruction*,[42] suggests five major stages and numerous sub-stages in the overall programme required (Table 1.6). Experience suggests that should a State set out to acquire an offensive biological weapons capability, it will examine the possibilities for attacking humans, animals and plants. Given the dangers involved in developing anti-personnel weapons, it is likely that efforts in this area will be more easily detected than in the others.[41] However, it would be unlikely for a State not to attempt to acquire an anti-personnel capability and it makes sense, therefore, to consider how such a capability might be detected. Clearly, the further through the process a State ventured, the more difficult it would be to conceal the results. But the earlier in the process that a State might be detected, the more likely it would be not even to start (i.e. it would be deterred). Such considerations point to the importance of the production stage. Though indications of research and development[42] might be obtained, for

Table 1.6 Stages in acquiring a militarily significant offensive biological weapons capability*

Stage	Sub-stage
1. Research and development	– Obtain seed stock(s) – (Maybe manipulate genetics) – Test suitability for weapons – Develop and pilot-test production – Mass produce and harvest agent – Induce spore formation/freeze-dry/ micro-enscapsulate – Store agent under refrigeration
2. Design, test and build munitions	– Area delivery spray system/point delivery cluster bomb or warhead – Field test – Mass produce – Fill munitions – (Stockpile filled munitions)
3. Acquire delivery system	– Adapt aircraft, missiles etc. – Integrate munitions with delivery system

4. Acquire operational capability	– Establish logistical network of support
	– Acquire individual and collective defence,
	  including vaccines
	– Develop battle plans
	– Train troops to use BW and to fight in a
	  BW contaminated environment
	– Integrate weapon systems into military
	  forces

5. Use	– Develop experience of use of weapons in the field[a]

Notes: *From Chapter 1, reference 42.
[a]Not included in Office of Technology Assessment listing.

example through literature analysis or human intelligence, many more signs would become available if production were undertaken.

A summary study produced for the US Armed Forces Medical Intelligence Center, *Signatures for Biological Warfare Facilities*, for example – though accepting the difficulty of finding clear indicators – argues that several could be suggestive.[43] The study looked at funding and personnel; facility design, equipment and security; technical considerations; safety; and process control. Within each of these categories, it contrasts what might be expected in a BW facility with what would be found in a legitimate facility. The example given for process flow is reproduced in Table 1.7. While it is true that such differences between a

Table 1.7 Stages in acquiring a militarily significant offensive biological weapons capability: Process Flow*

BW facility	Legitimate facility
1. Raw material consumption does not equal output.	1. Raw material consumption relates to output.
2. Large volume fermenters (greater than 500 litres), cell cultures (1000s of culture flasks/roller bottles), embryonated eggs (100s of thousands).[a]	2. Large or small-scale fermentation but cell culture and eggs in smaller volume.
3. Air pressure gradients keep microbes in vessel.	3. Air pressure gradients keep contaminants out of vessels.
4. Finished product – wet-stored at low temperature in sealed (often double packaging) containers – not readily identifiable.	4. Labeled by product, batch number, date, etc.
5. Milling equipment operated in biohazard protective suits.	5. Milling equipment is not operated in biohazard areas.
6. Storage – low temperature, high security, bunkers with containment.	6. Storage in temperature-controlled environment, clean warehouse conditions.
7. Munitions – special filling buildings and/or explosives handling facilities.	7. Not an issue.

Notes: *From Chapter 1, reference 43.
[a]Eggs and cell cultures would be for virus or rickettsiae production.

BW facility and a legitimate facility might be detectable, it is equally true that biotechnology is classically dual-use – legitimate civil technologies could be misused for offensive military purposes. So a verification regime could not afford to ignore *civil* capabilities.

Civil production

This point was made starkly by the former Deputy Director of the United States Central Intelligence Agency (CIA), Douglas MacEachin, in a discussion of the requirements for achieving effective compliance with the BTWC. In his view, 'Absent a regime for subjecting legitimate activities to a high degree of transparency, the best way for a violator to carry out a covert programme would be to bury it – piggy-back it – inside a legitimate programme ... '.[44] In that situation, only the illegal activity would have to be kept hidden and not the existence of the whole facility. No better example of this kind of evasion can be found than the offensive BW programme of the former Soviet Union.

In his book, *Biohazard*, published in 1999, the former senior member of the Soviet Union's offensive biological warfare programme, Ken Alibek, provided an appendix (number two) which summarized the 'Soviet Biological Warfare System'. Within that system one of the main elements Alibek describes is the Main Directorate Biopreparat. This, he states, was:

> Created in 1973 to provide civilian cover for advanced military research into biological weapons, the agency was originally attached to the Council of Ministers. The majority of its personnel came from the army's Fifteenth Directorate, which kept it effectively under military control... [45]

A government reorganization put Biopreparat under the Ministry of Medical and Microbiological Industries in the 1980s, but it remained autonomous. Officially, it was:

> responsible for civilian facilities around the country dedicated to the research and development of vaccines, biopesticides, and some laboratory and hospital equipment; but *many of its facilities doubled as BW development and production plants and were earmarked as 'reserve' or mobilisation units for use in case of war.* (emphasis added)

Table 1.8 gives details of Alibek's description of four of these facilities.

There can be no doubt of this duplicity. Many specialist authors in the West have made exactly the same point about the use of Biopreparat's civilian cover. Anthony Rimmington in the UK, for example, wrote in 1996:

> *Biopreparat* succeeded in building itself into the most powerful biotechnology organisation within the former Soviet Union... The organisation controls the world's second largest antibiotics industry and produces a range of biopharmaceuticals and veterinary products... However, until September 1992 *Biopreparat* was simultaneously being used as an ostensibly civil front for an elaborate military biological weapons programme...

A similar conclusion was reached, in a detailed 1996 analysis, by the American long-time analyst of biological weapons proliferation, Milton Leitenberg. [47]

Table 1.8 Some examples of Biopreparat facilities*

Facility	Description
1. Berdsk (production plant)	Mobilization (reserve) facility: plague, tularemia, glanders and brucellosis. Target capacity up to 100 tons of each weapon annually.
2. Koltsovo, Novosibirsk region, Institute of Molecular Biology, 'Vector'	Researched and developed viral weapons: smallpox, Ebola, Marburg ... Developed new production techniques for making smallpox and Marburg weapons ...
3. Obolensk, Moscow region, Institute of Applied Microbiology	Researched and developed plague, tularemia, glanders, anthrax. Developed drug-resistant and vaccine-resistant weapons ...
4. Stepnogorsk, Kazakhstan, Progress Scientific and Production Base	Mobilization (reserve) facility designated to produce 300 tons of modified form of anthrax BW over 250 days. Also designated for production of plague, glanders, and tularemia BW ...

Note: *From Chapter 1, reference 45.

After the Russian Federation admitted that it had had an illegal pro-gramme, a Trilateral Process was initiated between Russia, the United States and the United Kingdom in order to increase assurance that the programme had ended. The Trilateral Process involved visits by officials and scientists to facilities that might be of concern. The unfortunate con-sequences of Russian visits to the USA will be considered in Chapter 4. Here we should note what western inspectors saw at Biopreparat sites in the Russian Federation. While researching his book, *Plague Wars*, Tom Mangold talked to many of those involved in the inspections and pro-vides vivid descriptions of some of these visits. At the Berdsk facility, for example: 'the visitors saw an extensive fermentation capacity that was up and running.... Four huge 64,000-litre fermenters ... were in use'. What they also saw was an incomplete building where construction had been halted. In this building: 'the long, tall, central room had been pre-pared to hold four rows of 64,000-litre fermenters – with ten units in each row'. These fermenters were the largest made in the Soviet Union. The target capacity of the facility can be seen in Alibek's account (Table 1.8 here) to be 100 tons each of different agents each year.

It is, of course, unlikely that a small or medium-sized state prolifera-tor would be involved in such *massive* production activities. The impor-tant point is that accounts of proliferation in small and medium-sized states clearly also indicate the covert use of civilian facilities. This pattern is well-known from Iraq's illegal biological weapons programme,[48] but Leitenberg quotes from the 1994 US Arms Control and Disarmament Agency's report, *Adherence to and Compliance with Arms Control Agreements*, in regard to Iran. This report stated:

> The Iranian BW program has been embedded within Iran's extensive biotechnology and pharmaceutical industries so as to obscure its activities. The Iranian military has used medical, educational, and scientific research organizations for many aspects of BW procurement, research, and production...

It is quite obvious, therefore, that civil biotechnology facilities cannot possibly be exempt from an effective control mechanism for preventing the proliferation of biological weapons. As will become apparent, much of the debate has centred on how civilian biotechnology facilities can be brought within the remit of a verification protocol. In the next chapter the solution found for covering the civil chemical industry in the Chemical Weapons Convention (CWC) will be examined.

2
The Chemical Weapons Convention and the Worldwide Chemical Industry

Given the general Soviet position on verification, and the suspicions of the Cold War era, it is hardly surprising that there was considerable debate about the concept throughout that period of time. In a Stockholm International Peace Research Institute study published in 1977, for example, Andrzej Karkoszka, from Poland, argued that verification had five specific functions.[1] These are set out in what might be considered to be a descending order of importance in Table 2.1. It will be noted, first, that this is a very broad view of verification. More surprisingly, Karkoszka did not regard the deterrence of violations as the most important function of verification. In his view, reassurance was more fundamental. As he put the matter:

> Here the function of verification is seen mainly as a positive concept; the idea that verification is not merely a deterrent against violations in a negative sense, but that it is a means of … giving states reassurance that their security is not being jeopardized by the implementation of the treaty …

This is an important viewpoint, as is the associated idea that a verification system can form an important channel for low-level dispute settlement and a building block for future treaty development.

A similar point was made by Allan Krass in another SIPRI study a decade later.[2] In Krass' view verification has two main purposes: to deter violations by posing a credible threat of discovery and to build confidence in a treaty by demonstrating compliance …. These two functions overlap, and to an extent can be contradictory, but they have to be

Table 2.1   The functions of verification*

---

1. Deterrence of violation, inducing or enforcing compliance by the threat of discovery of violations.

2. Reassurance for the security of states through confirmation that a treaty is being implemented, or through a high probability of detecting violations if they occur; thus the function of confidence-building.

3. Channel of communication (through which states may identify and deal with potential disputes before they become too serious).

4. Precedent for subsequent, more advanced stages of disarmament.

5. Mechanism for distinguishing between major and minor violations (substantive violations, procedural violations and non-disarmament conduct).

Note: *From Chapter 2, reference 1.

balanced in any agreement. Krass' study is of interest because of its reference to the internal US debate about verification. The problem here, in his opinion, is that arguments about verification have frequently been surrogates for arguments about more fundamental disagreements on the validity of arms control and disarmament agreements as a means of seeking security. Thus he notes that concepts of the *adequacy* of verification which evolved in the United States in the 1960s and 1970s were tied to a view that the East–West military balance was robust and could not be disturbed by marginal changes. The then current American concepts of *effectiveness* of verification (in the early 1980s) were, in his view, linked to: '… a much more activist military-political doctrine which sees continued value in either the reality or the perception of marginal military superiority'. On the basis of his extensive study of verification, he concluded that the only verification system likely to stand the test of time was one based on the ability to detect militarily significant violations of an accord. This he linked to the concept of adequacy of verification. He argued that a very legalistic approach, which did not distinguish between possible levels of violations, would not withstand the political tensions it helped to engender.

Debates on verification were particularly important in relation to the Chemical Weapons Convention (CWC). As we saw in the last chapter, many participants in the negotiation of the BTWC felt that chemical and biological weapons should have been dealt with at the same time. The BTWC thus contains an article committing States Parties to the negotiation of an analogous ban on chemical weapons. In 1993, as the negotiations of the CWC were coming to a close, Jessica Stern wrote 'Verification was the single most contentious issue in the negotiations on the

Chemical Weapons Convention (CWC). *Disputes about on-site inspections dominated the negotiations for the 24 years they took...'*(emphasis added).[3] This dispute had a certain absurd quality. It began, of course, with the West arguing that a ban on chemical weapons was impossible without provision for 'anytime, anywhere' on-site inspections with no right of refusal, and the Soviet Union arguing that this would legitimize spying. When the Gorbachev regime accepted the West's proposal, in a reasonable confirmation of Myrdal's view that the previous opposition between East and West had been a charade,[4] the West altered its position. As Stern recounts: 'A policy review led the USA to conclude that "anytime, anywhere" on-site inspections with no right of refusal would pose sufficiently grave risks to sensitive facilities that the proposal for mandatory inspections should be dropped...'. Together with the UK, Japan and Australia, the United States then proposed '*less* intrusive inspections than those that the Soviet Union had supported'. Also, a number of Third World countries which had remained silent during the stalemate over verification came forward to express their own concerns over intrusive inspections. Thus the inspection system agreed, whilst being considerably stronger than previous regimes, was less stringent than the West had originally demanded. Some on the right of the political spectrum in the United States, moreover, felt that the system that the US had itself watered down was inadequate. One well-known critic, Kathleen Bailey,[5] suggested in 1992 that 'there are three very serious problems that may prove impossible to solve. The first problem is the unlikelihood that a CW treaty can be effectively verified with today's technology'.

Despite the reservations of such critics, President George Bush senior sent a dramatic message to the negotiators on 23 May 1991[6] which noted that the Gulf War had again raised the spectre of the use of chemical weapons. As Vice-President, in March 1984, Bush had introduced a working paper which contained a draft CWC with many of the elements that were to be retained in the final text.[7] That working paper had followed confirmation of chemical weapons use in the Iran/Iraq War. Now the President had a blunt response following the 1991 Gulf War: 'These stark events renew and reinforce my conviction, shared by responsible leaders around the world, that chemical weapons must be banned – everywhere in the world'. The statement then set out a number of steps that the United States was going to take, based on the assumption that the best way to achieve such a worldwide ban was to reach agreement on the CWC. The President stated that he had instructed his negotiators, for example, to make it clear that the United States would now formally foreswear the use of chemical weapons for any reason – including retaliation – against any State as soon as the CWC entered into force. The United States also unconditionally committed itself to the destruction of all its chemical weapons stocks within ten years of entry into force. Furthermore, President Bush said that America would call for a target date to be set for the conclusion of the negotiations, and for the negotiators to go into continuous session, if need be, to meet that target. With such an initiative from the United States, at the time of the ending of the Cold War, the negotiations did move quickly to a conclusion. What is of interest here is how the problem of verification was perceived by those involved and how they set about solving that problem. Given the length of time taken to achieve the agreement, we need first to look briefly at how the end-game was reached.

The protracted negotiations

In a detailed review of the successful negotiation of the CWC, the Stockholm International Peace Research Institute's *Yearbook* of 1993 pointed out that the roots of the agreement lay in two different sources: the long-held general abhorrence of the use of poison weapons and the changing politico-military calculations of the security value of chemical weapons.[8] What changed significantly in the 1960s was the second of these factors. After the Second World War, the impressive toxic characteristics of the newly-discovered nerve gases suggested that stocks of these chemicals would be of great value for major industrial states, both for dealing with human wave attacks from less sophisticated forces and as an 'in kind' deterrent against chemical attacks. However, by the 1960s, and in the presence of vast stocks of nuclear and other weapons, the technical limitations of chemical weapons had become more obvious to the industrialized states. More particularly, the dangers of pouring money and technical resources into chemical weaponry developments – which would then be taken up and used as effective force multipliers by developing states – began to be appreciated. Indeed, it was the suspected use of chemical weapons by Egypt in Yemen, as well as American use of herbicides and riot-control agents in Vietnam, that led Sweden, in 1968, to propose that chemical and biological weapons should be placed on the agenda of the Geneva multilateral disarmament conference.

The SIPRI account gives an overview of the efforts of the negotiating states to develop an acceptable agreement and of the many texts proposed – despite the vicissitudes of superpower relations – in the period from the late 1960s through to the late 1980s. Then in 1989, as the East–West thaw accelerated, President Bush announced a crucial change in American policy to the UN General Assembly. According to the SIPRI account: 'No longer would the United States judge the acceptability of chemical arms control in terms of whether it was or was not verifiable. Instead, it would seek a "level of verification that gives us confidence to go forward".' The SIPRI authors commented:

> The importance of this change lay in its express recognition of what had always been the case, that no international ban on chemical weapons could ever be fully verifiable. *This was so because a great many chemicals and chemical manufacturing technologies can be used as well for chemical warfare as for peaceful purposes*... (emphasis added)

We shall return to this point, but it has to be reiterated that the move towards finishing the CWC negotiations, made possible by this dramatic change in the American position, did not lead to a trouble-free endgame. In particular, the seeming settlement of East–West disagreements brought into the open differences between North and South over issues other than those directly connected with the problem of verification. These issues, including that of the Australia Group's export control system, and its continuation as the CWC entered into force, were settled, at least well enough to prevent failure, in a frantic round of bargaining in mid-1992.

It is not a requirement here to review the structure of the whole of the CWC,[9,10] nor is it necessary to assess the verification system for the destruction of CW stockpiles and CW production facilities because they have no parallel in the Protocol to the Biological and Toxin Weapons Convention. It is important, however, to understand how the negotiators of the CWC set about dealing with the problem of illegal new production of chemical weapons and in order to do that, the nature of modern chemical weapons and of modern civil production in the chemical industry must be considered.

Chemical weapons

In 1999, the organization set up to oversee the CWC – the Organization for the Prohibition of Chemical Weapons (OPCW) – issued a pamphlet entitled *Chemical Disarmament: Basic Facts*.[11] This pamphlet noted that, traditionally, a chemical weapon was viewed as a poisonous (toxic) chemical contained in some kind of delivery system. However, for the CWC, a broader definition was needed. This definition was in three parts:

> A toxic chemical that can cause death or injury through its chemical action is, of course, a central element in the definition of a chemical

weapon. If such a chemical is produced or stockpiled, and has no legitimate use for peaceful purposes, it meets the definition of a chemical weapon...

This also applies to the precursors (or building blocks) of such chemicals. The second element of the definition:

> relates to munitions and devices. Irrespective of whether they are filled or unfilled, such munitions and devices are also defined as chemical weapons if they have been specifically designed for the purpose of disseminating a chemical agent ...

A third element of the definition applies to equipment, such as multiple rocket launchers, which has been specifically produced for use directly in the employment of chemical weapons.

Prior to the end of the nineteenth century, many poisons were known but it was not possible to produce them in large quantities. This became feasible with the rise of the modern chemical industry at that time. The means of distributing or dispersing chemical weapons agents has clearly been revolutionized – from the simple opening of drums of chlorine to drift on the wind in the First World War, to delivery by missile warhead today – but the significant changes in chemical weapons development have been in the nature of the chemicals made available for use as the chemical industry has grown and evolved over the past century. The agents used throughout the last hundred years can be divided into two general types: harassing agents, which are generally not lethal; and lethal agents, which can be expected to kill. Harassing agents such as CS are used as riot control agents in domestic police operations. The CWC does not prevent such domestic use, but it does not permit use of these agents as a method of warfare (such as in an artillery bombardment to force unprotected soldiers from cover).[12] The early lethal agents were industrial chemicals such as chlorine and phosgene, and were already available in large quantities at the time of the First World War. However, an arms race rapidly developed in which new chemical agents specifically designed for the purpose became available.

Probably the most significant of these new agents was mustard gas, which destroys any skin or membrane surface it comes into contact with. It is still regarded as a potent threat today.[13] During the 1930s scientists in Germany discovered the first, extremely toxic, nerve agents (G-agents such as tabun, sarin and soman). In the 1950s, even more toxic nerve agents (V-agents such as VX) were developed.[14] These substances have well-known specific effects on the nervous system. A new non-lethal agent,

BZ – which has complex actions on the central nervous system – was also weaponized by the United States in the 1960s. Stocks were only finally destroyed in the early 1990s.[15] Parallel research on biological weapons had also resulted in the weaponization of some of the extremely potent toxins produced by living organisms (such as botulinal toxins). These non-living chemicals can now often also be produced by biotechnology manufacturing processes and are covered by both the CWC and the BTWC.

Two points are worth noting from this short account. First, there are many more substances that *could* be used as chemical weapons agents than those known to have been weaponized. This would be particularly the case if requirements on the need for reasonable storage life and condition and other properties of the agents were relaxed.[16] Indeed, over the last century a very large number of chemicals have been examined as potential agents from which those weaponized by a number of states at different times were selected, by setting storage and other criteria at various levels. Secondly, if the CWC had not been agreed, and should it not be universally and effectively implemented, the process of research and development can be expected to produce new agents and means of agent delivery, exemplified by binary weapons in which two relatively safe chemicals could be mixed in the munition just before use.

Production of chemical weapons agents

It is important to understand that the production processes required to produce chemical weapons agents are well-known *old* technology. For example, regarding the production of sulphur mustard gas, the US Office of Technology Assessment (OTA) study of 1993, *Technologies Underlying Weapons of Mass Destruction*, noted:[17]

> Nine production processes for sulfur mustard have been documented in the published chemical literature. During World War I, thousands of tons of mustard gas were produced from alcohol, bleaching powder, and sodium sulphite. During World War II, the two largest producers of mustard gas, the United States and the Soviet Union, used two common industrial chemicals – sulfur monochloride and ethylene – as starting materials...

The study points out that a mustard gas plant based on this latter method could be located in an oil refinery, where the precursors would be readily available. Indeed, it concludes that production of mustard gas is technically simple.

The first militarized nerve agent, tabun (GA), is the simplest to produce. The four precursor chemicals required – phosphorus oxychloride, sodium cyanide, dimethylamine and ethyl alcohol – are widely available. The major technical difficulty is the cyanation reaction (in which a cyanide group is added) because of the dangers of using the toxic hydrogen cyanide reagent. Sarin (GB) and soman (GD) can be made by a variety of methods, but all involve a difficult alkylation reaction: '...in which a methyl group (-CH₃) or an ethyl group (-CH₂CH₃) is added to the central phosphorus to form a P-C bond [phosphorus-carbon bond]...'. Besides being technically difficult, this step is not often used in the production of commercial pesticides, to which the nerve agents are related. There are at least three practical routes to synthesize VX, all of which also involve this difficult alkylation. However, production of VX does not involve the use of some of the very corrosive substances required to produce sarin and soman. In summary, the Office of Technology Assessment concluded: 'the technologies required for the production of mustard and nerve agents have been known for more than 40 years and are within the capabilities of any moderately advanced chemical or pharmaceutical industry...'. The most challenging technical production problems for nerve gases are shown in Table 2.2. But in the view of the OTA, while difficult and hazardous, even these 'would probably represent more of a nuisance than a true obstacle to a determined proliferant'.

In an early review of verification of the chemical industry under the newly agreed CWC, the Australian government expert, Robert Mathews, started from exactly the same viewpoint:[18]

the production of sulphur-mustard involves *condensation* and *chlorination* processes. The production of Sarin nerve agent involves *phosphorylation, alkylation, chlorination, fluorination,* and *esterification*. The production of BZ psychochemical agent involves *esterification*...

Table 2.2 Technical challenges in nerve gas production*

1. The cyanation reaction for tabun which involves the containment of a highly toxic gas.
2. The alkylation step for sarin, soman, and VX, which requires the use of high temperatures and results in corrosive and dangerous byproducts such as hot hydrochloric acid.
3. Careful temperature control, including cooling of the reactor vessel during heat-producing reactions, and heating to complete reactions or to remove unwanted byproducts.
4. Intermediates that react explosively with water, requiring the use of heat-exchangers based on fluids or oils rather than water.
5. A distillation step if high-purity agent is required.

Note: *From Chapter 2, reference 17.

He then showed how exactly the same procedures are involved in normal commercial production processes (Table 2.3). But he made a crucial additional point. Not only are the types of production equipment used in the civil chemical industry around the world also suitable for production of chemical weapons agents, but:

> This is especially the situation with 'multi-purpose' plants (MPPs), in which the reactors, associated pipework, pumps and valves are typically constructed from a corrosion-resistant material ... to enable the plant to be used for many different types of reaction, including those either consuming or producing corrosive chemicals ...

Moreover, the whole MPP system will be controlled by a readily (re)programmable computer system and will have effluent systems suitable for dealing with a range of toxic chemicals.

Table 2.3 Chemical production processes*

Production process	CW agents	Typical commercial products
Chlorination	Sulphur-mustard	Insecticides
	Nitrogen-mustard	Herbicides
	Lewisite	Polymers, dyes
	Sarin	Pharmaceuticals
	VX	Solvents
Fluorination	Sarin	Polymers, solvents
	Soman	Pharmaceuticals
		Pesticides, herbicides
		Refrigerant gases
		Anaesthetic gases
Esterification	Sarin	Insecticides
	Tabun	Solvents
	BZ	Flavours
		Pharmaceuticals
Phosphorylation	Sarin	Insecticides
	Tabun	Flame retardants
	VX	Oil additives
Alkylation	Sarin	Flame retardants
	Soman	Oil additives
	VX	Petrochemicals

Note: *From Chapter 2, reference 18.

The civil chemical industry

It follows logically, from the preceding two sections, that the civil chemical industry had to be incorporated within the verification system of the CWC. Yet this is a massive industry, with the top 50 companies having sales of some $356 billion in 1998. The largest companies, concentrated in the developed world, are household names: BASF (Germany); Du Pont (France); Shell (UK/Netherlands); ICI (UK); Hoechst (US); Exxon (US): Rhône-Poulenc (France) and so on.[19]

The importance of this diverse industry can be seen by looking at the chemical imports and exports figures by sector for the American economy.[20] These data are summarized in Table 2.4. Clearly, the chemical industry is crucial to the well-being of modern industrial societies. Moreover, the worldwide demand for chemicals is expected to grow from a level of $1500 billion in 1996 to $2400 billion in 2010. There is also expected to be an increasing use of biotechnology to produce chemicals and increasing use of combinatorial chemistry and computer modelling. The pharmaceutical sector in particular is expected to grow as the population of the developed world contains a larger proportion of older people.[21] Obviously, the opportunities provided by the biotechnology revolution are producing a massive restructuring in this industry as it inclines more towards the life sciences and away from traditional chemistry.[22]

Yet despite its size, its importance to modern economies, and the process of rapid change, it is clear that the chemical industry took a

Table 2.4   US trade in chemicals in 1998*

Sector	Exports ($ million)	Imports ($ million)
Organic chemicals	15 181	18 300
Inorganic chemicals	4 843	5 118
Dyeing, tanning and colouring materials	3 528	2 470
Medicinals and pharmaceuticals	9 661	10 885
Essential oils, perfumes, toilet and cleansing preparations	4 888	2 893
Fertilizers	3 282	1 568
Plastics in primary form	11 560	5 084
Plastics in nonprimary form	5 315	3 840
Other	11 014	4 822
TOTAL	69 272	54 620

Note: *From Chapter 2, reference 20.

deliberate and constructive role, over a protracted period, in the process of bringing the CWC into being. This is clearly demonstrated by the presence of industry representatives at detailed, non-governmental, discussions of how the CWC might be developed, long before the treaty was agreed.[23] Whilst there was certainly vociferous opposition to the CWC on the grounds of its costs to industry,[24] what is particularly striking in the historical record is the major constructive role played by the Chemical Manufacturers Association (CMA) in the United States. Moreover, the CMA has not been reluctant to demonstrate pride in its record, despite the difficulties of achieving ratification of the CWC in the United States. The President and Chief Executive of the CMA was asked about the CMA's role in a long interview in 1997. He stated:

It wasn't easy. When we got close to the ratification vote, many false accusations were made about the treaty…I am convinced the treaty would not have passed without strong chemical industry support. CMA goes back more than 15 years on this issue…'[25]

In an article supporting ratification earlier in 1996, he pointed out how the CMA's input had influenced the negotiations: 'We *carefully gauged the potential effect of the CWC on industry and negotiated a treaty that deters illegal proliferation activity and respects commercial interest'.[26] (emphasis added) How then was this accomplished?

Verification of the CWC

The Chemical Weapons Convention contains 24 Articles and three Annexes (on Chemicals, Verification and Protection of Confidential Information respectively). It is summarized in Table 2.5. Our main concern here is with the means crafted to prevent the future production of militarily significant quantities of chemical weapons – particularly in dual-use civilian production facilities – but, as Mathews pointed out at the time of the agreement, the effectiveness of the CWC would come about through a combination of its features. The verification system set up in Article VI (see Table 2.5) must be seen in the context of the whole package. A summary of Mathews' view of this package is shown in Table 2.6. By agreeing to the Convention, declaring and destroying its chemical weapons and production facilities, being willing to undertake consultations, co-operation and fact-finding (including the possibility of challenge inspections), providing assistance and accepting that sanctions can be applied to ensure compliance, *in addition to Article VI verification*, a

Table 2.5 The Chemical Weapons Convention*

PREAMBLE
ARTICLE I GENERAL OBLIGATIONS
ARTICLE II DEFINITIONS AND CRITERIA
ARTICLE III DECLARATIONS
ARTICLE IV CHEMICAL WEAPONS
ARTICLE V CHEMICAL WEAPONS PRODUCTION FACILITIES
ARTICLE VI ACTIVITIES NOT PROHIBITED UNDER THIS CONVENTION
ARTICLE VII NATIONAL IMPLEMENTATION MEASURES
ARTICLE VIII THE ORGANIZATION
ARTICLE IX CONSULTATIONS, COOPERATION AND FACT-FINDING
ARTICLE X ASSISTANCE AND PROTECTION AGAINST CHEMICAL WEAPONS
ARTICLE XI ECONOMIC AND TECHNOLOGICAL DEVELOPMENT
ARTICLE XII MEASURES TO REDRESS A SITUATION AND TO ENSURE COMPLIANCE
ARTICLE XIII RELATION TO OTHER INTERNATIONAL AGREEMENTS
ARTICLE XIV SETTLEMENT OF DISPUTES
ARTICLE XV AMENDMENTS
ARTICLE XVI DURATION AND WITHDRAWAL
ARTICLE XVII STATUS OF THE ANNEXES
ARTICLE XVIII SIGNATURE
ARTICLE XIX RATIFICATION
ARTICLE XX ACCESSION
ARTICLE XXI ENTRY INTO FORCE
ARTICLE XXII RESERVATIONS
ARTICLE XXIII DEPOSITARY
ARTICLE XXIV AUTHENTIC TEXTS
ANNEX ON CHEMICALS
ANNEX ON IMPLEMENTATION AND VERIFICATION ('VERIFICATION ANNEX')
ANNEX ON PROTECTION OF CONFIDENTIAL INFORMATION

Note: *From OPCW Website (opcw.org).

State Party provides a basis for others to have confidence that it is not undertaking illegal activities. We are therefore dealing here with a sophisticated view of verification which incorporates (re)assurance as well as deterrence.

Turning then to the system of verification itself, the CWC begins by adopting the concept of a 'General Purpose Criterion' from the BTWC. This defines chemical weapons, not in terms of their characteristics but in terms of the purposes for which they have been designed. Article II.1(a) defines them as: 'Toxic chemicals and their precursors, except where intended for purposes not prohibited under this Convention, as long as the types and quantities are consistent with such purposes...'. The purposes not prohibited under the Convention are then set out in Article II.9, and in Article II.2, a toxic chemical is defined as: 'Any chemical

Table 2.6 Mechanisms for building confidence in the CWC*

Under the provisions of:

Article I, each nation joining the treaty agrees, *inter alia*, never to develop, produce or use chemical weapons, nor to assist any other country to produce or use chemical weapons. And each State Party agrees not to use riot control agents and herbicides as a method of warfare;

Articles III, IV and V, each State Party currently possessing chemical weapons agrees to provide accurate declarations of all of its chemical weapons and chemical weapons production facilities, and to destroy them under international monitoring;

Article VI, each State Party agrees to provide data on the activities of a large part of its chemical industry, and allow international teams to inspect these activities.

Article IX (Consultations, co-operation and fact-finding), each State Party agrees to allow a challenge inspection of any facility or location within its territory if another State Party is concerned about its compliance;

Article X (Assistance and protection against chemical weapons), each State Party agrees to provide assistance in the form of protection against chemical weapons (for example, detection equipment, protective clothing and medical treatment) to another treaty member who has been attacked (or is under serious risk of attack) with chemical weapons; and

Article XII (Measures to redress a situation, and to ensure compliance, including sanctions), each treaty member is aware that sanctions may be imposed against it if it contravenes the provisions of this treaty.

Note: *From Chapter 2, reference 18.

which through its chemical action on life processes can cause death, temporary incapacitation or permanent harm to humans or animals...'. One long-term observer of the CWC negotiations, Julian Perry Robinson, has commented:

> A chemical weapon in the sense of the CWC is therefore a considerably broader concept than the chemical weapon of, say, common military parlance. Without that breadth, chemical-warfare agents of novel but still-secret chemical identity, or toxic chemicals not yet discovered or made newly accessible through manufacturing innovation, would be unaffected by the strictures of the treaty...[27]

In short, the CWC cannot be circumvented by technological change; it applies to *all possible* toxic chemicals.

In order to give effect to this General Purpose Criterion – including allowing the peaceful non-prohibited purposes set out in Article II.9 – the

CWC divides responsibility between the international Organization for the Prohibition of Chemical Weapons (OPCW) and the required national authorities of the States Parties. As Perry Robinson has been at pains to point out, the primary responsibility is put on the States Parties. Article VI.2 states:

> Each State Party shall adopt the necessary measures to ensure that toxic chemicals and their precursors are only developed, produced, otherwise acquired, retained, transferred, or used within its territory or in any place under its jurisdiction or control for purposes not prohibited under this Convention ...

Only then, in regard to the chemicals listed in the schedules of the Annex on Chemicals, does the Convention go on to specify how this obligation shall be implemented by the international organization. For the vast majority of chemicals covered by the General Purpose Criterion, and not on the schedules, it is the national authorities which must oversee the implementation of the treaty. This crucial point is often overlooked. By way of illustration, it can be seen that two toxins, ricin and saxitoxin, appear in the Schedule 1 (the most dangerous) list of chemicals in the CWC Annex on Chemicals.[10] Yet it is quite clear that there are many other toxins – for example, botulinal toxin – of equal concern.[28] Thus the chemicals listed in the CWC schedules do not, indeed cannot, constitute a definitive list of chemical weapons.

Before turning our attention to these schedules and the international aspect of the verification system, it is as well to remember that the negotiators had a very long period over which to develop the CWC. Governments had time to carry out extensive analyses and to evolve their own approaches to feed into the negotiations. An example of this can be seen in the mid-1980s review by Graham Cooper of the UK series of papers previously presented to the Conference on Disarmament in Geneva.[29] Another example concerns the many trial inspections carried out by States Parties[30] and the practice challenge inspections carried out jointly by States Parties.[31] The extensive work reported by the United States on trial inspection exercises should also be noted.[32] It can hardly be argued, therefore, that the States Parties to the CWC did not have a very good idea of the architecture of the verification system they were constructing.

This architecture consists of *mandatory declarations, routine inspections* and the possibility of *challenge inspections* in the event of a well-founded case of concern over non-compliance. However, it should be noted that while such a challenge investigation would be governed by a 'red-light' procedure in which a vote of the Executive Council of the OPCW would have to be taken in order to prevent the investigation, Article IX of the CWC – on Consultations, Cooperation and Fact-Finding – gives many other means of clarifying issues to the States Parties before such a challenge would be considered.[33] In regard to the possible misuse of chemical industry facilities:

> Article VI provides for the declarations of industrial rather than chemical-weapons data. The original negotiators intended the declarations of industrial information as a means for identifying facilities whose 'dual-use' attributes rendered them a particular threat ... in other words facilities that might be especially attractive to potential cheaters seeking to conceal production of chemical-warfare agents behind a façade of legitimate industrial activity ...[27]

Such facilities would thus be subject to mandatory declarations and routine inspections which would force potential cheaters to undertake their illegal activities elsewhere, but such illegal activities would be potentially open to challenge inspection and would therefore have to be completely and expensively hidden.

For the purpose of these Article VI declarations, the Annex on Chemicals sets out three schedules of chemicals. Schedule I chemicals pose a high risk to the objectives and purpose of the Convention, Schedule II chemicals a significant risk and Schedule III chemicals a lesser risk. The scheduling also reflects the amount of industrial use of the chemicals, with Schedule III chemicals being produced in large quantities and those on Schedule I having little or no use for purposes not prohibited. It is obvious from the foregoing that the schedules are, in fact, *negotiated lists*. Altogether, 43 species or families of chemicals are contained in the schedules: 12 in Schedule I, 14 in Schedule II and 17 in Schedule III. Of the 43, 27 are precursors and 16 are toxicants. Some details provided for illustration by the OPCW are shown in Table 2.7.

The declarations triggered are of two types – one concerned with the chemicals themselves and the other with the facilities associated with production of the chemicals. The amount of detail required is greatest for Schedule I and least for Schedule III chemicals. The facilities needing to be declared are those in which more than certain defined quantities of the chemicals are produced or, for Schedule I and II chemicals, processed or consumed. Facility declarations are also required for plant sites where other unscheduled, discrete, organic chemicals are produced by synthesis above certain quantities.

If the annual quantity of scheduled chemical processed, consumed and/ or produced in a declared facility exceeds a certain threshold the facility

Table 2.7   Chemicals controlled by the OPCW*

Schedule 1 chemicals include those that have been or can be easily used as chemical weapons and which have very limited, if any, uses for peaceful purposes. These chemicals are subject to very stringent restrictions, including a ceiling on production, in total, of 1 tonne per annum per state party, a ceiling on total possession at any given time at 1 tonne per state party, licensing requirements, and restrictions on transfers. These restrictions will apply to the relatively few industrial facilities that use Schedule 1 chemicals. Some Schedule 1 chemicals are used as ingredients in pharmaceutical preparations or as diagnostics. For example, treatments for certain types of cancer contain nitrogen mustard. Another Schedule 1 chemical, saxitoxin, is used as a calibration standard in monitoring programmes for paralytic shellfish poisoning, and is also used in neurological research. Ricin, yet another Schedule 1 chemical, is a valuable research tool. Other Schedule 1 chemicals are usually produced and used for protective purposes, such as for testing protective equipment and chemical agent alarms.

Schedule 2 chemicals include those that are precursors to, or that, in some cases, can themselves be used as chemical weapons agents, but which have a number of other commercial uses (such as ingredients in insecticides, herbicides, lubricants and some pharmaceutical products). Some Schedule 2 chemicals can be found in applications quite unrelated to chemical weapons, and even in household products. For example, BZ is a neurotoxic chemical listed under Schedule 2 which has been used as a chemical weapon, but is also an industrial intermediate in the manufacture of a pharmaceutical product. ... thiodiglycol is both a mustard gas precursor as well as an ingredient in water-based inks, dyes and some pesticides. Another such example is DMMP, a chemical related to certain nerve agent precursors which is used as a flame retardant in polyurethane foam.

Schedule 3 chemicals include those that can be used to produce, or that, in some cases, can themselves be used as, chemical weapons, but which are widely used for peaceful purposes (including in herbicides, insecticides, paints, coatings, textiles and lubricants). Among the toxic chemicals listed under Schedule 3 are phosgene and hydrogen cyanide, which have been used as chemical weapons, but are also intermediates in the manufacture of certain plastics. Triethanolamine, a precursor chemical for nitrogen mustard gas, is found in a variety of detergents (including shampoos, bubble baths and household cleaners) as well as in industrial lubricants and surfactants.

Discrete organic chemicals
In addition to the chemicals included in the three Schedules, the Convention also puts into place a reporting and verification requirement for production facilities making a wide variety of organic chemicals, with particular emphasis on plants that make organic chemicals containing the elements phosphorus, sulfur or fluorine.

Note: *From Chapter 2, reference 11.

Table 2.8 The chemical control regimes under the CWC*

Elements of control regime	For Schedule 1 chemicals	For Schedule 2 chemicals	For Schedule 3 chemicals	For unscheduled discrete organic chemicals
Production limit	No more than 1000 kg of all types may be held by a State Party	None specified, but all production must be for and in quantities consistent with purposes not prohibited under the Convention		
Data reporting (initial and annual)	Yes: detailed information on production, use, import and export	Yes: for each one, aggregate national data on production, use, import and export	Yes: for each one, aggregate national data on production, import and export	No, except for plant specific data (as with the scheduled chemicals)
Inspection of facilities producing more than threshold quantities	Yes: highly stringent and augmented with instrumented monitoring	Yes	Yes: less stringent	Not until EIF+3 yrs, if then approved by the Conference of the States Parties
Export control	Exports permitted only to States Parties, with advance notification of OPCW	End-use certification required until EIF+3yrs, after which exports permitted only to States Parties	End-use certification required; and possibility of other measures after EIF +5 yrs	None specified

Note: *From Chapter 2, reference 27.

becomes liable to routine inspection by the OPCW. The routine inspection system was worked out in co-operation with the representatives of the chemical industry and is therefore tightly constrained. There are stringent requirements for the protection of confidential proprietary information, a limit on the number of inspections that a State Party is required to receive at declared facilities in any one year and a requirement for a negotiated facility agreement for every routine inspection. As Perry Robinson has noted:

These facility agreements limit access by OPCW inspectors solely to those particular areas of a plant site that had been declared as producing or otherwise handling, a scheduled chemical; the facility agreement precludes access to other areas...

Thus the routine inspection system is there only to check the accuracy of the facility declaration. The intrusiveness of the access does, however, vary from schedule to schedule. Nevertheless, it is again obvious that confidence in the compliance of a State Party cannot come about because *all* relevant activities are being monitored by the international inspectorate. Inspection of part of a multipurpose chemical plant cannot, by definition, demonstrate what is going on in the uninspected part of the plant. A summary of the chemical control regimes under the CWC is shown in Table 2.8.

The initial stages of implementation of the CWC

Following the agreement of the CWC, it had a difficult passage through the Russian Duma, and particularly through the United States Senate, where a series of reservations were added.[34] Undoubtedly, the delay in enacting US implementation legislation, and the consequent lack of routine inspections in US facilities, led to feelings of inequality amongst large chemical industries in other countries. Yet the general view appears to be that implementation of the CWC has proved to be acceptable to the international community. As one commentator noted in late 1999:

> All things considered, the CWC's first two years have proceeded relatively smoothly. The inspectorate has set into motion a complex arms control verification system, visiting hundreds of military and commercial facilities and analysing thousands of pages of declarations. The inspection process has unfolded more efficiently than originally envisaged. No earth-shattering clashes have emerged among member states...[35]

So though we are still in the early days of the life of the CWC, it appears we can conclude that, despite the difficult problem of the dual-use chemical industry, a successful solution has been found in the structure of the Convention.

3
Developing the BTWC, 1975–1995

At a seminar in March 2000, to celebrate the 25th anniversary of the entry into force of the BTWC, Nicholas Sims noted: 'Looking back over our Convention's first 25 years in force, we find, not a simple linear progress ever onward and upward, but a more complicated history...'.[1] In his view, the Convention's first quarter-century has been complicated by 'vicissitudes of reputation and credibility'. He felt that in particular the Convention had: 'suffered from the failure of some States Parties to demonstrate their compliance with its obligations credibly and consistently, and the failure of the States Parties collectively to get to grips with the problem...'. Getting to grips with that problem is what the BTWC Protocol has to do, and that is the core of our concern here. Sims also noted, however, that over the last 25 years there had been progress.

On entry into force there were 46 original parties to the Convention. By March 2000 almost 100 further states had joined. Furthermore, through its five-yearly Review Conferences the Convention had generated a treaty regime with a built-in mechanism for its own development. The evolution of the regime has been the subject of detailed studies which it is not necessary to recapitulate in full here.[2,3] What needs to be done, nevertheless, is to review the key elements in the efforts made to strengthen the Convention prior to the commencement of the work of the Ad Hoc Group mandated, from 1995, to negotiate the BTWC Protocol. Three sets of issues are of interest: efforts to develop the unsatisfactory provisions related to verification in Articles V and VI of the BTWC; efforts to develop greater transparency through Confidence-Building Measures (CBMs); and the initial stages of current attempts to develop a Protocol carried out in the VEREX investigation of the possibility of verification for the BTWC in 1992–3 (leading up to the 1994 Special Conference which mandated the work of the present Ad Hoc Group).

Enhanced consultation

As we saw in Chapter 1, experienced diplomats such as Barend ter Haar had concerns about the verification element of the BTWC from the initial stages of the development of the text. Sweden was certainly concerned about the final outcome of the decisions on Article V and Article VI (see Appendix 1). As Sims states, in his detailed account of the 1980 First Review Conference, in 1979 Sweden gave notice of its intention: 'to use the Review Conference as an occasion for launching the amendment process, using Article Eleven to amend either Article Five (in respect of consultation) or Article Six (in respect of complaint)'.[2] The objections to Article VI included the disproportionate power given to the Security Council, which Alva Myrdal had argued against in 1971.

In the event, however, the efforts to develop the BTWC centred on Article V, not Article VI, and rather than the difficult amendment process, the Final Declarations of successive Review Conferences were used to elaborate and specify what could be done under the Article V consultation procedure. Thus the Final Declaration of the First Review Conference in 1980 noted, in part:

> The Conference considers that the flexibility of the provisions concerning consultation and co-operation on any problems which may arise in relation to the objective, or the application of the provisions of, the Convention, enables interested States Parties to use various international procedures which would make it possible to ensure effectively and adequately the implementation of the Convention provisions... [4]

The declaration then added the new element that: 'These procedures include, *inter alia*, the right of any State Party subsequently to request that a *consultative meeting* open to all States Parties be convened at expert level'. (emphasis added) Finally, in regard to Article V, the declaration added: 'The Conference, noting the concerns and differing views expressed on the adequacy of Article V, believes that this question should be further considered at an appropriate time'. So whilst Sweden had failed in its efforts to insert into the BTWC a Consultative Committee of Experts along the lines of that in the 1976 En-Mod Convention,[5] the door for further development had been kept open.

In the 1986 Final Declaration of the Second Review Conference, under Article V, it was agreed:

> – that a consultative meeting shall be promptly convened when requested by a State Party,

- that a consultative meeting may consider any problems which may arise in relation to the objective of, or in the application of the provisions of the Convention, suggest ways and means for further clarifying, *inter alia*, with the assistance of technical experts, any matter considered ambiguous or unresolved, as well as initiate appropriate international procedures within the framework of the United Nations and in accordance with its Charter,
- that the consultative meeting or any State Party, may request specialised assistance in solving any problems which may arise in relation to the objective of, or in the application of the provisions of, the Convention ... [6]

Whilst this wording indicated, for example, that the consultative meeting would be held promptly, and that it would have wide terms of reference, it left much else undefined. How, for instance, was the meeting to reach any decisions?

Such issues were clarified, to an extent, at the Third Review Conference in 1991 where it was noted, in part, that:

- A formal consultative meeting could be preceded by bilateral or other consultations by agreement among those States parties involved in the problems which had arisen;
- Requests for the convening of a consultative meeting shall be addressed to the Depositaries, who shall immediately inform all States parties of the request and shall convene within 30 days an informal meeting of interested States parties to discuss the arrangements for the formal consultative meeting, which shall be convened within 60 days of receipt of the request;
- With regard to the taking of decisions, the consultative meeting shall proceed in accordance with rule 28 of the rules of procedure of the Review Conference. [7]

So almost two decades after the negotiation of the BTWC a consultative mechanism appeared to be in place. However, the only time when the procedure has been used, when Cuba accused the United States of using the agricultural pest *Thrips palmi* against it in 1997, the chairman of the formal consultative meeting concluded that: 'due *inter alia* to the technical complexity of the subject and the passage of time, it has not proved possible to reach a definitive conclusion with regard to the concerns raised by the Government of Cuba'.[8] However, the Third Review

Conference did note, in regard to Article V (and Article VI) of the BTWC, the useful progress made in:

> United Nations Security Council resolution 620 of 1988, which encourages the United Nations Secretary-General to carry out prompt investigations, in response to allegations brought to his attention by any Member State concerning the possible use of chemical and bacteriological (biological) or toxin weapons.[7]

In the section of the Final Declaration dealing with Article V the conference also stated that it:

> welcomes the proposals set out in annex I of United Nations document A/44/561 developed by a group of qualified experts and endorsed by the United Nations General Assembly in 1990 in its resolution 45/57/C for technical guidelines and procedures to guide the United Nations Secretary-General in the timely and efficient investigation of reports of the possible use of chemical and bacteriological (biological) or toxin weapons...

The concerns of the international community over the use of these weapons of mass destruction, concerns which had certainly grown during the 1980s, were therefore beginning to have an impact on the evolution of the BTWC.

Confidence-Building Measures (CBMs)

The Second Review Conference of the BTWC was held in the same month of 1986 as the Stockholm Conference[5] at which the first signs of the end of the long East–West Cold War began to appear, and mechanisms of gaining trust, such as Confidence-Building Measures (CBMs), were on the international agenda. Thus, in the Final Declaration of the review, in regard to Article V, parties agreed to implement measures: 'in order to prevent or reduce the occurrence of ambiguities, doubts and suspicions, and in order to improve international co-operation in the field of peaceful bacteriological (biological) activities'.[6] The agreed measures, which amounted to voluntary (politically, not legally binding) annual data exchanges, are summarized in Table 3.1. The Review Conference also decided that a group of scientific and technical experts should meet in the following year to work out the details of the data exchange.

Table 3.1 Summary of the confidence-building measures agreed in 1986*

1. Exchange of data on research centres and laboratories that have very high safety standards in handling biological materials that pose a high risk.
2. Exchange of information on outbreaks of infectious diseases and similar occurrences caused by toxins that appear to be different from normal.
3. Encouragement of publication of results directly related to the convention and promotion of the use of such knowledge for permitted purposes.
4. Active promotion of contacts between scientists engaged in research directly related to the convention, including exchanges for joint research.

Note: *From Chapter 3, reference 3.

Our concern here is with the first two CBMs, rather than those concerned with international co-operation. The experts' meeting in 1987 agreed:

> that data should be provided on each research centre or laboratory, within the territory of a State Party, under its jurisdiction or under its control anywhere,
>
> (a) which has maximum containment unit(s) meeting the criteria for a 'maximum containment laboratory' as specified in the 1983 WHO Laboratory Biosafety Manual (Annex IV), such as those designated as Biosafety Level 4 (BL4) or P4, or equivalent standard; or
>
> (b) which has containment unit(s) and specialises in research or development for prophylactic or protective purposes against possible hostile use of microbial and/or other biological agents or toxins.[9]

Commenting on this specification, Erhard Geissler noted in 1990 that:

> The idea behind this proposed measure was the awareness that at least some important stages of design and development of BW and TW agents must be done in high-containment laboratories. Several experts have therefore concluded that high-containment laboratories are obvious subjects of and targets for verification measures.[10]

Similarly, he noted:

> The idea behind the exchange of information on outbreaks of infectious diseases and similar occurrences caused by toxins was that in the past private sources or even officials have occasionally related outbreaks to activities forbidden either by the Convention or the 1925 Geneva Protocol...

An obvious example cited was the outbreak of anthrax in the Soviet city of Sverdlovsk.

The experts at the meeting consulted the World Health Organization (WHO) and accepted that:

> An outbreak or epidemic is the occurrence of an unusually large or unexpected number of cases of an illness or health-related event in a given place at a given time. The number of cases considered as unusual will vary according to the illness or event and the community concerned.[9]

The experts attempted to give further precision to what needed to be reported in the CBM and in particular suggested that outbreaks with certain defined characteristics should be considered especially important. These characteristics are shown in Table 3.2.

Unfortunately, as Geissler reported prior to the Third Review Conference of the BTWC in 1991, the results of the first three rounds of data exchange were disappointing. Indeed, the majority of the States Parties to the BTWC did not participate at all in the information exchange.[11] Nevertheless, the Third Review Conference attempted to improve the previously agreed measures and to add to them. The CBMs agreed in 1991 are set out in Table 3.3. Reviewing these new measures in 1992, Geissler certainly had some criticisms over remaining deficiencies, but he also thought there were significant advances. In his view: 'The most significant decision taken by the Conference was to amend

Table 3.2   Characteristics of particularly important outbreaks*

– When the cause of the outbreak cannot be readily determined or the causative agent (including organisms made pathogenic by molecular biology techniques) is difficult to diagnose.

– When the disease may be caused by organisms which meet the criteria for risk groups III or IV, according to the classification in the 1983 WHO Laboratory Biosafety Manual.

– When the causative agent is exotic to a given region.

– When the disease follows an unusual pattern of development.

– When the disease occurs in the vicinity of research centres and laboratories subject to exchange of data under item A.**

– When suspicions arise of the possible occurrence of a new disease.

Notes: *From Chapter 3, reference 9.
　　　　**The first item of Table 3.1.

Table 3.3 Summary of the confidence-building measures agreed in 1991*

Declaration form stating 'Nothing to declare' or 'Nothing new to declare'.

CBM A
    Part 1 Exchange of data on research centres and laboratories.
    Part 2 Exchange of information on national biological defence research and development programmes.

CBM B Exchange of information on outbreaks of infectious diseases and similar occurrences caused by toxins.
CBM C Encouragement of publication of results and promotion of use of knowledge.
CBM D Active promotion of contacts.
CBM E Declaration of legislation, regulations and other measures.
CBM F Declaration of past activities in offensive and/or defensive biological research and development programmes.
CBM G Declaration of vaccine production facilities.

Note: *From Chapter 3, reference 3.

the exchange of data on research centers and to request the provision of detailed information on national biological defense research and development programs...'.[12] This new measure was important, he felt, because:

> ... it represents a first step towards *covering research* by the Convention, because it constitutes an important prerequisite for the establishment of verification measures, and because it will provide information on military programs for the development of vaccines. ... In addition, this measure will provide information on *all* facilities, governmental and non-governmental, which are involved in defense R&D programs...

Unfortunately, a detailed study of the CBM returns carried out in 1996, prior to the Fourth Review Conference of the BTWC, showed that the level of State participation was still far from adequate. Only eleven States Parties had taken part in all nine rounds of annual data exchange and only half of the States Parties had made at least one annual declaration.[13]

VEREX

Against this background, and the fears expressed over the possible use of biological weapons by Iraq in the 1991 Gulf War, it is perhaps not surprising that another approach to strengthening the BTWC was taken at the Third Review Conference.[7] In addition to the improved CBMs, the States Parties, in the consideration of Article V, agreed to a process in which potential verification measures were to be identified and examined from a scientific and technical standpoint. It was also agreed that the Ad Hoc Group of Government Experts involved would meet in Geneva in early 1992 under the chairmanship of Ambassador Tibor Tóth of Hungary. Further meetings were to be held as necessary with a view to finishing the work before the end of 1993. Eventually, four of these meetings, which became known as VEREX, were held – in March/April and November/December 1992, and May/June and September 1993. A final report was agreed at the last meeting and circulated to all States Parties.

The mandate issued by the Third Review Conference, for the government experts in the VEREX meetings, stated that the group should try to identify measures which could determine:

Whether a State party is developing, producing, stockpiling, acquiring or retaining microbial or other biological agents or toxins, of types and in quantities that have no justification for prophylactic, protective or other peaceful purposes;

Whether a State party is developing, producing, stockpiling, acquiring or retaining weapons, equipment or means of delivery designed to use such agents or toxins for hostile purposes or in armed conflict.[7]

These measures, which clearly relate to the scope of the BTWC set out in Article I (Appendix I), could be addressed singly or in combination. Specifically, the group was to evaluate potential verification measures: 'taking into account the broad range of types and quantities of microbial and other biological agents and toxins, whether naturally occurring or altered, which are capable of being used as means of warfare'. The criteria that the group were instructed to use are summarized in Table 3.4.

It is important to note the restrictions placed on the work of the government experts. The mandate stated:

The Group shall adopt by *consensus* a report taking into account views expressed in the course of its work. The report of the group shall be *a description of its work* on the identification and examination of potential verification measures *from a scientific and technical standpoint* ... (emphases added)

Table 3.4 Main criteria used for the evaluation of potential verification measures in VEREX*

Their strengths and weaknesses based on, but not limited to, the amount and quality of information they provide, and fail to provide.

Their ability to differentiate between prohibited and permitted activities.

Their ability to resolve ambiguities about compliance.

Their technology, material, manpower and equipment requirements.

Their financial, legal, safety and organisational implications.

Their impact on scientific research, scientific co-operation, industrial development and other permitted activities, and their implications for the confidentiality of commercial proprietary information.

Note: *From Chapter 3, reference 7.

So in no sense was VEREX a process of negotiation of verification measures. This limited mandate is hardly surprising because the representative of the United States told the 8th Meeting of the States at the Review Conference: 'his Government has made it clear at an earlier stage that it believed that the Convention was not effectively verifiable ... '.[7] It should be noted that it is *effective* verification that appears to be denied as possible (see Preface). The possibility of an *adequate* verification of the Convention appears to be left open. It was also agreed that after the report of the VEREX meetings had been circulated:

> If a majority of States Parties ask for the convening of a conference to examine the report, by submitting a proposal to this effect to the Depositary Governments, such a conference will be convened. *In such a case the conference shall decide on any further action* ... (emphasis added)

Those who believed that the BTWC could be strengthened through the addition of verification measures thus also had a means of moving forward from VEREX, if they could persuade enough other States Parties.

In 1994 Ambassador Tóth co-authored a review of the work of VEREX.[14] This began by pointing out the differences of approach to verification amongst those involved, but concluded:

> In any case, verification under the BWC must serve to deter a possible violator from seeking to acquire biological weapons and provide a degree of assurance that any such violation is likely to be detected by these verification measures ...

Additionally, the authors pointed out that:

> an independent international authority must have the power to evaluate verification results and to draw conclusions about compliance or non-compliance. Conducting such verification on an international level will require both resources and personnel.

The concept of verification being discussed here therefore involves both deterrence and reassurance (as in the more sophisticated views discussed in previous chapters) and clearly involves the setting up of an international body requiring a certain level of financial support and personnel.

Ambassador Tóth and his co-authors then briefly reviewed the outcome of the VEREX meetings. In VEREX I the focus was on the identification of the relevant measures and a series of 21 measures were identified for further examination. These measures are shown in Table 3.5. Interestingly, the authors pointed out that:

> Not surprisingly, the subcategory 'on-site inspections' presents the greatest number of practical procedures and activities. They range from interviewing staff and authorities to visual inspection of facilities and equipment, from identification of key equipment to auditing procedures...

The idea that verification requires international personnel to have onsite access in order to really gain an understanding of whether there is non-compliance is a key point that will be taken up again in later chapters.

In the VEREX II and VEREX III meetings the advantages and disadvantages of the application of the 21 verification measures were evaluated against the set of criteria. Tóth and his co-authors noted that at these meetings it became clear that: 'from a technical and scientific standpoint, no single measure is able to distinguish conclusively between activities permitted or prohibited by the BWC...'. At VEREX III, therefore, the measures were evaluated to some extent in combination and it was concluded that combinations of several measures produced synergistic effects. These conclusions are summarized in Table 3.6.

As noted previously, the agreement of the CWC was preceded by States Parties carrying out extensive trials of inspections. In VEREX III also:

> the group discussed the experiences gained by trial inspections carried out by Canada, the Netherlands and the UK, and considered *a Swiss study on Q-fever... which showed that the inspection scheme used in that study could identify a violation of the BWC with a high degree of reliability.* (emphasis added)

Table 3.5 Potential verification measures identified in VEREX I*

Off-site measures

Information monitoring
Surveillance of publications
Surveillance of legislation
Data on transfers and transfer requests and on production
Multilateral information sharing
Exchange visits

Data exchange
Declarations (including notifications, data on transfers and transfer requests and on production)

Remote sensing
Surveillance by satellite
Surveillance by aircraft
Ground-based surveillance

Inspections
Sampling and identification
Observation
Auditing

On-site measures

Exchange visits
International arrangements

Inspections
Interviewing
Visual inspections (including observation and surveillance by aircraft)
Identification of key equipment
Auditing
Sampling and identification
Medical examination

Continuous monitoring
By instruments (including ground-based surveillance)
By personnel

Note: *From Chapter 3, reference 14.

The VEREX group considered, in fact, some 200 working papers in which such studies and views were reported by States Parties.

It was in the light of all this work, over an extended period of 18 months, that the group met in VEREX IV to prepare its final consensus report. Tóth and his co-authors concluded, in part, that: 'potential verification measures as identified and evaluated could be useful to varying

Table 3.6 Examples of combinations of measures producing synergistic effects*

Combination A
Declarations + multilateral information sharing + satellite surveillance +
visual inspection.

Combination B
Information monitoring (surveillance of publications + surveillance of
legislation + data on transfers, transfer requests and production + multilateral
information sharing + exchange visits).

Combination C
On-site inspection (interviewing + visual inspections, identification of key
equipment + auditing + sampling and identification).

Combination D
Declarations + multilateral information sharing + on-site inspection.

Combination E
Declarations + information monitoring.

Note: *From Chapter 3, reference 14.

degrees in enhancing confidence, through increased transparency, that
States Parties were fulfilling their obligations under the BWC...'[15] and that:

> some measures in combination could provide enhanced capabilities
> by increasing, for example, the focus and improving the quality of
> information thereby improving the possibility of differentiating
> between prohibited and permitted activities and of resolving ambi-
> guities about compliance.

According to the mandate, the final report was circulated to all States
Parties. By February 1994, Ambassador Tóth and his colleagues concluded that, since 67 countries had requested that a Special Conference
be held (two more than the 65 then required), a start had been made to
convening a Special Conference.

A Special Conference was held in September 1994 and mandated the
work of the current Ad Hoc Group (which is the focus of following
chapters). After considering the VEREX final report, the Special Conference issued a complex set of instructions to the Ad Hoc Group. In
particular, the final declaration argued for:

> the establishment of a coherent regime to enhance the effectiveness
> of and improve compliance with the Convention. This regime would
> include, *inter alia*, potential verification measures, as well as agreed

procedures and mechanisms for their efficient implementation and measures for the investigation of alleged use…[16]

Thus the objective of the Ad Hoc Group was: 'to consider appropriate measures, *including possible verification measures*, and draft proposals to strengthen the Convention, to be included, as appropriate, *in a legally binding instrument…*' (emphases added). So this marked a clear change of approach. The aim now was to embed *verification measures* in a legally binding (i.e. compulsory, rather than voluntary) instrument.

The Ad Hoc Group was instructed to consider a number of aspects relevant to its task. These are summarized in Table 3.7. Clearly, since it was the requirement to enhance the effectiveness and improve compliance with the Convention, it was appropriate that measures related to Article X of the Convention (on international co-operation and economic development) were included in the mandate. Moreover, protection of sensitive commercial proprietary information and legitimate security needs and avoidance of negative impacts on scientific research and industrial development would be necessary in order to ensure widespread acceptance of the measures agreed.

From the point of view of ensuring confidence that Article I of the Convention was not being broken, however, the key issue was the instruction to consider:

A system of measures to promote compliance with the Convention, including, as appropriate, measures identified, examined and evaluated in the VEREX Report. *Such measures should apply to all relevant facilities and activities, be reliable, cost-effective, non-discriminatory and as non-intrusive as possible, consistent with the effective implementation* of the system and should not lead to abuse. (emphases added)

Table 3.7 Summary of the essential elements of the Protocol to be considered by the Ad Hoc Group*

– Definition of terms and objective criteria.

– Enhanced confidence-building and transparency measures.

– A system of measures to promote compliance.

– Specific measures to ensure effective and full implementation of Article X.

– Protection of sensitive commercial proprietary information and legitimate national security needs.

– Avoidance of any negative impact on scientific research, international cooperation and industrial development.

Note: *From Chapter 3, reference 16.

In this regard also it was obvious that there would be a requirement to add specificity to the measures agreed, through:

> *Definitions of terms and objective criteria*, such as lists of bacteriological (biological) agents and toxins, their threshold quantities, as well as equipment and types of activities, *where relevant for specific measures designed to strengthen the Convention*. (emphases added)

The amplification in the latter part of the instruction, 'where relevant for specific measures', was crucial in order to avoid any implication that the definitions and objective criteria in any way restricted the all-encompassing General Purpose Criterion of the Convention itself. They were to relate only to the specific measures agreed for the additional instrument.

It should be clearly understood that the mandate given by the 1994 Special Conference to the Ad Hoc Group was agreed by consensus. For example, the US delegate, Mr Mahley, argued during the Conference that:

> the ad hoc committee should focus on developing a legally binding regime based on the measures proposed by the VEREX Group and the conclusions reported to States parties ... the selection process should consider both off-site measures, such as mandatory declarations, and on-site measures, such as facility visits, providing a solid foundation for the verification regime.[16]

Indeed, Mr Mahley went on to suggest there should be a programme of work which would allow completion of the draft Protocol in time for consideration and action at the Fourth Review Conference in 1996.

The objective of verification

It is obvious from this brief history that the work of the current Ad Hoc Group engaged in negotiation of the Protocol to the BTWC runs on directly from that of the group of government experts in the VEREX process. It is useful, therefore, before considering the Ad Hoc Group's efforts, to ask what those experts engaged in the VEREX process believed they were trying to achieve when they began their work.

It is also useful, before examining some of the early working papers produced in the VEREX process, to ask whether States Parties considered it, at least theoretically, possible to identify militarily significant quantities of biological weapons agents during an on-site inspection. A paper produced for a NATO Advanced Research Workshop in Budapest in

1996 by Dr John Bartlett, Senior Scientific Advisor for Non-Proliferation at Porton Down, the UK's centre of expertise on chemical and biological warfare, attempted to provide a *quantitative answer* to that question.[17] The paper asked 'How much is a militarily significant quantity?' Bartlett began by accepting that small quantities of a biological agent might be used to attack a command headquarters or in terrorist attacks on civilians, but did not accept that a biological weapons capability would be acquired just for such purposes. A more credible military scenario, he argued: 'is one in which the attacker seeks to exploit the fact that an extremely small amount of BW [biological warfare] agent material is needed to infect unprotected victims by mounting a clandestine stand-off attack at night...'. He continued: 'Making reasonable assumptions it can be shown that for a single attack of this type, the attacker will need to release of the order of 10^{12} ID_{50} into the atmosphere in such an attack...'. ID_{50} is the amount of material needed to infect half of the people exposed. Bartlett went on to argue that a similar figure could be obtained for other credible military scenarios. Thus, 'for normal purposes, an aggressor will need to produce more than about 10^{12} ID_{50}, or one trillion doses'. This could simply be termed the *trillion dose criterion*. Table 3.8 shows how this dose criterion is derived for the stand-off attack scenario used by Bartlett.

Table 3.8   Derivation of the trillion dose criterion*

Dose received
$$D = Q \times b/h \times u$$
– Where

Q = source strength (units/m)
b = breathing rate (volume/min)
h = depth of (air) mixing layer
u = mean surface wind speed

Typical values
$b = 20$ litres/min $= 2 \times 10^{-2} m^3 min^{-1}$
$h = 1 km$ $= 10^3 m$
$u = 5 m/s$ $= 3 \times 10^2 m\,min^{-1}$

For $D = 10\ ID_{50}$ (ID_{50} is the dose required to infect 50% of those exposed)
$Q = D \times h \times u/b$
$Q = 10 \times 10^3 \times 3 \times 10^2 / 2 \times 10^{-2} = 1.5 \times 10^8 ID_{50}$

Attacker needs to achieve approximately $10^8 \times ID_{50}/m$
For a source 10 km long, this is equivalent to $10^4 \times 10^8 = 10^{12} ID_{50}$

Note: *From Chapter 3, reference 17.

The second question, then, is what fermentation capacity is needed to produce such an amount of agent? Bartlett's paper suggests that the simplest method would be to grow a bacterium in a fermenter and use the resulting liquid suspension. The proliferator could be confident of achieving a concentration of about 10^8 bacterial cells per millilitre of liquid in the fermenter. It would therefore be necessary to produce:

$10^{12} \times$ (No. of cells equivalent to 1 ID_{50})/$10^8 \times 1000$ litres of suspension even if no allowance is made for loss of viability of the agent in storage.

Bartlett then used the best-known agent, anthrax, as an example:

In the case of *B. anthracis*, the very stable causative agent for anthrax, the ID_{50} for man is estimated to be about 10^4 cells. *Hence the total quantity of culture required under the above assumptions would be about 100,000 litres.* (emphasis added)

Such a quantity could be produced from, for example, 10 runs of 10 fermenters each with a capacity of 1000 litres. Bartlett comments that the space occupied by such a set of fermenters and the necessary ancillary equipment: 'is not very small and is certainly large enough to be included within the facilities examined by a team of inspectors in a Challenge inspection of the type planned under the Chemical Weapons Convention...'. Bartlett concludes his analysis by stating: 'In other words, any proliferator possessing such a production capability on a challenged site would have to demonstrate that it was being used for purposes which did not contravene the Convention'. Other bacterial agents might have a lower ID_{50} than anthrax, but this would likely be offset by greater losses in storage and rapid decay in the atmosphere after release. Viral agents would certainly be more difficult to produce and would need a greater amount of ancillary equipment, in Bartlett's opinion.

Finally, in his consideration of militarily significant illegal activities, Bartlett notes:

if the aggressor wishes to have some flexibility in the way he uses his BW agents, he will need to consider more than one type of delivery system and to ensure that agents and their means of delivery are supported by a subtle logistic system. All of these aspects are potentially detectable in on-site inspections and cannot easily be changed at very short notice.

So if we consider militarily significant proliferation, it is simply not correct to argue that detection is impossible. The view that detection of a militarily significant programme is indeed possible is reinforced by considering western views of the Soviet offensive programme in the 1980s. It will be recalled that the official US document, *Soviet Military Power*, stated in 1987:[18]

> The Soviet offensive BW programme has been monitored by the US for decades.... Although the BWC bans the development, production, and stockpiling of biological agents and toxins for hostile purposes, no reduction in Soviet offensive BW activity has been observed...

Significantly, the publication added a paragraph later:

> A number of installations capable of producing disease agents and toxins on a largescale basis *and placing them in munitions and delivery/dissemination systems* have also been identified. These installations have been established by the Ministry of Defense and are under its control...

So by the mid-1980s clear public statements were indicating Soviet establishments with *weaponization* capabilities.

The point is reinforced by, amongst others, the former UK defence intelligence scientist, Dr Christopher Davis. In an interview for US Public Service Broadcasting in 1998 he stated: '[W]e were firmly of the opinion, by the time we reached the mid-to-late 80s, that the Soviet Union had a substantial clandestine offensive biological weapons program'.[19] Given the kinds of satellite photographs likely to have been available at that time,[20] such a conclusion was surely not surprising. It is noteworthy also that in the second half of his paper Bartlett[17] concludes that revealing illegal activities in an arms control regime which also protects the interests of legitimate commercial companies is an achievable task. When the VEREX process began, how were the States Parties thinking this might be brought about?

Some 200 working papers were produced in the VEREX process. Of interest here are the first four (WP.1–WP.4) produced by States Parties for the first meeting in March/April 1992. Their contents are shown in Table 3.9. In addition to the length and detail of these four papers, especially interesting are the common elements of approach. Whilst none saw the differentiation of illegal use of dual-use biotechnology from legal use as

Table 3.9   Initial State Party VEREX working papers*

No.	State	Title	Length (pages)
WP.1	UK	Verification of the BWC: Possible Directions	16
WP.2	France	Verification of the Biological Weapons Convention	16
WP.3	Netherlands	Discussion Paper	8
WP.4	Germany	Options for the Verification of the BWC	8

Note: *From Chapter 3, references 21–24.

a simple matter, all conveyed the impression of the task being a matter of proper practical organization. The United Kingdom's WP.1, for example, noted:

> As the primary operational objective is to detect non-compliance, candidate regimes should be evaluated in terms of their ability to achieve a reasonable probability of detecting non-compliance in a reasonable proportion of evasion scenarios ... [21]

But it went on to add: 'However, a verification scheme aimed at detecting evasion that even performs only moderately well, is likely to have a significant deterrent effect on potential evaders...' The paper then set out the main stages of a militarily significant programme and what elements should sensibly be targeted by the verification system. The paper then reviewed what might be learned from other verification regimes, paying particular attention to declarations and means of checking such declarations. A detailed annex (Annex B) of the paper reviewed what kinds of features in a facility inspectors would have to take into account when assessing compliance.

The paper from France[22] conveyed a similar message, stating that the 'aim would be to establish, on the basis of a number of convergent indicators, that a state was pursuing activities forbidden under the 1972 Convention'. Again, it was backed up by detailed consideration of the characteristics which would permit detection of an illegal programme. The paper from France stands out, however, by recalling that France did not initially join the BTWC because of the inadequacy of its verification provisions and later by noting that: '[S]ight must not be lost of the ultimate objective of the Group's work, namely, the elaboration of a set of measures resulting in the preparation of a *verification protocol*' (emphasis added). The paper concluded with proposals on how the Group of Experts might best organize their work to achieve this outcome.

The Netherlands paper similarly attempted to set the work of the government experts in a wider context, suggesting a phased approach to developing a BW verification regime, including:

  i. Expert group on technical matters;
 ii. Drafting and signing of an inspection protocol;
iii. Ratification, establishment of institutions;
 iv. Entry into force, operational phase.[23]

For the first – technical – phase, it then listed and began to address some of the significant questions such as the stages of a BW programme that should be targeted by a verification regime and what sources of information were presently available or could be developed.

The paper from Germany was again very clear on the aim: 'a possible verification regime will aim ... towards the detection of militarily significant biological weapons programs and the possible utilization of dual-use facilities and equipment for such programs ... '.[24] The paper went on to suggest that the way to solve the problem might be a regime consisting of:

– transparency of national biological and biotechnological programs by annual declaration of research and development and production activities,
– exchange of information gained from monitoring of biological agents and toxins as well as of relevant equipment for the production of biological materials,
– inspections at laboratories, production and storage facilities ...
– inspections at sites where an accidental or deliberate use of BW has taken place.

The paper ended with an attempt to produce an ordered list of keywords extracted from other studies/regimes which might be used as starting points in further discussions. This listing illustrates the extent to which thinking in 1992 was to foreshadow what later developed in the BTWC Protocol negotiations and the extent of detailed understanding of what would be required in an effective regime already present at that stage.

However, it would be a mistake to think that the consensus agreed for the Ad Hoc Group mandate indicated that all State Parties favouring a Protocol agreed about what should be possible. A working paper presented by South Africa to the 1994 Special Conference, for example, argued that declarations should form the nucleus of any verification regime, but that these were of little value if they were not verified in some way. The paper went on to argue that:

> Confirmation of security provisions at a facility, the nature of containment facilities, the presence of equipment for declared activities and changes in previously declared status, are all areas of useful information which can be verified during on-site visits without threatening commercial confidentiality.[25]

Furthermore, the paper suggested that if more intrusive measures were required for the investigation of suspect activities these would not be routine and the investigated party would be protected by an appeals procedure.

In a similar vein, a working paper presented by the UK reported on its programme of trial visits to four different facilities with characteristics that might be of concern. The objective was to: 'test whether sufficient access within the plant and to documentation could be given to demonstrate compliance with the BTWC, without unacceptable compromise to commercial confidentiality'.[26] The paper concluded, in part, that:

> Provided the inspection team is given sufficient access, and the definition of this will vary fron site to site, it is possible to determine with confidence that no non-compliant activities are being concealed. The degree of confidence depends on the nature and extent of access provided.

> Whenever inspectors can establish the internal consistency, technical and commercial plausibility of the evidence and explanations provided across as broad a range of site activities as possible, then the confidence in compliance increases dramatically.

Moreover, all of this was considered possible without great threat to commercial confidentiality.

In view of what was to happen later it is important to try to understand the position of the United States at this juncture. The tangled history of US official thinking from the Reagan years onwards has been described by Chevrier.[27] As we saw in Chapter 2, the CWC was made possible by a variation in the US position on verification so that it would accept a 'level of verification that gives a confidence to go forward'. In regard to the BTWC the US appeared still to be at odds with parties such as the UK and South Africa, which were to play a significant role in the coming negotiations. Table 3.10 sets out extracts from a US working paper presented at the 1994 Special Conference.[28]

Table 3.10   The US position at the 1994 Special Conference*

Extract A
The U.S. believes that the term 'effective verification' in the specialised context of formal arms control, refers to a set of measures designed to verify compliance with the provisions of a treaty with sufficient confidence to detect any militarily significant violation in time for other states parties to take appropriate countermeasures. In addition, an effective verification regime should safeguard non-relevant national security and industrial proprietary information and provide a net benefit to states parties' national security …

Extract B
This definition further assumes that measures are developed with an ability to distinguish between treaty prohibited and permitted activities with a minimum of ambiguity. The Ad Hoc Group of Experts [VEREX] recognised the great difficulty in meeting this condition but 'concluded that potential measures as identified and evaluated could be useful to varying degrees in enhancing confidence, through increased transparency, that states parties were fulfilling their obligations under the BWC'. Further, 'The group considered, from the scientific and technical standpoint, that some of the verification measures would contribute to strengthening the effectiveness and improve the implementation of the Convention'.

Even under this relaxed definition of verification: i.e., compliance enhancement, it is an extremely complex task to define as well as distinguish between 'treaty prohibited' and 'permitted activities' …

Note: *From Chapter 3, reference 28.

From extract A it would seem that the meanings of 'effective' and 'adequate' verification in standard US official discourse had been elided (see Preface). However, another possibility is that what the US chose to regard as militarily significant was activity on a far smaller scale than envisaged by States Parties such as the UK and South Africa. For whatever reason, it is quite clear from extract B that the US viewed the Protocol as to be constructed under a 'relaxed definition of verification: i.e. compliance enhancement' and even this was seen as being very difficult to achieve. So it would appear that from the outset the US was at odds with many States Parties which were looking to construct a much tighter regime to much higher standards of verification than the US thought advisable.

As we are particularly concerned here with the potential misuse of modern biotechnology as the genomics revolution spreads around the world, that industry and its possible future will be reviewed in the next chapter before a return to considering the negotiation of the BTWC Protocol by the Ad Hoc Group.

4
Genomics and the New Biotechnology

On 27 June 2000 the quality press struggled to find headlines adequate to mark the announcement that a draft of the whole human genetic code had been completed. In London *The Times* had the headline, 'Opening the book of life'[1] and the *Daily Telegraph*, 'All human life is here'.[2] The *International Herald Tribune* noted in its front-page story: 'The announcement was hailed almost universally as an achievement that ranks with the invention of the printing press and the splitting of the atom ... '.[3] John Sulston, director of the Sanger Centre in Cambridge which had played a major role in the research, was quoted as saying: 'Over the decades and centuries to come, this sequence will inform all of medicine, all of biology, and will lead us to a total understanding of not only human beings but all of life.'[4] There appeared to be little dissension from this viewpoint in the vast media coverage. Yet there were concerns expressed. The *International Herald Tribune*, for example, pointed out that: 'the question of how to regulate this powerful information is likely to challenge society for years to come, scientists and politicians said ... '. However, almost without exception, the question of regulation was raised in the quality press in regard to *civil* applications of the new knowledge. An altogether darker point was made by Professor Matthew Meselson, of the Department of Molecular and Cellular Biology at Harvard University, in the June 2000 edition of the *Chemical and Biological Weapons Conventions Bulletin*.[5] Meselson argued that every major new technology has been exploited intensively for *hostile purposes* as well as for peaceful ones. He then raised the crucial question, 'Must this also happen with biotechnology, certain to be a dominant technology of the twenty-first century?'

The view of the human blueprint becoming the basis for a vast new industry was made time and again in the media coverage of the first draft of the DNA sequence. The *Financial Times* front-page story had a second paragraph reading: 'The completion of a first draft of the DNA blueprint is set to open up new frontiers in medical science, accelerate the commercial use of biotechnology and pave the way for new treatments for inherited disease.'[6] On its inside pages the same paper had an article on the commercial exploitation of the human genome sequence entitled 'Stand by for a gene-rush'.[7] This article was written by the paper's pharmaceutical correspondent. He began by reviewing the key aspects of interest commercially, and how companies were responding to the new opportunities. Significantly, he ended by discussing the merger of Glaxo Wellcome and Smith Kline Beecham – and summarized as follows: 'In other words, the biggest pharmaceutical merger of all time was the direct result of the genetic Klondike. Glaxo Smith Kline is now preparing to throw a staggering $4bn a year at prizing golden nuggets from the genome.' As we saw in Chapter 2, the worldwide chemical industry is a massive mature enterprise, and the periodic table of chemical elements on which it is founded was elucidated long ago between 1869 and 1889.[8] The Human Genome Project's production of the sequence of human (and other) DNA is quite new, and it can hardly be of any surprise if the biotechnology industry on which it will impact is in a different situation, and perhaps state of mind, from the chemical industry during the recent negotiation of the Chemical Weapons Convention.

The 'old' biotechnology

One recent account of biotechnology put its aims rather succinctly:

> The biological sciences are dedicated to the exploration and comprehension of natural phenomena; biotechnology is about using these sciences as a basis for industry and commerce ... *biotechnology is fundamentally about making money with biology* ...[9] (emphasis added)

Biotechnology for making bread, cheese and alcoholic beverages dates back into prehistory.[10] Over the longer term it is possible to divide the development of the technology into a series of stages as the basic science and engineering knowledge was developed (Table 4.1). We can thus see that the development of modern microbiology at the end of the nineteenth century led to the rapid development of a new kind of technology increasingly capable of the specific manipulation of microorganisms for commercial purposes, first under non-sterile conditions, then under sterile conditions during the 1940s.

Table 4.1   The historical development of biotechnology*

1. *Biotechnological production of foods and beverages* (from prehistorical times through to the beginnings of scientific microbiology at the end of the nineteenth century).

2. *Biotechnological processes initially developed under non-sterile conditions* (production of ethanol, acetic acid etc. in open fermentation; waste-water and sewage treatment).

3. *Introduction of sterility to biotechnological processes* (required in the production of antibiotics, vaccines etc. as capabilities developed in the 1940s).

4. *Applied genetics and recombinant DNA* (traditional strain improvement of micro-organisms overtaken by capabilities to programme biological properties of organisms).

Note: *From Chapter 4, reference 10.

Table 4.2   Major products and worldwide market value in US$ millions in 1981 before commercial application of genetic engineering*

Alcoholic beverages	36 800
Cheese	23 800
Antibiotics	7 900
Industrial ethanol	3 625
High-fructose syrups	1 360
Amino-acids	1 275
Baker's yeast	920
Steroids	850
Vitamins	560
Citric acid	360
Enzymes	340
Vaccines	225
Polysaccharide gums	100

Note: *From Chapter 4, reference 11.

There is no doubt, however, that the decisive break came when genetic engineering – the ability to move genes between different species and have them function in the new genomes – was introduced in the early 1970s. Prior to the commercial application of genetic engineering, biotechnology was, of course, an industry of major significance worldwide (Table 4.2). All the products shown in Table 4.2 remain important, although many manufacturing processes have changed because of genetic engineering. The period since the first production of insulin from bacteria in 1982, however: 'is remarkable for the appearance in

Table 4.3 Examples of human proteins cloned in *E. coli* (bacteria)*

Erythropoietin	–	Stimulates hematopoiesis and is used to treat anaemia.
Growth hormone-releasing factor	–	Stimulates secretion of growth hormone and therefore promotes growth.
Serum albumin	–	Major protein of blood plasma used to supplement plasma.

Note: *From Chapter 4, reference 11.

rapid succession of widely used protein therapeutic agents whose production depends entirely on recombinant DNA technology'.[11] Some of these novel products are shown in Table 4.3.

Understanding the 'new' biotechnology

For most of human history what science there was had little connection with technology and production. These were craft skills which developed without the benefit of scientific understanding.[12] The modern world of the last few centuries has been shaped, on the other hand, by the application by technologists of a series of scientific revolutions in steam power, electricity, internal combustion engines, oil-based chemicals and electronic computing.

Students of such revolutions have stressed the complex social and institutional changes that are necessary, in addition to scientific knowledge, technological application and economic activity, in order for a new revolution to arise.[13] Yet it was becoming clear well before the first draft of the human genome sequence was produced that the new biotechnology was likely to be a core technology shaping human society in the early decades of the twenty-first century.[14] What is more, though the initial impact of this revolution was clearly seen to be in the healthcare sector, applications in agriculture, waste treatment, etc. were viewed as likely to be of major future importance.[15]

Humanity's potential future in the next 100 years, under the impact of this revolution, has perhaps been most eloquently predicted by Jeremy Rifkin: 'The Biotech Century brings with it a new resource base, a new set of transforming technologies, new forms of commercial protection to spur commerce, a global trading market to reseed the Earth with an artificial second Genesis…'[16] and, he continued, 'an emerging eugenics science, a new supporting sociology, a new communication tool to organize and manage economic activity at the genetic level, and a new cosmological narrative to accompany the journey…'. The main features of what Rifkin calls this new 'operational matrix' are set out in Table 4.4. It is not difficult to understand the excitement of those involved in this activity, even if one is concerned about the potential implications of such massive and rapid change.

Whilst Rifkin's description of the impact of this new scientific revolution may seem overly dramatic, there can be no doubt that the capabilities of biologists have undergone a fundamental change within a very short period of time. The key point is this: 'Life as we know it is specified by genomes. Every organism possesses a genome that contains the biological information needed to construct and maintain a living example of that organism ... '.[17] So by understanding, first, the structure of genomes, and then moving on to an understanding of how they function in the living organism, biologists will increasingly be able to modify an organism's operation in specific ways. This will be particularly true as the revolution in biology is progressively linked to the revolution in information technology.

The point was clearly made in a recent major review, 'Genomic medicine and the future of health care', in which the author noted: 'Decoding the genome – describing the connection between gene sequences and macroscopic life phenomena – is thus fundamentally a problem of describing and modelling biological information processes...'.[18] He went on to state: 'In practice, this implies the generation, processing, and analysis of large data sets. The outcome will be a quantitative and predictive understanding of life processes, from molecular detail to

Table 4.4   The new operational matrix in the biotech century*

- The ability to isolate, identify and recombine genes makes the gene pool available as a primary resource for economic activity.

- The awarding of patents in genes, tissues and organisms provides incentives to exploit these resources.

- The globalization of commerce and trade allows giant life science companies to wield enormous power over the world's biological resources.

- The mapping of the human genome and associated technologies opens up the possible future wholesale alteration of the human species.

- New scientific studies stress the importance of 'nature over nurture' and provide the cultural context for the acceptance of the new technologies.

- The information technology revolution and genetic technologies have fused to provide powerful new means of manipulation of genomic information.

- Our understanding of evolution is being reshaped to suggest that the new operational matrix is 'natural' and thus acceptable.

Note: *From Chapter 4, reference 16.

macroscopic phenotype, *that is a new predictive biology.*'(emphasis added) In short, we can say that biology will become a mechanistic science rather like classical physics. There will obviously be many new technological opportunities available, notably, in the first instance, in medicine and health care.

This is a particularly important issue in relation to the problem of strengthening the BTWC because the already powerful worldwide pharmaceutical industry is certain to expand to take advantage of these new opportunities. We know that the development of drugs, initially based on the new understanding of chemistry, has been a key feature of the progress of medicine over the last century. Then, in the mid-twentieth century, the discovery and development of penicillin began a new burst of expansion: 'After the discovery of penicillin and subsequently of other antibiotics, many drug companies established departments of microbiology and fermentation units which added to their technological scope ...'.[19] Yet modern understanding, more and more at the molecular level, suggests that there are many, many more targets for drugs than are presently being exploited. The new knowledge of genomes, the link with information technology and associated developments in the study of the structure of cellular proteins therefore seem likely, as with the initial developments one hundred years ago, to spawn a major new industrial revolution.

The pharmaceutical industry

In October 1991 the greatly esteemed, but now defunct, US Congress Office of Technology Assessment produced a study entitled *Biotechnology in the Global Economy.*[20] In line with the thrust of arguments presented here, the report stated: 'Biotechnology is not an industry. It is, instead, a set of biological techniques, developed through decades of basic research, that are now being applied to research and product development in several existing industrial sectors ...'. It went on to review in some detail major industrial sectors where biotechnology is being significantly employed. These sectors are the pharmaceutical industry, agriculture, the chemical industry and the environment.

The report then discussed industrial competitiveness and concluded:

> By many measures, the United States remains preeminent in biotechnology, based on strong research programs and well-established foundations in pharmaceuticals and agriculture. Broad-based, federally funded basic research – especially in biomedicine – is the hallmark of US capability in biotechnology ...

In addition to huge federal support, the US was also characterized by having many dedicated biotechnology companies and much available venture capital. Japan was seen as having strengths in biotechnology, even if it did not have such a strong research base. Additionally, in the view of the report's authors, 'Europe's strengths in pharmaceuticals and agriculture lend themselves to the adoption of biotechnology'. By this, of course, they meant the 'new' biotechnology based on genetic engineering and associated techniques.

These areas of concentrated strength obviously remain today, but genomics will have a worldwide impact on a growing pharmaceutical industry. The *Financial Times* reported in 1997, for example, that India was the world's second largest pharmaceutical market by volume of sales even though by value of sales it was only in thirteenth place.[21] Moreover, the article continued:

> drug consumption has been clipping along at an annual [growth] rate of 15 per cent for more than a decade...
> If it continues to grow at the same pace, as urbanisation and economic growth bring more people within reach of western medicine, India could overtake European countries such as Italy... within 10 years.

Many local Indian companies are likely to find it difficult to survive as pressure from the World Trade Organization brings India's patent laws into line with international standards, but there is no doubt that a number of indigenous companies will grow and thrive over coming decades.

The pharmaceutical companies of individual countries are often linked together in national associations such as the Association of the British Pharmaceutical Industry (ABPI). This association has as its main function the representation of the industry in the UK, in order to create: 'a favourable political and economic environment that encourages innovative research and development and affords fair commercial returns'.[22] Many national organizations are also linked together in the International Federation of Pharmaceutical Manufacturers Associations (IFPMA) which is based in Geneva. This federation deals with matters of common interest among its member organizations, promotes the development of the industry, and aims: 'to contribute expertise to and cooperation with national and international, governmental or nongovernmental, organizations'.[23] IFPMA was founded in 1968 and held its 19th Assembly in 1998 in Cape Town, South Africa. Thus the pharmaceutical industry is a well-established economic force worldwide and, as in the chemical industry, many of the pharmaceutical companies are household names. It will become clear in later chapters, however, that it is the American pharmaceutical industry which particularly concerns us here.

The US pharmaceutical industry

There is no agreed definition of what the biotechnology industry includes. In order, therefore, to carry out a census of potentially relevant US facilities in relation to strengthening the BTWC, Taylor and Johnson decided to: 'identify those industrial sectors and products that involve the use of key equipment and materials listed in the VEREX report'.[24] They then used the Standard Industrial Classification (SIC) codes to identify the relevant sectors. This approach produced the list of sectors shown in Table 4.5. The study explains that the first set of categories, in the drugs group, were chosen because they clearly contain terms of direct concern such as toxins, and involve processes using key items of equipment. Although in the food category, other products in the dairy industry involve fermentation, yoghurt production was chosen because of the large-scale methods in general use. Under the agriculture category, ethanol production was of interest – again because of the fermentation processes involved. Microbial pesticides were obviously also chosen because of the key equipment and materials involved.

The study concluded that in these industrial sectors at least 2000 facilities in the United States could be affected by the measures being

Table 4.5 Industrial categories of potential relevance to the BTWC*

	No.**
Drugs	
– Medicinal chemicals and botanical products	250
– Pharmaceutical preparations	750
– *In vitro* and *in vivo* diagnostic substances	236
– Biological products (except the diagnostics above)	268
Food	
– Yoghurt	143
– Beer	480
Agriculture	
– Fuel ethanol	57
– Microbial pesticides	12

Notes: *From Chapter 4, reference 24.

**The authors stress the approximate nature of these figures, it not being clear, for example, whether a company cited has more than one facility.

considered, but noted that the final number would depend on how discriminatory the measures were. The figures given in the study are included in Table 4.5 to give some indication of the upper limits of what might be involved. It is no surprise to find that these industrial sectors have associations devoted to guarding the common interests of the companies within them. For example:

> The International Dairy Foods Association (IDFA) is a Washington, DC-based dairy foods trade association that provides government relations, regulatory affairs ... and a host of other services to all facets of the industry ...

The IDFA is, in fact, an umbrella organization for three groups dealing with milk, cheese and ice-cream products.

The association of particular interest here, because it has taken a leading role and interest in the problem of strengthening the BTWC, is the Pharmaceutical Research and Manufacturers of America (PhRMA). This association was founded in 1958 and in 1997 it listed 61 major companies as members.[26] These included Eli Lilly, Merck and Pfizer. PhRMA's publicity material makes clear America's leading position in drug innovation in the world.[27] As shown in Table 4.6, some 45 per cent of drugs developed between 1975 and 1994 were from the United States. PhRMA also clearly believes that this pre-eminent position is based on an American system which fosters innovation, whereas many other countries have controls which discourage pharmaceutical research and development.

Table 4.6 Development of 152 global drugs by country of origin, 1975–1994*

	%
US	45
UK	14
Switzerland	9
Germany	7
Japan	7
Others	6
Belgium	5
Sweden	4
France	3

Note: *From Chapter 4, reference 27.

It is not, of course, the case that the pharmaceutical industries in developed countries lack regulation. Indeed, they are very highly regulated by governments which have a major interest in the safety of drugs put on sale by the healthcare sector.[28] Pharmaceutical production is subject to frequent and very intrusive government inspection and, if sales are to be made in other developed countries, often also to international inspection through reciprocal agreements.[29]

What characterizes the pharmaceutical industry, in the United States in particular, is the view that the very high costs of research and development and the relatively small number of drugs that actually make it to market through the long development process, mean a need for patent protection for some years after the drug becomes available in order that profits are made at the end of the process. PhRMA publications make this point quite emphatically. They argue that research-based pharmaceutical companies (that is, those innovating new drugs) have research and development costs of 20.8 per cent as a percentage of sales as opposed to, for example, 4.1 per cent in the automotive industry.[30] Moreover, even among those drugs which reach the market, only three out of ten produce revenues that match or exceed the average research and development costs.[31] As PhRMA notes, 'In other words, given the high costs and high risk of drug research, companies must rely on a limited number of highly successful products to finance their continuing R&D'. Without patent protection, it is argued, the finance to continue such research and development would simply not be forthcoming. The industry's concern over patent protection, and commercial confidentiality in general,[32] are thus not unexpected.

An added problem for the industry is that market forces have been driving a wave of mergers and consolidations. The standard chemistry-based techniques for producing small-molecule drugs have not been subject to radical improvement and keeping up productivity and investment, therefore, by the steady introduction of new drugs has not been easy to achieve.[33] But the switch to new technologies is very expensive. As the *Financial Times* noted, one major reason for consolidation: 'is the escalating cost of R&D, thanks largely to the proliferation of new technologies for discovering disease mechanisms and potential drugs ... '.[34] Even the biggest companies such as Merck, Pfizer, Bristol-Myers Squibb and Glaxo, this 1999 article suggested, 'cannot hope to compete across every disease area'. Indeed, it has been argued that genomics is already forcing a vast restructuring, not only of US pharmaceutical companies but also of major segments of other industries such as the chemical industry, and not just in the United States but around the world.[35]

What is of concern?

Given the combination of opportunity, threat and very rapid, large-scale change in the industry, it would hardly be surprising if the problem of strengthening the BTWC was not exactly the centre of attention for those involved in the US pharmaceutical industry or the new biotechnology in general.

Yet the activities of such industries must be of central concern to the BTWC strengthening process. To give just one simple example: most people would understand the word 'fermentation' to imply a process such as the production of alcohol by yeast cells growing, and thereby breaking down organic substances, in a bioreactor vessel.[36] However, such a bioreactor might also be used to grow a micro-organism into which a foreign toxin gene had been inserted, with the intention of obtaining large quantities of the toxin as the process was scaled up from laboratory through to pilot and then industrial-scale production.

This is not, of course, to argue that every activity and facility engaged in biotechnology would be of equal concern. Those facilities with expertise in handling dangerous pathogens or those with advanced capabilities which could be rapidly and effectively switched between different activities would surely be of greater concern to those hoping to prevent proliferation than a standard brewery or dairy plant. Clearly, the anti-proliferation authorities of major states would be careful not to announce too explicitly what would really be of concern to them, but we do have one recent example that can help to illuminate the problem.

During the 1991 Gulf War with Iraq, senior commanders were clearly worried that Iraq might use biological weapons against coalition forces. After the war the United Nations, in Security Council Resolution 687 (1991), established detailed measures for the ceasefire following Iraq's defeat. Section C of the resolution was concerned with the removal of Iraq's weapons of mass destruction, and with measures to prevent it obtaining such weapons again. Iraq was required to have items of concern destroyed or rendered harmless. These items included: 'All chemical and biological weapons and all stocks of agents and all related subsystems and components and all research, development, support and manufacturing facilities.'[37] Security Council Resolution 715 of October 1991 set out the plan for ongoing monitoring and verification to ensure Iraq's compliance.

In a recent detailed analysis of UNSCOM's efforts, Graham Pearson noted:

> Given the nature of biological weapons, effective monitoring in the biological area required monitoring of Iraq's basic biological research

potential, its stocks of micro-organisms and complex growth media, its biological production capability (i.e. fermenters and incubators), its ability to isolate micro-organisms from fermenter slurry (i.e. spray and drum driers) and to create particles of a size appropriate for biological warfare (milling machines), its ability to fill containers with biological materials and its ability to disperse such materials...

It must be stressed that Iraq was a country which had been defeated after waging an aggressive war and shown to have been attempting to obtain a range of weapons of mass destruction and related delivery systems. What was thought necessary to monitor in Iraq, therefore, has to be seen as the most *extreme* set of requirements. To reassure fellow States Parties to an international arms control agreement, arrived at voluntarily by participating states, would therefore require less than this set for regular monitoring, particularly if backed up with an element allowing investigation of suspicions.

In Pearson's view, the capabilities needing to be monitored in Iraq could be found in: 'biological laboratories (found in hospitals, universities and the food industry), biological production facilities (e.g. single-cell protein production, vaccine production, drug formulation and production, breweries and distilleries), and agricultural crop sprayers...'. Monitoring finally began in earnest in 1995, after many difficulties with Iraq, and Pearson states that 79 sites throughout Iraq were included in the monitoring related to biological weapons. The categories of sites are shown in Table 4.7. Nine of these sites were chosen for the most intensive monitoring, as they presumably presented the greatest danger, and 45 for the least intensive monitoring. Clearly, therefore, there is the

Table 4.7 Categories of sites chosen for monitoring in Iraq*

- Five sites currently known to have played a significant role in Iraq's past biological weapons programme.
- Five vaccine or pharmaceutical facilities.
- 35 research and university sites which have significant technology or equipment.
- 13 breweries, distilleries and dairies with dual-purpose capabilities.
- Eight diagnostic laboratories.
- Five acquisition and distribution sites of biological supplies/equipment.
- Four facilities associated with biological equipment development.
- Four product development organizations.

Note: *From Chapter 4, reference 37.

potential for a more discriminating approach in an arms control agreement focusing attention on the most critical sub-set of such a listing.

The absolute necessity of including civilian production sites in that sub-set was underlined once again in a paper in late 2000 by the Federation of American Scientists (FAS). They pointed out that:[38]

> It is now known that South Africa's former secret BW program had planned and intended to build a production facility with a single, 300 litre fermenter, as part of a 'front' company that conducted commercial contract research. Profit was not a serious concern ...

In the view of the FAS, 'If exempted from declaration, such facilities would make ideal covers for a BW program. This fact underscores the importance of requiring declaration of commercial production facilities'.

We turn now to the negotiations in Geneva which, in part, have tried to find a discriminating means to strengthen verification of the Biological and Toxin Weapons Convention through an agreement to monitor what would clearly be of most concern.

5
The Negotiation of the BTWC Protocol

As we saw in Chapter 3, the mandate given to the Ad Hoc Group (AHG) was complex, and it was recognized by the 1994 Special Conference that reaching a satisfactory agreement would not be straightforward.[1] A further level of complexity was due to the negotiations being genuinely multilateral. There are over 140 States Parties to the BTWC and it is clear, from the Procedural Reports[2] of the AHG, that at least one-third of them were regularly represented at the meetings of the AHG right from the start of the negotiations (Table 5.1).

Analysis of the early stages of negotiation also demonstrates that, despite the predominance of two States Parties (South Africa and the UK), a wide range of the participants produced working papers on particular aspects of the issues confronting the negotiators (Table 5.2). Notwithstanding a tendency for various groups of states to craft common positions on issues of concern, with so many active participants the achievement of a final agreement is obviously more difficult than in a bilateral negotiation. Furthermore, the required mode of operation is that a consensus has to be reached, and nothing is agreed until everything is agreed. In such circumstances, complex compromises have to be reached across a range of issues and there is plenty of opportunity for intended or unintended delay of the process.

A final difficulty in these negotiations is also apparent from analyses of the early stages of the negotiations.[3] The various States Parties had vastly different resources – as measured by the size of their delegations – to contribute to the AHG meetings. At the twelfth session in the autumn of 1998, for example, the delegation listed for the United States totalled 21 people. Other states had smaller delegations, and most had *much* smaller levels of representation (Table 5.3). Moreover, quite unlike the situation in many other arms control negotiations, there were very

Table 5.1   Participation of States Parties in the early meetings of the Ad Hoc Group*

Session	Participation	
	States parties	*Signatory states*[a]
I	51	—
II	52	1
III	52	1
IV	51	2
V	51	3
VI	51	2
VII	54	2
VIII	58	3
IX	54	3
X	49	3
XI	50	2
XII	57	3

Notes: *From Chapter 5, reference 2.
[a]Signatory states have signed but, unlike States Parties, not ratified the BTWC.

Table 5.2   Working Papers produced by various States Parties in early meetings of the AHG*[a]

Country	No. of working papers
South Africa	57
United Kingdom	41
Russian Federation	20
Japan	11
Canada, France, USA	10 each
Cuba	9
Brazil	8
Netherlands, Sweden	7 each
Australia, Iran	6 each
Argentina, Austria, China, Czech Republic, Germany, Indonesia, Italy, Korea, New Zealand, Switzerland, Turkey, Ukraine	5 or fewer each

Notes: *From Chapter 5, reference 2.
[a]As nearly all State Working Papers are produced by single states, and most of the rest by two states acting together, the very small number of multiple-authored State Working Papers are not included here.

Table 5.3 Numbers of delegates representing States Parties at the AHG in the 12th (XII) Session*

Size of delegation	Number of delegations of this size
1	7
2	11
3	12
4	6
5	6
6	5
7	2
8	1
9	2
10	2
11	2
12	3
12(+)	1

Note: *From Chapter 5, reference 3.

few well-informed non-governmental organizations (NGOs) providing independent ideas and analyses relevant to these negotiations. The deficit probably arose in good part from the traditional lack of interest in arms control shown by most biologists, and the almost total lack of knowledge of biology among most arms control specialists in NGOs and academia. The United Nations Institute for Disarmament Research (UNIDIR) in Geneva has traditionally provided information on biological arms control issues,[4] the Federation of American Scientists has long had a group interested in biological arms control,[5] and the Department of Peace Studies at Bradford University has taken an intensive interest in the work of the AHG,[6] but there has been little other long-term outside interest or involvement. The two major exceptions to this general rule, of course, have been the sustained involvement of the Pugwash CBW Study Group[7] and the work of the Harvard/Sussex Program on CB Armament and Arms Limitation.[8]

With that background, it is hardly surprising that there has been very little coverage of the AHG negotiations in the mass media. The overwhelming impression from the beginning has been that the AHG was carrying out an 'orphaned' negotiation, often overshadowed by other arms control issues involving chemical weapons, nuclear weapons, landmines, small arms and so on. In such circumstances there has been obvious concern over whether sustained high-level political interest could be maintained in major capitals around the world if the negotiations dragged on for a protracted period.[2,3]

The structure of the negotiation process

At its first meeting in January 1995, the AHG agreed rules of procedure and further decided that: 'for each session a report of a procedural nature should be prepared, which would have an annex containing the results of the work of the Ad Hoc Group'.[9] The negotiations can therefore be followed through the series of procedural reports and their associated annexes. Also at this first meeting, the Chairman, Ambassador Tibor Tóth of Hungary, indicated his intention to appoint Friends of the Chair (FOCs) to 'assist him in his consultations and negotiations on particular issues'. These issues addressed the four points stressed in the mandate and the (States Parties) groups from which the various FOCs were to be drawn were also indicated:

- Definition of Terms and Objective Criteria (Members of the Non-Aligned Movement);
- Confidence-Building and Transparency Measures (Eastern European Group);
- Measures to Promote Compliance (Western Group);
- Measures related to Article X (Members of the Non-Aligned Movement).

This process of using FOCs to deal with particular issues continued through the next five years. The list of FOCs at the 21st Session in December 2000[10] is set out in Table 5.4A. The number of FOCs obviously grew as the issues addressed by the AHG evolved and by that time it had also proved necessary to appoint a number of 'Facilitators' to assist the Ad Hoc Group in certain areas (Table 5.4B).

At the second session of the AHG in July 1995 the first four FOCs were appointed to cover the areas agreed at the first session. The group held 21 meetings and the FOCs reported on the separate topics in papers which were: 'without prejudice to the positions of the delegations on the issues under consideration in the Ad Hoc Group and [which did] not imply agreement on the scope or content...'.[11] The FOCs' papers, nevertheless, reflect the progress of the discussions on each of the topics.

Writing in the *CBW Conventions Bulletin* in December 1999, Ambassador Tóth suggested that the work of the AHG had gone through three stages: 'First, from 1995 to mid-1997 the preliminary work of the AHG

Table 5.4A Friends of the Chair at the 21st session*

Preamble
– Mr Malik Azhar Ellahi (Pakistan)

General Provisions
– Ambassador Hubert de La Fortelle (France)

Definitions of Terms and Objective Criteria
– Dr Ali A. Mohammadi (Islamic Republic of Iran)

Measures to Promote Compliance
– Ambassador Ian Soutar (United Kingdom of Great Britain and Northern Ireland)

Investigations
– Mr Peter Goosen (South Africa)

Confidentiality Issues
– Ambassador Dr Gunther Seibert (Germany)

Legal Issues
– Ambassador Leslie Luck (Australia)

Measures Related to Article X
– Mr Antonio de Aguiar Patriota (Brazil)

Declaration Formats
– Dr Anthony Phillips (United Kingdom of Great Britain and Northern Ireland)

Seat of the Organization
– Ambassador Seiichiro Noboru (Japan).

Note: *From Chapter 5, reference 10.

Table 5.4B Facilitators at the 21st session*

Harmonization of timelines for activities and measures in the Protocol
– Ambassador Ali Ashgar Soltanieh (Islamic Republic of Iran)

Structural harmonization of issues in the Protocol
– Ambassador Henrik Salander (Sweden)

Editorial issues in the Protocol
– Dr Ben Steyn (South Africa) and Dr John Walker (United Kingdom of Great Britain and Northern Ireland)

Decision on the establishment of a Preparatory Commission
– Mr Peter Goosen (South Africa), Mr Fu Zhigang (China) and Mr Gennady A. Loutai (Russian Federation)

The Headquarters Agreement with the Host Country
– Ambassador Donald A. Mahley (United States of America) who shall be assisted by Ambassador Krzysztof Jakubowski (Poland), Mr Adrian White (Australia), Mr Malik Azhar Ellahi (Pakistan), Ms Katarina Rangnitt (Sweden) and Sra Anayansi Rodriguez Camejo (Cuba) as well as additional personnel as considered necessary

Harmonization of legal aspects of the Protocol
– (to be appointed)

Note: *From Chapter 5, reference 10.

built upon the VEREX negotiations and final report to identify elements of a Protocol...'.[12] Then:

> The July–August 1997 session of the AHG witnessed the transition to a rolling text of the draft Protocol and initiated the second phase of the negotiations; the inclusion of detailed provisions in the Protocol and an intensification of the work of the AHG...

The move to a rolling text and an intensification of the work of the AHG had been called for at the Fourth Review Conference of the BTWC itself, in late 1996. Finally, according to Ambassador Tóth: '...January 1999 saw the third phase of the negotiations, the move to a final framework for the Protocol and the detailed negotiation on key elements'. It is helpful to examine separately what happened in each of these different phases.

The initial phase of negotiations

If the procedural reports of the first six sessions of the AHG (that is, before the Chairman produced the first version of the rolling text) are examined[3] it is clear that the dominant issue considered in the formal meetings was 'Measures to Promote Compliance'. Thirty-seven formal meetings were devoted to this matter alone while another four considered it alongside 'Definition of Terms and Objective Criteria'. The latter topic was second in importance as measured by number of meetings, 28 formal meetings being devoted to it. There were 18 meetings on 'Measures Related to Article X' and eight on 'Confidence-Building Measures' (Table 5.5).

If the papers produced by the various FOCs in Annex 1 of the procedural reports of Sessions II–VI are taken as another index of the differential importance of the different topics, it is obvious (Table 5.6) that 'Measures to Promote Compliance' stand out. 'Confidence-Building Measures', on the other hand, were of the least importance, and also appeared to be declining in importance. 'Definition of Terms and Objective Criteria' and 'Measures Related to Article X' each had about half the amount of accumulated text that was taken up by compliance measures. The number of Working Papers produced by the States Parties and Friends of the Chair on these four topics during the first six sessions produced a similar picture of concentration on the compliance measures aspect of the negotiation (Table 5.7).

Table 5.5 Formal meetings of the AHG on mandate topics during sessions I–VI[*]

Topic	Sessions					Topic Total
	II[a]	III	IV	V	VI	
Measures to promote compliance	9	6	7	7	8	37
Definition of terms and objective criteria	7	5	6[b]	4[b]	6	28
Measures related to Article X	2	4	3[b]	4[b]	5	18
Confidence-Building Measures	2	2	2[b]	2[b]	—	8
Consultation with international organisations	—	—	1	—	—	1
Joint meetings on Measures to Promote Compliance/Definition of Terms and Objective Criteria	—	—	—	—	4[b]	4
Technical issues	—	—	—	—	6	6
Session Total	21	20	20	20	30	

Notes: [*]From Chapter 5, reference 3.
[a]Where individual topic totals do not match stated overall totals, plenary meeting are assumed to make up the difference.
[b]Procedural reports also note some informal meetings/consultations on these topics.

Table 5.6 Number of pages of text on the FOC's topics in Annex I of procedural reports for sessions I–VI[*]

Topic	Sessions					Topic Total
	II	III	IV	V	VI	
Measures to promote compliance	17	30	36	13	40	136
Definition of terms and objective criteria	10	7	15	20	18	70
Measures related to Article X	10	6	16	28	11	71
Confidence-Building Measures	5	13	14	14	—	46
Session Total	42	56	81	75	59	

Note: [*]From Chapter 5, reference 3.

Table 5.7   Number of working papers produced by States Parties and Friends of the Chair on the topics under discussion in AHG sessions I–VI*

Topic	Sessions					Topic Total
	II[a]	III	IV	V	VI	
Measures to promote complianceb	10	21	17	12	25	85
Definition of terms and objective criteria	12	13	13	7	6	51
Measures related to Article X	5	10	3	2	5	25
Confidence-Building Measures	1	6	3	—	—	10
Other	—	1	1	—	1	3
Session Total	28	51	37	21	37	

Notes: *From Chapter 5, reference 3.
   aIncludes one paper from First Session. Nomenclature of papers changes in first three sessions but all have been included here.
   bInvestigations of alleged use have been included under compliance measures in this table.

The Fourth Review Conference of the BTWC

At its fifth session in the autumn of 1996, the AHG agreed to report to the Review Conference that:

> The Ad Hoc Group has made significant progress towards fulfilling the mandate given by the Special Conference including by identifying a preliminary framework and elaborating potential basic elements of a legally-binding instrument to strengthen the Convention.[13]

However, the report continued:

> Nevertheless, the Ad Hoc Group was not able to complete its work and submit its report including a draft of the future legally-binding instrument to the States Parties for consideration at the Fourth Review Conference. ... In order to fulfil its mandate the Ad Hoc Group has decided to intensify its work with a view to completing it as soon as possible before the commencement of the Fifth Review Conference ...

And, as we saw from Ambassador Tóth's review in 1999, the Fourth Review Conference welcomed the decision of the AHG to intensify its work. Indeed the conference declaration added: 'The Conference encourages the Ad Hoc Group to review its method of work and *to move to a negotiating format* in order to fulfil its mandate.'[1] (emphasis added) That agreement to move to a rolling text did, however, conceal some strong differences in perspective.

John Holum, Director of the US Arms Control and Disarmament Agency, asked:

> What about the pace of this work? The Ad Hoc Group itself recently decided upon a more rigorous approach, to intensify its efforts with a view towards completing its work as soon as possible before the Fifth Review Conference in 2001. But let me suggest that in the light of the mounting BW danger, such a timetable is still inappropriately relaxed. ... *most of the States Parties here today could identify and write down the essential elements for a protocol.*[14] (emphasis added)

Mr Berdennikov, head of the Russian delegation, on the other hand argued:

> Russia is in favour of intensifying the Group's activities. We are in favour of a full-scale negotiation process. At the same time we are against an artificial forcing of events that would be prejudicial to the final results, *we do not consider justified the attempts to impose artificial time frames for the Group's work.* The activities of the Ad Hoc Group should end when it completes its mandate in full.[15] (emphasis added)

Similarly, Ambassador Tarmidzi of Indonesia stated:

> Some delegations have already stated that they wish to see the Ad Hoc Group of the States Parties to the Convention complete the verification protocol in 1998. While fully sharing their concern that the absence of a verification regime would render the Convention ineffective. ... *A predetermined deadline, particularly one which has not been agreed by all participating states, would only prevent us from achieving the universality of the verification regime in the future...*[16] (emphasis added)

Such differences reflected divisions both about wider disarmament problems and about how the protocol to the BTWC was to be constructed. The fact that an agreement was not reached in 1998, in 1999, nor even in 2000, indicates just how deep were the divisions that existed.

The first stages of rolling text development, 1997–1998

Given the prominence of South Africa's input to the work of the AHG, it is perhaps not surprising that there was some impatience in the statement of its representative to the Fourth Review Conference:

> Although South Africa agrees that the intensification of the work of the Ad Hoc Group would require an increase in the amount of time allocated to the group, the mandate of the group, in our view, will only be fulfilled through the improvement of the Group's working methods and through greater commitment by all States Parties. Since the work completed so far has reached an advanced stage, we wish to encourage the Ad Hoc Group to move towards a 'rolling text' format as soon as possible.[17]

South Africa then proposed, not surprisingly, the first outline structure of the protocol at the sixth session of the AHG in early 1997.[18] The procedural report noted:

> The Ad Hoc Group in its informal consultations considered as well the possible structural elements of a legally binding instrument to the Biological Weapons Convention. The outcome of the discussion on that issue is reflected in a paper annexed to the present report (Annex II)...[19]

The Chairman of the AHG presented the first version of the 'rolling text' at the seventh session in mid-1997,[20] and by the end of 1998 a further five substantive versions of this text had been produced.[3]

The basic structure of the intended protocol remained essentially the same throughout this period. This structure can be seen in the listing of the Articles, Annexes and Appendices in the sixth version of the rolling text (Table 5.8) from the 12th session.[21] Nevertheless, the rolling text was substantially developed, growing from some 18 000 to 76 000 words between the first and sixth versions. Yet within the overall expansion there were great variations (Table 5.9). Article I (General Provisions), Article VIII (Confidence-Building Measures), Annexes C (Measures to Strengthen the Implementation of Article III) and F (Scientific and Technological Exchange for Peaceful Purposes and Technical Cooperation), for example, still had no text by the end of 1998. On the other hand, the administrative Articles XI–XXIII had been agreed early on. Steady expansion of text clearly had taken place in regard to Article III

Table 5.8 Structure of the verification Protocol*

Preamble	
Article I	General Provisions
Article II	[Definitions]
Article III	Compliance Measures
Article IV	Confidentiality Provisions
Article V	Measures to Redress a Situation and Ensure Compliance
Article VI	Assistance and Protection Against Biological and Toxin Weapons
Article VII	[Scientific and Technological Exchange for Peaceful Purposes] [Implementation Assistance] and Technical Cooperation
Article VIII	Confidence-Building Measures
Article IX	[The Organization] [and Implementation Arrangements]
Article X	National Implementation Measures
Article XI	Relationship of the Protocol to the BWC and Other International Agreements
Article XII	Settlement of Disputes
Article XIII	Review of the Protocol
Article XIV	Amendments
Article XV	Duration and Withdrawal
Article XVI	Status of the Annexes and Appendices
Article XVII	Signature, XVIII Ratification, XIX Accession, XX Entry into Force, XXI Reservations, XXII Depositary(ies), XXIII Authentic Texts.

Annexes
  A. Declarations
  B. [Visits]
  C. [Measures to Strengthen the Implementation of Article III]
  D. Investigations
  E. Confidentiality Provisions
  F. Scientific and Technological Exchange for Peaceful Purposes and Technical Cooperation
  G. Confidence-Building Measures

Appendices
  A. [Information to be Provided in Declarations of Past Biological and Toxins Offensive and/or Defensive Research and Development Programmes]
  B. [Information to be Provided in Declarations of [Biological] Defence Programmes [Against Biological Weapons]]
  C. Information to be Provided in Declarations of Facilities
  D. [List of Approved Investigation/Visit Equipment]

Note: *From Chapter 5, reference 21.

(Compliance Measures), Annex A (Declarations), Annex D (Investigations) and the Appendices, with some expansion in other areas such as Article VII and IX early on and Annex B at later stages.

Despite such development of the rolling text, it was clearly far from a complete, agreed document by the end of 1998. As noted in the

Table 5.9 Number of pages of text on the articles, annexes and appendices of the six versions of the rolling text of the verification Protocol, 1997–98*

Topic	Version					
	I (35)[a]	II (36)	III (38)	IV (39)	V (41)	VI (43)
Preamble	1	4	4	4	4	4
Articles						
I	1	1	1	1	1	1
II	—	5	6	7	9	9
III	29	31	36	37	47	58
IV	1	1	2	3	3	3
V	1	1	1	1	1	1
VI	1	1	3	3	3	3
VII	8	9	10	9	10	10
VIII	1	1	1	1	1	1
IX	1	18	14	15	15	14
X	1	1	1	1	1	1
XI–XIII	12	15	17	17	16	13
Annexes						
A	14	24	26	30	37	24
B	1	1	1	6	6	11
C	1	1	1	1	1	1
D	6	25	64	40	40	41
E	1	1	3	16	11	12
F	1	1	1	1	1	1
G	15	13	12	17	18	16
H	—	—	10	11	—	—
Appendices	12	8	18	16	22	44
Total[b]	114	172	247	247	257	283

Notes: *From the relevant versions of the 'Rolling Text' as shown in brackets.
   [a] The first version of the 'Rolling Text' had Article I (Basic Obligations), Article II (Compliance Measures). A new Article II (Definitions) was inserted in the second version. I have re-ordered the Articles of the first version to fit the later scheme.
   [b] As some pages are blank, the total of pages can sometimes differ from the sum of the sections of text.

Procedural Report of the twelfth session (and all other reports pertaining to the rolling text):

The results of the discussions are attached to this report (Annex I) [containing the rolling text]. In addition to the statement of the Chairman that the position of delegations is not prejudiced by this paper, individual brackets have been introduced to cover specific preliminary concerns of delegations and it is recognised that further and detailed consideration of all elements will be required at future sessions.[21]

It will be seen (Table 5.8) that the elements bracketed in late 1998 extended even to the titles of some articles of the proposed text.

However, the Procedural Report for the eleventh session of June–July 1998[22] had contained an attached Working Paper 293 on Annex D – Investigations, by the Friend of the Chair, 'to provide delegations with the opportunity to study the proposals therein during the intersessional period'. As one commentator noted:

> There was also evidence that text is now being consolidated and developed with a move towards production by the Friends of the Chair of clean texts in which language without square brackets was being prepared. An indication of this is provided by the working paper (WP.293) prepared by the Friend of the Chair on the Investigations Annex...[23]

This process was taken further in the twelfth session. The Procedural Report notes:

> 7. Proposals for future consideration from the Chairman and Friends of the Chair on the respective parts of the Rolling Text regarding the work undertaken in the respective areas are attached in Annex IV without prejudice to the positions of the delegations...[21]

The papers produced in this Annex IV are shown in Table 5.10. It must be emphasized, however, that the Procedural Report noted right after item 7 quoted above that, '[I]t was reaffirmed that the Rolling Text is the only basis for negotiations in the Ad Hoc Group'. There was clearly still a long way to go.

The later stages of the negotiations, 1999–2000

Though the negotiations of the Protocol to the BTWC featured rarely in the mass media, the later stages of the negotiations are somewhat easier to follow since a regular review by Graham Pearson[24] appeared in the *CBW Conventions Bulletin*, and *Disarmament Diplomacy*[25] also carried a regular report, first by Henrietta Wilson, and then by Jenni Rissanen. Thus the technical and academic material concerned with the negotiations that was available in the public record gradually became more and more substantial. The negotiators also continued to develop and produce

Table 5.10   Friends of the Chair papers, October 1998*

Title	Reference
Proposals for further consideration by the Friend of the Chair on the Investigations Annex	BWC/AD HOC GROUP/FOC/1
Proposals for further consideration by the Friend of the Chair on Measures to Promote Compliance	BWC/AD HOC GROUP/FOC/2
Proposals for further consideration by the Friend of the Chair on Confidentiality	BWC/AD HOC GROUP/FOC/3
Proposals for further consideration by the Chairman on Organization/ Implementational Arrangements	BWC/AD HOC GROUP/FOC/4
Proposals for further consideration by the Friend of the Chair on Legal Issues	BWC/AD HOC GROUP/FOC/5
Proposals for further consideration by the Friend of the Chair on Measures Related to Article X	BWC/AD HOC GROUP/FOC/6
Proposals for further consideration by the Friend of the Chair on Measures to Promote Compliance	BWC/AD HOC GROUP/FOC/7

Note: *From Chapter 5, reference 21.

new versions of the rolling text (Table 5.11). Additionally, from the October 1998 Report (BWC/AD HOC GROUP/43) onwards an annex in Part II also contained papers prepared by the Friends of the Chair containing proposals for further consideration in which the rolling text was modified in a transparent way. In the June/July 1999 session: 'For the first time, the 177 page Part II ... text reflects the structure of the Protocol with Friends of the Chair proposed language for the Articles, Annexes and Appendices of the Protocol ... '.[26] Pearson noted that the FOCs' text provided a 'vision' of how the Protocol might eventually look.

Nevertheless, the only official text remained the developing rolling text, but even there confusion could easily arise. As one of the earlier *Quarterly Reports* pointed out:

> It is important to emphasise that each new version of the rolling text is made up of relatively small sections with new language surrounded by much larger sections of older text which are *not* revised because there is insufficient time in the session for each FOC to review in his meetings all of the text for which he is responsible ...[27]

Table 5.11 Later versions of the rolling text*

Year	Version	Procedural report
2000		
November/Dec.	14	BWC/AD HOC GROUP/54
July/August	13	BWC/AD HOC GROUP/52
April	12	BWC/AD HOC GROUP/51
February	11	BWC/AD HOC GROUP/50
1999		
October	10	BWC/AD HOC GROUP/47
July	9	BWC/AD HOC GROUP/46
April	8	BWC/AD HOC GROUP/45
January	7	BWC/AD HOC GROUP/44
1998		
September/October	6	BWC/AD HOC GROUP/43
June/July	5	BWC/AD HOC GROUP/41
February	4	BWC/AD HOC GROUP/39

Note: *From Chapter 5, reference 24.

By way of illustration, the review went on to point out that the rolling text of January 1999 contained language in Article III on a variety of different kinds of visits and that this language had arisen from a range of sources (indicated in brackets):

Randomly-selected Visits (new):

Clarification Procedures and Voluntary Visit/Declaration Clarification Procedures (WP.338/WP.347 respectively):

Voluntary visits (as in the previous rolling text);

Voluntary Confidence-Building (as in the previous rolling text together with new South African text on voluntary visits from WP.336).

As the review commented, 'It is therefore easy to be confused about the latest terminology if the language in the rolling text is taken at its face value without giving due consideration to which is the most recent text'.

In addition to the rolling text, States Parties continued to contribute Working Papers on aspects of the negotiations. By the end of 2000 there were some 451 Working Papers in total.[24] As was noted for the earlier period alone, the South Africans had produced most papers (76 in total) and the UK had produced the second largest total (43). Russia had produced 27 Working Papers and eight other States Parties had produced 10 or more. By the end of the year 2000, however, there were very clear signs that the technical development of the text had come to an end. Political decisions on complex compromises would be required to bring the negotiations to closure.

One further complication that needs to be borne in mind when considering the development of the Protocol negotiations is that different parts of the text had developed at different rates. For example, by June 1999 the *Quarterly Review* had noted: 'The overall assessment that emerges is that in a number of areas such as legal issues, confidentiality, organization, national implementation, assistance and Annex D. Investigations the text for the Protocol is well developed'.[28] It continued, though: 'There are three principal areas – Article III Compliance Measures (and its associated Annexes and Appendices), Article VII Technical Cooperation and Article III [Definitions] – where more work remains to be done...'. The Friend of the Chair dealing with the 100 pages concerned with the whole issue of Compliance Measures clearly faced the largest task.

Nevertheless, by December 1999 the *Quarterly Review*[29] was noting that in the September–October session there had been a sharp reduction (from 31 to 11) in the number of sessional Working Papers produced. This trend continued, with only three new Working Papers being produced in the December 1999 session. As the *Quarterly Review* pointed out: '[T]his continued reduction shows that everything that is needed is *already* in the draft Protocol, and there is no need for additional Working Papers to add additional ideas or alternative language'.[30] This trend went further in the January–February 2000 session of the AHG, with only two Working Papers being submitted.

At the end of January 2000, as noted by the *Quarterly Review*, Chairman Tóth pointed out to a meeting in Paris: 'the draft Protocol already had 60 per cent fewer square brackets proportionally than the CTBT text had some 3.5 months before the CTBT negotiation had been completed'.[30] The Chairman therefore argued that the Protocol could be completed in 2000 and urged the negotiators to undertake more joint efforts to reach this conclusion. This theme of the possibility of, and need for, completion of the Protocol was much in evidence in the March 2000 19th session of the AHG as it coincided with the 25th anniversary of the entry-into-force of the BTWC. Numerous political statements and two NGO seminars reiterated the theme. Moreover, as the *Quarterly Review* noted, one NGO presentation included a paper entitled *The BTWC Protocol: Proposed Complete Text for an Integrated Regime* which had: 'a complete clear text for the Protocol which sought to introduce realism and to strike a balance between the different aspirations so as to arrive at a worthwhile and valuable Protocol acceptable to all states parties'.[31] This paper was widely distributed to delegations, as were two updated versions later in the year.

The July–August 2000 20th session of the AHG saw a further indication of the approaching end of the negotiations as the Chairman: '... initiated a series of bilateral consultations with the representatives of the states parties...to address those issues...on which there were strong conceptual differences in views...'.[32] These differences had been delineated at the March 2000 session when the Friends of the Chair had categorized differences as they saw them, in the February AHG/50 (Part I) rolling text, into three groups. Category I were seen as involving little controversy and being easy to resolve, Category II as involving medium levels of disagreement and Category III as involving strong conceptual differences in views. A marked text became available in which the increasing levels of difficulty in relevant areas of text were indicated in yellow (Category I), green (Category II), and red (Category III). The Chairman conducted some 90 bilateral meetings in the four-week session on the Category III issues while the Friends of the Chair dealt with the Category I and II issues.

This change in working methods was continued in the November–December 2000 21st session of the AHG, with the *Quarterly Review* suggesting that:

> the previous more formal methods of work have achieved as much as possible in developing agreed text and in the removal of square brackets, and there is a need now to explore new informal and formal ways of reaching solutions that will attract wide support.[24]

At this session the Chairman also appointed a number of Facilitators additional to the Friends of the Chair in order to consider matters such as harmonization of timelines and editorial issues necessary for completion of the Protocol. Further indication of the end of the negotiations was the presentation, on the penultimate day, of the cases for the two candidates – the Netherlands and Switzerland – for the seat of the future organization.

As if to finalize this transition to an entirely different mode of operation, the December 2000 *Quarterly Review* noted: 'The outcome of the July/August session was produced as a complete update of the Protocol issued as Annex 1 of the procedural report (BWC/AD HOC GROUP/54). This was thus the fourteenth version of the rolling text...'.[24] It also pointed out that: 'unlike in previous procedural reports there was no Part II containing papers prepared by the Friends of the Chair of proposals for modified text for further consideration ... '. The review went on to argue that this reflected the changing form of the negotiations.

There was clearly now a variety of methods being used to bring the negotiations to closure including, for example, 'bracket bazaars' in which proposals that looked as if they could attract wide support were brought before the AHG for approval. In particular, the review noted that in the November–December session:

> the Chairman has provided delegations with written elements related to certain parts of the text in order for delegations to look at these and consider the ideas contained in them so as to come back to him with their views for how the text may be developed so as to attract wide support ... [24]

These written elements were stated to include some from 'declarations, declaration follow-up procedures, investigations, transfers. ... cooperation', that is, from areas where major differences remained.

Despite all these hopeful indicators of progress towards a conclusion to the negotiations, it was also evident to experienced commentators that much more work was required. One person who had been deeply involved in the endgame of the Chemical Weapons Convention negotiation, Robert Mathews, suggested that, in addition to the change to a less formalistic negotiation in the AHG, a range of 'capital-based activities' (that is, work in the ministries of major countries) was also required.[33] These included surveys of relevant facilities, practice visits, practice investigations, interactions with the biotechnology industry, BWC national authority preparations and regional activities. It was alarming that it was necessary for such suggestions to be made by an informed commentator in early 2000 – after five years of work by the AHG. It strongly suggested that some key states were less than enthusiastic supporters of an early, effective conclusion to the negotiations.

In his opening remarks to the 22nd session of the AHG in February 2001, the Chairman was quite blunt in his assessment of the situation:

> I have given considerable thought to the working methods of the Ad Hoc Group over the last eight weeks. I stated in my concluding remarks at the last session that the preliminary figures on square brackets indicated numerical stagnation in terms of un-bracketing, or

cleaning up, the rolling text. More comprehensive figures available now confirm this stagnation. Indeed, in certain areas and places we are going backwards...[34]

Later in his remarks Ambassador Tóth pointed out that:

> We have nine weeks to complete our work and such work includes not only finalizing the rolling text and agreeing on a Protocol that is acceptable to all. We also have to draft our own report, consider in detail issues relating to the Preparatory Committee for the future Organization and convene a Special Conference to adopt the report before November 2001. Let us not underestimate the scale of the task before us...

Turning finally to what, in his judgement, was required of the delegations, he concluded:

> I stated at the end of the last session that in my own judgement delegations should return in 2001 with instructions and proposals that lead us to the necessary compromises. If, as individuals, delegations and as the Ad Hoc Group we are serious about completing our work in the timeframe before us, then the time for expecting other delegations to move in a certain direction while you stand still – that time is over. Every single delegation, in my judgement, here now has to move from its long-standing favoured options towards a middle-ground that brings an acceptable compromise to all delegations...

Serious issues and differences between the different delegations obviously remained at the start of the year 2001.

In his analysis of early 2000 Mathews had argued[33] that it would help to conclude negotiations in that year if the Chairman could provide a clean text to 'help focus minds on how the eventual Protocol might look'. At the 22nd AHG meeting in February 2001, it was reported that, following on from Ambassador Tóth's opening statement, South Africa's representative took the floor and suggested that:

> the moment had now arrived for a new methodology to be adopted, and for the Chair to issue his 'best guestimate' of the compromises that should be considered as the basis for concluding the negotiations: a complete vision text through which delegations could see the full picture...[35]

South Africa's position was reported to be strongly supported by some delegations and opposed by others. This commentary by Jenni Rissanen ended by putting forward a very pessimistic possibility:

> With only nine weeks of negotiations this year [2001], Tóth is under extreme pressure. There is a general feeling that this session will not see the introduction of the vision text, but that this may happen in the period between this and the next session, due to begin on April 23rd. If it is not issued by then, some may argue that the AHG deadline is certain to be missed, and *perhaps the whole game lost.* (emphasis added)

What then were the strong differences blocking compromise?

The strong conceptual differences

The overall configuration of the Protocol just prior to the initiation of the new methods of working in mid-2000 as just described can be obtained from the structure of the rolling text in the document BWC/ AD HOC GROUP/54 – the fourteenth version (Table 5.12). While this gives a good picture, for example, of the dominating importance of Compliance Measures (Article III), it does not give an obvious insight into the nature of the differences dividing the States Parties to the negotiations.

This information can, though, be gathered from the categorized version of the earlier text (BWC/AD HOC GROUP/50 Part I) in which, as noted previously, the levels of differences were picked out in various colours in an electronic version. The areas of strong conceptual differences were listed in three sub-categories by Pearson et al. in an introduction to their second version of a complete Protocol text in mid-2000.[36]

The three sub-categories used were: A. Key Issues; B. Other Issues; and C. Further Issues. The first eleven issues identified were these:

A. Key Issues
1. Red light/green light initiation procedure for investigations;
2. Randomly-selected visits to all declared facilities;
3. Thresholds;
4. Modification, particularly to Article I of the BTWC...;
5. Transfer guidelines (Article III of the BTWC...);
6. Cooperation Committee role;
7. Biodefence in Article VII of the Protocol;

Table 5.12 Articles, annexes and appendices of the rolling text in BWC/AD HOC GROUP/54*

		Number of pages
Preamble		3
Article I	[General Provisions]	3
Article II	Definitions	8
Article III	Compliance Measures	69
Article IV	Confidentiality Provisions	2
Article V	Measures to Redress a Situation and to Ensure Compliance	1
Article VI	Assistance and Protection Against Biological and Toxin Weapons	3
Article VII	Scientific and Technological Exchange for Peaceful Purposes and Technical Cooperation	12
Article VIII	Confidence-Building Measures	1
Article IX	The Organization	14
Article X	National Implementation Measures	1
Article XI	Relationship of the Protocol to the BTWC	1
Article XII	Settlement of Disputes	1
Article XIII	Review of the Protocol	1
Article XIV	Amendments, Article XV Duration and Withdrawal, Article XVI Status of the Annexes and Appendices, Article XVII Signature, XVIII Ratification, XIX Accession, XX Entry into Force, XXI Reservations, XXII Depositary(ies), XXIII Authentic Texts	12

Annexes

A.	Declarations	18
B.	[Measures to Strengthen the Implementation of Article III]	1
C.	Investigations	42
D.	Confidentiality Provisions	7
E.	Scientific and Technological Exchange for Peaceful Purposes and Technical Cooperation	1
F.	Confidence-Building Measures	13

Appendices

A.	Declarations of Offensive and/or Defensive Biological and Toxin Programmes and/or Activities Conducted Prior to Entry into Force of the Protocol for Each State Party	11
B.	Declarations of Defensive Biological and Toxin Programmes and/or Activities Conducted During the Previous Year	7
C.	Facilities	40
[D.	Listing of Facilities Participating in Biological Defensive Activities]	1
[E.	Facilities Existing on the Territory of a State Party but Falling under the Jurisdiction or Control of Another State Party/State]	3
F.	Information to be Provided in the Declarations Required under Paragraphs ... of Article VII	1
G.	[List of Approved Investigation/Visit Equipment]	4
[H.	Standardized Formats for Reporting International Transfers of Equipment]	1
	Total Pages	281

Note: *From Chapter 5, reference 10.

8. Clarification procedures regarding facilities that appear to meet guidelines for declaration and have not been declared;

B. Other Issues

1. Declaration Triggers (BL-3, Work with Listed Agents, Other Production Facilities, Other Facilities, Outbreaks);
2. Date for initial declarations (1925, 1946, 1975);
3. Documentation availability during visits/investigations;

This was clearly a diverse set of issues reflecting the fact that various States Parties were pursuing different outcomes across a range of topics.

Some analyses in the open literature have attempted to gather together the different issues under coherent headings and to specify where the fracture planes lay between the different parties or groups of parties.[37] One specific problem concerned *Transfer/Export Control Regimes*, where many developing countries wished to see a rapid dismantling of export controls in order to increase the availability of technology for development, but where many developed countries feared that a rapid relaxation of export controls would open up new avenues for proliferation. This clearly became an emotive issue in the negotiations where it was difficult to find pragmatic compromises despite the overall move towards international regulation of transfers of much dual-use material.[38]

The envisaged Protocol would have to have *declarations* of a range of relevant facilities and activities. However, there was obviously much room for disagreement over precisely how the triggers (which would determine which facilities should be declared) should be designed. Again there were differences between the developed and developing worlds. 'The developed countries are aiming for the triggers to strike the right balance so that the most relevant facilities are declared in all countries without placing a disproportionate burden on themselves...'.[37] On the other hand: 'The developing countries, however, want to see the burden placed primarily on the developed countries, who have the most facilities of concern to the BWC, and therefore advocate triggers that would accomplish such a result.' Additionally, though it is generally agreed that some form of *declaration follow-up procedures* are needed, there are differences over what should be visited:

Some non-aligned states suggest that only biodefence and maximum containment facilities should receive randomly selected/transparency visits – effectively ensuring that only facilities in the developed countries would be subject to these visits...[37]

Morover, some non-aligned states argue that *clarification visits* should not apply to facilities that appear to meet the criteria for declaration but have not been declared, whereas the Western Group of states believe that an effective regime requires that such facilities should be subject to clarification visits.

Besides the differences between major groups of states, there were manifestly also differences within groups. Though South Africa was within the Non-Aligned Group it obviously and consistently played a very much more proactive role in attempting to achieve a protocol than other states in the group, which were considerably more concerned about the outcomes and thus much more willing to take whatever time was required. In the Western Group there were also differences that surfaced in the public domain. In regard to the crucial issue of *initiation of investigations*:[37]

> European states and most others in the Western Group, though not the United States, favour a strong regime in which a requested investigation would take place unless a majority of the executive council votes to *stop* it (the so-called red-light procedure)... (emphasis added)

This would be equivalent to the agreed process in the CWC (which, it will be recalled, also covers two toxins – saxitoxin and ricin). However:

> some of the non-aligned countries and the United States argue for a much weaker regime in which a requested investigation would not take place unless a majority of the executive council votes *for* it to take place (the so-called green-light procedure)... (emphasis added)

This position of the United States is perhaps somewhat surprising, given the views of its representative Ambassador Holum quoted earlier in the chapter.

Another difference was between Russia and most other states. Most states appear to be very cautious about the danger of *defining terms* in the Protocol in such a way as to appear to restrict the General Purpose Criterion of the Convention itself, but:

> this has not prevented some states, notably Russia and the Ukraine, from proposing definitions that would effectively modify basic prohibitions laid out in Article I of the convention – terms such as 'biological weapons', 'biological agents', and 'hostile purposes'...[37]

Similarly, some states have argued for the use of *threshold quantities* below which it would be permitted to retain agents. But given the ability to rapidly grow such agents, this approach is not acceptable to most delegations.

It can therefore be seen that there are many important issues that need tracing in detail in order to determine precisely what happened in the negotiations and why. In the next two chapters one such set of issues – declarations and visits – will be pursued because it seems absolutely critical for the attainment of an effective agreement controlling the most relevant facilities and activities. This will lead to a detailed examination of the positions taken by some states and other interested parties. It should be noted, however, that equally searching investigations would be appropriate in regard to the other issues highlighted above.[38]

6

Compliance Measures: Declarations and Visits

As we saw in Chapter 5, the long decade of investigations and negotiations since the Third Review Conference of 1991 had, by December 2000, produced an almost 300-page document constructed with enormous effort by various States Parties in an attempt to meet the requirements of the mandate to strengthen the Convention. Yet there were clearly differences in the views of various states over how quickly the work should be carried out and over the relative importance of the different objectives. Indeed it was possible to discern a number of different objectives, and different perceptions of the importance of various aspects of the Protocol, amongst the States Parties negotiating in the AHG. In an article written in 1998 and devoted mainly to the evolution of US policy, Jonathan Tucker suggested that there were eight issues of major importance (Table 6.1).[1]

This listing gives a good picture of the diversity of interests brought to bear on the negotiations, but it also suggests that it may be difficult to

Table 6.1 Major issues in the BTWC Protocol*

1. Definitions, lists and criteria.
2. Declarations.
3. Challenge inspections of facilities suspected of a treaty violation.
4. Field investigations of unusual disease outbreaks (possibly associated with the covert use of biological weapons or an accidental leak from a clandestine development or production facility).
5. Non-challenge visits to declared facilities.
6. Protection of confidential information.
7. Scientific and technological cooperation in the peaceful uses of biotechnology.
8. The non-transfer of equipment and know-how needed for the production of biological weapons.

Note: *From Chapter 6, reference 1.

obtain a coherent grasp of what was happening in the negotiations and which aspects were of critical importance. This is actually not a correct viewpoint. Clearly, item 1 of Table 6.1 is related to concerns which some states had that there should be precise definitions of what was required to comply with the Convention, while others were concerned to ensure that the Convention's General Purpose Criterion was in no way affected by the measures taken to implement the Protocol. Item 4 was of concern to some states which felt that there should be no role for the BTWC in dealing with natural outbreaks of disease and to others who felt that the BTWC did have a role if outbreaks were suspicious. Items 7 and 8 were related to the long-running debate over the place of export control regimes outside of the Convention for States Parties which signed up to the Protocol. The rest of the items related to differing views about the extent of intrusiveness of the central compliance measures.

That all these divisions were fairly obvious is not surprising because they reflect long-standing differences between States Parties. It is rare for states' policies to undergo seismic shifts. For the most part the policies brought to bear in such multilateral negotiations are the product of detailed internal studies based on a long-term understanding of major foreign policy interests. This stability and persistence of policy is obvious in the area of central concern here – compliance measures – and is demonstrated in the proposals consistently advocated by the European Union (EU) and associated states. For example, the Ambassador of Portugal, speaking on behalf of the EU at the 19th Session of the AHG on 13 March 2000, stated in part:

> The EU favours a *comprehensive declaration regime* that will capture in a balanced way all facilities and activities relevant to the Convention. The EU maintains that it is essential that biodefensive activities and facilities, vaccine production, maximum biological containment, work with listed agents and/or toxins, and other production be declared annually...

> The Protocol must contain *an effective mechanism for follow-up of declarations in the form of visits.* The concept of visits based on random selection that is now widely accepted is an important step forward. The EU emphasizes its belief that a visit regime must include such visits, selected on the basis of appropriate mechanisms of random selection ... we believe that these visits must apply to all declared facilities.

> The Protocol must contain *appropriate clarification procedures.* Most cases can be solved through consultations or, if necessary, through

clarification visits based on a voluntary invitation. But clarification procedures must go beyond that ... Appropriate clarification procedures also apply whenever a facility meeting the criteria for declaration ought to have been declared but was not.

The Protocol must include provisions for *rapid and effective investigations* ...[2] (emphasis added)

Now it can reasonably be assumed that Challenge Investigations will be a rarely-used, politically extremely sensitive, final (but essential) back-up to the whole set of compliance measures.[3] What is of importance here, therefore, is the set of declarations and visits which are the real heart of the compliance measures. Table 6.2 provides a summary of the EU's position as set out by the Portuguese Ambassador in March 2000.

What we see here is a compliance architecture for dealing with a dual-use problem which is modelled on the Chemical Weapons Convention – for the good reason that the CWC attempted to deal with the same general dual-use problem. There is, of course, no equivalent in the BTWC Protocol to the chemical weapons destruction requirements of

Table 6.2 The stated position of the EU in March 2000*

1. Comprehensive *declaration regime* to capture all facilities and activities of relevance. Encompass
     – Biodefensive activities and facilities;
     – Vaccine production;
     – Maximum biological containment work;
     – Work with listed agents and/or toxins;
     – Other production.
   All to be declared annually.

2. Effective mechanism to follow-up declarations in the form of *visits*:
     – Random selection;
     – To promote accuracy of declarations;
     – To enhance transparency of all declared facilities;
     – To ensure fulfilment of declaration obligations.
   Must apply to all declared facilities.

3. Appropriate *clarification procedures*, including:
     – Consultations;
     – Voluntary (invitation) visits;
     – Clarification visits (where an invitation is not made but is considered necessary).
   Must apply to all declared facilities, and to facilities meeting the criteria for declaration but which were not declared.

Note: *From Chapter 6, reference 2.

the CWC because the BTWC itself requires such destruction in Article II (and destruction of biological agents, unlike chemical agents, is simple and not dangerous). Then, as MacEachin argued (see Chapter 1), the parties are required to declare the most relevant facilities and activities and to have those declarations checked out, thus rendering it unlikely that such facilities will be misused. Should there be misuse in another facility, that would have to be kept entirely secret because it could be the subject of a challenge investigation if it came to the notice of other parties. Additionally, in the BTWC Protocol, and unlike the CWC, a facility that looked as if it should have been declared could also be subject to a lesser, but still formal, clarification procedure. Furthermore, as we shall see, the BTWC Protocol has also incorporated measures to ensure submission of declarations at the appropriate time in order to underpin the viability of the regime.[4]

This gives a reasonable picture of the EU's public position towards the end of five years of negotiation, after it had surely had time to consider alternatives put forward by other States Parties. What, though, did the Protocol text itself state in regard to Article III Compliance Measures at the end of 2000?

The structure of Article III

As can be seen in the rolling text set out in BWC/AD HOC GROUP/54,[5] there were eight major sections of Article III at that stage, but a number even of the titles were still in square brackets (Table 6.3). The first three sections, lists and criteria (agents and toxins), equipment and thresholds, and the last section on additional provisions, are ancillary to the main compliance measures. As might be expected from the discussion of the differences between States Parties in Chapter 5, section (F) of Article III dealing with the implementation of Article III of the Convention (on transfers) was heavily bracketed.[6] Yet the key aspects of Declarations (D), Consultation, Clarification and Cooperation (E) and Investigations (G) were not bracketed to this extent. Furthermore, Article III was the largest Article in the text and Section D was by far the largest part of this Article, comprising 42 of the total 69 pages.

The first sub-section of Article III D. Declarations, is concerned with *I. Submission of Declarations*. This is further sub-divided into Initial Declarations and Annual Declarations. The major options under Initial Declarations are shown in Table 6.4. It would obviously help to provide transparency and thereby increase confidence if activities conducted

Table 6.3 Article III compliance measures*

Section	Pages
A. [Lists and Criteria (Agents and Toxins)]	1
B. [Equipment]	1
C. [Thresholds]	2
D. Declarations	42
E. Consultation, Clarification and Cooperation	3
[F. [Measures to Strengthen the Implementation of Article III]]	6
G. Investigations	9
[H. Additional Provisions]	3

Note: *From Chapter 6, reference 5.

Table 6.4 Article III D declarations: I. submission of declarations: initial declarations*

[(A) Offensive Biological and Toxin Programmes and/or Activities Conducted Prior to Entry into Force of the Protocol for Each State Party]
[(B) Defensive Biological and Toxin Programmes and/or Activities Conducted Prior to Entry into Force of the Protocol for Each State Party]
OR
[(A) Offensive and/or Defensive Biological and Toxin Programmes and/or Activities Conducted Prior to Entry into Force of the Protocol for Each State Party]

Note: *From Chapter 6, reference 5.

prior to entry into force of the Protocol were clarified, but there remained differences over the detail of how this should best be done. The major sub-divisions of the Annual Declarations are set out in Table 6.5. Here it can be seen that there is agreement on some of the main categories of concern – defensive programmes, vaccine production facilities, maximum biological containment, and work with listed agents, but much disagreement about other main categories.

The second sub-section of Article III Section D. Declarations is entitled *II. Follow-Up After Submission of Declarations*. The main divisions of the text under this sub-section are shown in Table 6.6. This part of the text, dealing as it does with the crucial issue of visits, will be discussed in more detail later in the chapter.

The third sub-section of Article III Section D. Declarations is entitled *III. Measures to Ensure Submission of Declarations* and, as noted above, sets out a range of possible actions that might be taken following non-submission of declarations.

Table 6.5 Article III D declarations: I. submission of declarations: annual declarations*

(C) Defensive Biological and Toxin Programmes and/or Activities Conducted
    during the Previous Year
(D) Vaccine Production Facilities
(E) Maximum Biological Containment [(BL-4-WHO [and OIE] Classification]
    Facilities
[(F) High Biological Containment [(BL-3-WHO [and OIE] Classification]
    Facilities...]
[(G) Plant Pathogen Containment...]
(H) Work with Listed Agents and/or Toxins
[(I) Other Production Facilities...]
[(J) Other Facilities...]
[(K) Transfers...]
[(L) Declarations on the Implementation of Article X of the Convention and
    Article VII of the Protocol...]
[Notifications...]

Note: *From Chapter 6, reference 5.

Table 6.6 Article III D declarations: II. follow-up after submission of declarations*

(A) [Randomly-Selected Visits] [Transparency Visits]
    Pre-Visit Activities
    Activities upon Arrival of the Visiting Team
    Conduct of the Visit
    Post-Visit Activities
    Reports
(B) Declaration Clarification Procedures
    [Voluntary Clarification Visit]
    Pre-Visit Activities
    Activities Upon Arrival of the Visiting Team
    Conduct of the Visit
    Post-Visit Activities
    Report
(C) Voluntary Assistance Visits

Note: *From Chapter 6, reference 5.

The associated annexes and appendices

The Articles of the rolling text in BWC/AD HOC GROUP/54 are followed by a series of associated Annexes and Appendices (see Table 5.12). For example, the first section of Article III Compliance Measures is A.

[Lists and Criteria (Agents and Toxins)]. This reads as follows:

> [Each State Party shall declare agents and toxins from the lists set out in Annex A, section I, in accordance with the formats for declarations of facilities, activities and transfers referred to in Annex A, section IV.][5]

The relevant formats for declarations are detailed in the Appendices, but of particular interest here are the agents and toxins noted in Annex A, section I.

Annex A. Declarations I. Lists and Criteria (Agents and Toxins) begins with a discussion of the criteria that were used to draw up the lists – for example, whether the agents or toxins are known to have been previously developed, produced or used as a weapon, or whether they have severe public health and/or socioeconomic effects. A mechanism for revising the list is also set out and, importantly, it is noted in paragraph 4 that:

> The list is not exhaustive, it does not exclude the relevance for the Protocol of unlisted microbial or other biological agents or toxins which potentially can be used as weapons or vectors.[5]

This means that the lists are *illustrative* of what may be misused, but they do not in any way limit the scope of the General Purpose Criterion set out in Article I of the Biological and Toxin Weapons Convention.

The lists of agents are divided into three groups: human and zoonotic (infectious agents which affect humans, but whose reservoir source is an animal population) pathogens; animal pathogens; and plant pathogens. There is also a fourth list of toxins. The list of human and zoonotic pathogens contains 15 viruses, 11 bacteria and two protozoan species (both in brackets) (Table 6.7 gives some well-known illustrative examples). The list of animal pathogens is divided into five groups affecting different types of animals and contains 11 pathogenic species. However, most are in brackets – only Rinderpest virus and Newcastle disease virus are out of brackets, and even the latter virus has a footnote suggesting that it will be subject to further discussion. The list of plant pathogens is divided into four groups concerned with: cereal pathogens; sugar cane pathogens; cash crop pathogens; and forest pathogens. Of the 11 species of pathogen listed, only one is in brackets and one footnoted as requiring more discussion. Eleven toxins are listed and these are divided into bacteriotoxins, phycotoxins, mycotoxins, phytotoxins, and zootoxins. Well-known examples are the bacterial toxins such as botulinum toxin and staphylococcal enterotoxins and the phytotoxins such as abrins and ricins.

Table 6.7   Examples from the list of human and zoonotic pathogens*

Viruses
  6. Lassa fever virus
  8. Marburg virus
11. Variola major virus (Smallpox virus)
12. Venezuelan equine encephalitis virus

Bacteria
  1. *Bacillus anthracis*
  7. *Francisella tularensis*
  8. *Yersinia pestis*
  9. *Coxiella burnetii*

Note: *From Chapter 6, reference 5.

This listing may appear relatively clear and reasonable, but it has only emerged after extensive discussions. One indicator of their complexity can be gained from the listing of one of the criteria to be applied for selection of agents and toxins as (paragraph 2 (b)):[5] 'Scientific and technological developments that may affect the potential of individual agents or toxins for use as weapons'.[5] In this context the footnote (number 59) to this first section of the Annex is important. The footnote, in part, reads:

> The view was expressed that further consideration needs to be given to micro-organisms carrying nucleic acid sequences coding for pathogenic properties of listed agents and toxins.
>   Another view was expressed that further consideration also needs to be given to nucleic acid sequences coding for toxins...

So there is a concern that genes for pathogenic properties or toxins from the list could be introduced into other organisms not on the list.

Follow-up after submission of declarations

The second sub-section of Article III Section D. Declarations is titled *II. Follow-Up After Submission of Declarations* (Table 6.6). This begins clearly enough with a first paragraph which states:

> The Technical Secretariat [of the organization to be set up to run the operation of the Protocol] shall receive, process, analyse, and store declarations submitted by States Parties in accordance with the provisions of this Protocol.[5]

Paragraph 2 of the section then goes on to show how, once a State Party has submitted its own declarations, it gains access to those of other States Parties.

The disagreements described in outline in Chapter 5, however, do not take long to surface in the text. Paragraph 3 is heavily bracketed and begins:

[3. In order to [determine that the declarations submitted by States Parties are complete and accurate] [promote the accurate fulfilment of the declaration obligations under this Protocol], in accordance with the provisions set out in this Protocol, the technical secretariat shall ...

Before we turn to the following list of actions in the text that might be required of the Technical Secretariat in order to follow up the declarations, it is noteworthy that the two bracketed alternatives proposed offer a very different view of what the aim is: either to determine that the declarations are complete and accurate or to promote their accurate fulfilment. Clearly, the Protocol would be much stronger if the former aim were to be implemented.

Paragraph 3 continues with the actions of the Technical Secretariat:

[(a) Process and analyse the declarations;]

(b) Conduct a limited number of [randomly-selected] visits to [declared] [biodefence and BL4 with the principle of proportionality] [BL4] facilities [declared pursuant to Article III, section D, subsection I, parts (C), (D), (E), [(G)], (H) and (I)] [in accordance with the procedures set out in part A below];

(The reference to 'part A below' here refers to the succeeding paragraphs (10–46) under the heading '[(A) [Randomly-Selected Visits] [Transparency Visits]' as shown in Table 6.6.) What is evident in the passage quoted above are some of the disagreements pointed out in the previous chapter about the scope of the visits. The second set of square brackets under (b) alone would limit visits just to declared facilities and the third set of square brackets just to biodefence and BL4 facilities. The problem with limiting visits in this way would be that very few visits would be possible. We can see that this would be the case by referring back to the triggers for the annual declarations set out under *I. Submission of Declarations*: Annual Declarations (see Table 6.5). We know from the 1997 Confidence-Building Measures responses under the Convention itself that: 'some 43 biological defence facilities were declared by 15 countries, some 49 maximum containment facilities declared by 22 countries and some 162 vaccine production facilities declared by 36 countries ...'.[7] It follows logically from these data that:

> biological defence facilities are only likely to be declared in a small number of countries (15), and [that] the addition of maximum containment facilities only increases the number of countries by seven. It is only when vaccine production facilities are considered that the number of countries increases by another 14 to a total of 36 ...

So if the aim is to have a strong Protocol which increases transparency substantially, there is a clear need to expand the range of triggers so that it includes vaccine production, other triggers such as work with listed agents and toxins, and other production facilities. It also follows logically that the scope of the visits regime should not be restricted.

Paragraph 3 continues with the duties of the Technical Secretariat:

> [(c) If it, in its analysis pursuant to paragraph 3 (a) above, identifies any ambiguity, uncertainty, anomaly or omission [of a purely technical nature] related solely to the content of the declaration, [it should] seek clarification from the State Party concerned, in accordance with the procedures set out in part B below;][5]

(The reference here to 'part B' is to paragraphs 48–104 under the heading (B) Declaration Clarification Procedures, as shown in Table 6.6.) Paragraph 3 continues:

> [... (d) Provide technical assistance to States Parties to help them compile individual facility and national declarations including, if requested, by means of visiting a State Party, in accordance with the procedures set out in part C below.]

(The reference here to 'part C' is to paragraphs 105–13 under the heading (C) Voluntary Assistance Visits, as shown in Table 6.6.)

The whole of paragraph 3 is in brackets but it is followed by paragraph 4 which is not in brackets. This paragraph states:

> 4. A State Party which identifies any ambiguity, uncertainty, anomaly or omission in the declaration of another State Party may seek clarification from the State Party concerned, in accordance with the provisions of section E of this Article, or it may initiate the clarification process set out in part B above.

We have already noted 'part B'. Section E of Article III is titled E. Consultation, Clarification and Cooperation (see Table 6.3). Its seven paragraphs will be discussed briefly at the end of this chapter, but at this point it is worth noting that it lies somewhere between the non-confrontational declarations/visits process and the highly political investigation process (Article III G. Investigations, see Table 6.3), and that it could involve the Technical Secretariat making a visit to resolve a concern about a declaration obligation.

The visit schedule

The consideration of the follow-up after the submission of declarations then deals with the visit schedule in paragraphs 5 to 9. Paragraph 5 states:

> 5. The total number of all visits conducted pursuant to this Article [shall be approved by the [First] Conference of States Parties and] shall not exceed [30] [70] [140] [...] in each calendar year.[5]

It is therefore clear that very large numbers of visits in each calendar year are not envisaged and particularly clear – given the 140-plus States Parties to the Convention – that large numbers of visits to individual countries are most unlikely, since unbalanced distribution mechanisms will not be approved. Paragraph 6 states that the number of visits under paragraph 3 (b) – that is, randomly-selected visits – should comprise at least half of the total number of visits. That would mean an even smaller number of these crucial, randomly-selected, visits (which would be analogous to the non-challenge inspections under the Chemical Weapons Convention). Paragraph 6, however, ends with another proposal:

> [All visits in any year resulting from the procedures set forth in paragraphs 3 (c), 3 (d), and 4 shall be deducted from the total number allocated in paragraph 5. The resultant number, once all deductions are made, will be the new number of visits pursuant to paragraph 3 (b)]].

So this proposal would set no floor under which the number of randomly-selected visits could not go. Should the number of voluntary assistance visits under 3(d) escalate, for instance, there might be no room for *any* randomly-selected visits at all.

Randomly-selected visits

It is apparent, from what we have already discussed, that the whole concept of randomly-selected visits to really check declarations remains in doubt. It is even contested in the alternative heading of 'Transparency Visits' (Table 6.6) and this becomes increasingly obvious in paragraphs 10 and 11 which (in two alternative formulations) set out the purpose envisaged for these visits. This material was formulated in a more straightforward way in a suggested text by a group of academics:

> 10. The Technical Secretariat shall conduct visits pursuant to paragraph 3 (b) of this subsection which shall be confidence-building in nature. These visits shall, through cooperation with the visited State Party, promote the overall objectives of the Protocol by:
>
> (a) Increasing confidence in the consistency of declarations submitted by States Parties and encouraging submission of comprehensive declarations; and also by
>
> (b) Enhancing transparency of facilities and helping the Technical Secretariat, subject to the provisions of this section, to acquire and retain a comprehensive and up-to-date understanding of the facilities and activities declared globally.[8]

One expert commented on this formulation:

> As you can see, the purpose is not the verification of the declaration as such even if some elements of verification of the consistency of the declaration are there. *This purpose seems to be already the final compromise ...*[9] (emphasis added)

We can see clearly here that we do not have a strong system in which the randomly-selected visit is there to determine that the declaration is complete and accurate.

Declaration clarification procedures

The text following on deals with (B) Declaration Clarification Procedures, the first paragraph under this heading (number 48) reading:

> 48. Concerns related to the declaration of a State Party [concerning any facility pursuant to Article III, section D, subsection I, parts (C), (D), (E), [G;] (H) and (I)] shall [, as a rule,] be sought to be resolved either through the process of consultation, clarification and cooperation as provided for in paragraphs 1 (a) and 3 of section E of this Article, or through the procedures set out in this section ...[5]

It may well be determined, as has previously been suggested, that the consultation, clarification and cooperation process under Article III, section E is best used:

> to address any matter which may be raised relating to the object and purpose of the Convention, or the implementation of the provisions of the Protocol and to clarify and resolve any matter which may cause concern about possible non-compliance with the obligations of this Protocol or the Convention ...[8]

This would have the advantage of leaving Section D. *II Follow-Up After the Submission of Declarations* (B) Declaration Clarification Procedures a lower-key matter dealing just with declaration issues.

In this set of procedures paragraph 48 goes on to state that '[T]he State Party to which the concern is related may volunteer for the Technical Secretariat to conduct a visit in accordance with the provisions set out in this section to the facility in question with a view to resolving the concern'. Thus there is a means by which a State Party may volunteer to have a visit made to the facility of concern in order to resolve the problem.

The next paragraph sets out the means by which the clarification process should be initiated:

> [49. When a State Party considers that there is an ambiguity, uncertainty, anomaly or omission in the declaration [concerning any declared facility or activity] of another State Party, [or identifies any facility which it believes meets the criteria for declaration as set forth in Article III, section D, and that facility has not been included in the declaration(s) concerned,] it shall seek clarification from the other State Party... through... section E of this Article, *or it may submit a request in writing to the Director-General to initiate the clarification procedures set out in this section on its behalf* ...[4] (emphasis added)

One expert has noted that (provided the brackets are removed from this section): 'It is important to note that this procedure allows clarification of concern either for a declared facility or for a facility that should have been declared ...'.[9] The process initiated requires the Director-General to begin by writing to the State Party causing the concern, requesting clarification. A reply has to be sent within 20 days of receipt of the request. If the reply is not deemed satisfactory then the clarification process can proceed to a consultative meeting between staff of the Technical Secretariat and representatives of the State Party causing the concern.

If the matter still cannot be resolved, paragraph 70 provides that:

[70. If the Director-General has initiated a clarification process pursuant to paragraph 53 and considers that the consultative meeting has not resolved the matter, he/she shall submit a proposal to conduct a clarification visit within seven days after the conclusion of the consultative meeting ...

Now it is clear from the following Protocol text that the State Party causing concern can refuse the request. But the matter then goes forward for consideration by the Executive Council of the organization and this could clearly lead to further action. Paragraph 74 notes:

74. If the requested State Party declines to offer a clarification visit, the Director-General shall inform the Executive Council which shall consider the matter at its next regular session and may decide, *inter alia* ...

and the eight options then set out range from taking no further action to, for example, referring the matter to a special session of the (governing) Conference of States Parties.

Summary

From this brief review of the Compliance Measures in the Protocol it is obvious that what will eventually be decided upon, if a Protocol is agreed, will not be the greatest possible strengthening of the Convention. In the next chapter there will be an exploration of *how* some of this weakening of the initial ideals of some parties came about. In Chapter 8 an attempt will be made to discover *why* the weakening happened. This leads on, in Chapter 9, to an assessment of the Protocol and the question of whether it still matches our needs. Finally, in Chapter 10 these developments in biological arms control are set in the wider context of developments in international security at the turn of the twenty-first century.

7
The Debate on Visits

The negotiations to produce a Protocol to the Biological and Toxin Weapons Convention (BTWC) have been followed carefully by a number of scholars and activists in different countries despite the apparent lack of interest among scientists, the general public and the mass media. Amy Smithson probably reflected a view held by many such activists and scholars when she suggested that: 'Strengthening the BWC is unquestionably necessary to enhance international security, but this treaty is orders of magnitude more difficult to monitor than nuclear, chemical, or conventional arms control accords ... '.[1] However, it is important to understand that the task is not considered impossible by those who have looked very carefully at the problem. Stephen Black, for example, reflecting on the difficult task UNSCOM had in Iraq, concluded:

> Some have suggested that the goal of designing a BW verification mechanism, which can detect noncompliance, is unattainable. The Special Commission has proven that it is not impossible to detect a concealed BW program, even when it is carefully hidden. While it took several years and significant effort, UNSCOM was able to build a case that could have only one outcome – Iraq's admission of an offensive BW program ... [2]

What is of particular interest is Black's later comment that:

> UNSCOM showed the value of a systems approach to biological arms verification, rather than looking for single elements and discrete actions. ... It was the combination and obvious direction of Iraq's dual-use capabilities that convinced the world of Iraq's deceit.

The beginning of the attempt to develop a mechanism for assuring compliance with the BTWC in the early 1990s obviously overlapped with the successful conclusion of such a 'systems approach' agreement for the Chemical Weapons Convention (CWC).

The CWC includes the destruction of chemical weapons and chemical weapons production facilities, a proviso which has no parallel in the BTWC, but it is widely accepted that the CWC is of the greatest relevance to the emerging BTWC regime. Both regimes are concerned with the total prohibition of agents which attack humans and animals through the air and the two regimes overlap in that both cover toxins.[3] Jonathan Tucker considered how far the provisions of the CWC might fit the specific requirements of the BTWC. His discriminating analysis led him to suggest that:

> Taken together, the various elements of the CWC verification regime provide a useful model for a workable BWC compliance protocol. Depending on the specific issue, however, the CWC model is sometimes readily adaptable, sometimes in need of adjustment for the BW context, and sometimes incapable of meeting the unique challenges of monitoring biological weapons activities.[4]

The CWC includes two types of verification inspections: routine and challenge. According to Tucker, routine inspections are: 'periodic, pre-announced visits to declared government and commercial facilities to check the accuracy of declarations and to verify the *absence* of undeclared illicit production of chemical agents or the diversion of dual-use chemicals for military purposes ... '. The frequency and intrusiveness of routine inspections is related to the types of chemicals at the facility, with the depth of the inspection being highest for Schedule 1 and lowest for Schedule 3 facilities. As Tucker comments: 'By keeping declared facilities continually at risk of inspection, the regime seeks to force potential cheaters to move any illicit production to clandestine facilities, increasing the costs and risks of noncompliance and helping to deter violations.' He also seems to accept that this approach, with suitable modifications, would be reasonable for the BTWC:

> *Relevance to the BWC protocol.* Under a BWC protocol, routine or 'non-challenge' visits to declared facilities would assess whether the observed activities are consistent with the declared ones. ...Conducting the inspections on short-notice and without right of refusal would help to deter illicit development or production at all such sites.

Writing late in the 1990s Tucker went on to point out that no consensus on this aspect of the protocol had been agreed in the Ad Hoc Group (AHG).

Before moving on to discuss the activities of the AHG in this regard, it is necessary to stress again that the nature of the CWC verification regime is widely misunderstood. Firstly, though the General Purpose Criterion bans *all* misuse of chemicals, it is the responsibility of the States Parties to ensure that this ban is enacted in their territories. Then, amongst the enormous number of chemicals that *could* be misused, the international system focuses on an agreed sub-set – the scheduled chemicals – for monitoring. Moreover, visits are strictly circumscribed by facility agreements that severely limit what the inspectors can monitor – only the particular areas of the plant handling the scheduled chemical. Thus: 'Verification, confidence and trust does not come about in the CWC regime because all relevant items are monitored'.[5]

This point becomes particularly clear if the CWC negotiations are examined in more detail. As one of those involved has recently explained, events in the late 1980s – for example, Iraq's use of pesticide and multi-purpose production plants in its CW programme – gradually led to:

> an appreciation by the Geneva negotiators that to restrict the coverage of on-site verification activity only to facilities producing Schedule 1 and 2 chemicals, while ignoring Schedule 3 facilities and other facilities which could be readily adaptable to chemical weapons production, would be to build a serious deficiency into the Convention (the 'Verification Gap') ...[6]

It thus became clear that inspection of Schedule 3 or discrete organic chemical (DOC) – the politically acceptable codewords to cover CW-capable – facilities would be needed. However, since there are several thousand such facilities in the world, 'it was recognised that the declaration of DOC facilities was a transparency/confidence building measure' and not every such facility would need to be visited to build an increasing level of assurance of compliance over a number of years of implementation. To date, however, there have been very few DOC inspections and this insider account ends by stressing the importance of such inspections for the future of the regime: 'It should be borne in mind that the principal aims of routine inspections of DOC plant sites will be to check that the activities on-site are consistent with the information provided in the declarations ... '. The OPCW inspectorate has to adjust its procedures to this new task, but it is essential to do this because it is crucial to the overall success of the verification regime. It is important not to be confused by the quantification of some aspects of the CWC verification regime. This quantification takes place within a much more 'qualitative' systems approach in which a variety of different methods – including different methods of conducting visits – are used to achieve the goal of increasing confidence in compliance.

The Ad Hoc Group beginnings

It will be recalled from Chapter 5 that Ambassador Tibor Tóth, Chairman of the Ad Hoc Group, argued that the negotiation of the Protocol could be considered to have had three distinct phases:

1995 to mid-1997	– Identification of elements of the Protocol;
Mid-1997 to 1998	– Incorporation of detailed provisions into the rolling text;
1999 onwards	– Detailed negotiations on the key elements within the final framework.

In terms of the sessions of the negotiations we can think of Phase 1 as consisting of sessions 1–7, Phase 2 of sessions 8–12, and Phase 3 of session 13 onwards.

The negotiators certainly entered the first phase of the negotiations against a background of growing success of the CWC, but probably much more directly relevant was the continuity of the negotiations with the previous two years of the VEREX process. This is perfectly obvious from the early working papers submitted to the AHG. A paper produced by the UK in June 1995, for example, argued that two observations from the VEREX final report would be helpful to the group in carrying out its work in a practical and focused manner: 'Firstly, it noted that the measure described under the heading "*Declarations*" had been most frequently identified for application in combination with other measures ... '[7] (emphasis added) and 'secondly, that some *combinations* of potential verification measures, both on-site and off-site, could provide information which could be useful for the main objective of the Biological Weapons Convention ... ' (emphasis added). The paper argued that these two observations should guide the work of the AHG. Similarly, another paper of July 1995, submitted by Australia, began:

> During VEREX, *declarations* were identified as one of the central measures in verifying compliance with the BWC. Although unable,

on their own, to provide sufficient information, declarations were the measure most frequently identified, *in combination* with others, as providing a means for compliance ... [8] (emphasis added)

So declarations in combination with some other measures were a clear focus of attention from the start.

The role and objectives of visits were discussed in considerable detail in another UK paper of July 1995 which argued that the nature of biological weapons and the close relationship of illegal to legitimate activities required a fundamentally different approach to the design of an effective compliance mechanism: 'Although declarations and inspections are essential, a different conceptual framework is required to incorporate these elements into a BTWC compliance protocol ... '.[9] The paper argued that the close links of illegal to legitimate microbiology constrained what could be done because too heavy a burden could not be placed on the pharmaceutical and biotechnology industry. However, as there were such political sensitivities over challenge inspections, a system based solely on declarations and challenge inspections would not suffice:

There are also grounds for doubting whether such an arrangement would be as effective as a package of interrelated measures consisting of declarations, short-notice validation/information inspections/visits (*subsequently referred to in this paper as visits*), challenge inspections and procedures for investigating alleged use.[9] (emphasis added)

The paper then made a series of observations about the nature of such visits.

Granted the ease with which biological agents could be grown, it was not sensible to consider an approach based on material balances and quantities of agent held: 'It is thus not appropriate to think in terms of 'routine inspections' as understood in the CWC, CFE and INF Treaties for example. A BW inspection or visit, in contrast, requires a more *qualitative approach* ... '[9] (emphasis added). Such an approach was then outlined:

In practice this means that inspectors have to make an evaluation of a broad range of interrelated factors such as the scale of specific facilities and the explanations provided for their use. *A judgement needs to be formed on whether or not the facilities and activities are consistent with their stated purpose, with descriptions of the development of the site and with the BTWC itself.* (emphasis added)

A later paragraph emphasized the view that 'Visits ... would therefore have completely different objectives from those of comparable inspections under other arms control agreements'. The paper went on to argue that visits should be seen as part of an integrated package of measures and that they would bring five interrelated benefits. These potential benefits are shown in Table 7.1.

A further working paper, from Sweden, in July 1995 reinforced the view that the work of VEREX was crucial. It began:

> From the work of VEREX it can be concluded that potential verification measures have been comprehensively identified and evaluated from a scientific and technical standpoint and that this part of the governmental experts' work now is finished ... [10]

and went on to argue that the minimum requirements for a verification regime were a well-focused declarations scheme, on-site inspections and multilateral information-sharing. In the view of the Swedish authors:

> These measures are required, as there must be a mechanism to verify the accuracy of the information supplied in the declarations and for this some type of on-site inspection is needed. ... One objective of an inspection is to verify that facilities are in compliance with declared activities ...

In regard to how the verification was to be achieved, the paper suggested that: 'The basic measures required for on-site inspections are

Table 7.1   The potential benefits of visits*

1. Providing an opportunity to validate declarations in the context of the site activities and hence encourage State Parties to make accurate declarations.
2. Facilitating transparency of national microbiological activities related to the BTWC.
3. Providing an understanding of how national safety, genetic engineering, quality control, GMP, etc., rules and regulations operate and how they are implemented in practice.
4. Facilitating the relationship between the State Party and the Organization on issues such as national requests for assistance on declarations; and an opportunity to review declaration procedures with individual State Parties.
5. Contributing to deterring potential proliferators.

Note: *From Chapter 7, reference 9.

visual inspection, interviewing, identification of key equipment and auditing ... '. Whilst still mainly employing the term 'inspections' rather than 'visits', this early paper still pointed up the difference from routine CWC inspections:

> In comparison with the CWC it is proposed that on-site inspections of a routine type for validation of declarations and information gathering for the BTWC should be strongly restricted in frequency and intensity to a small number of inspections/visits per year to keep inspectors and an inspectorate well trained and give them adequate experience but at the same time limiting the costs ...

Another paper from Sweden in November 1995 took the conceptualization of visits a stage further. This paper referred back specifically to the UK paper of July 1995 (reference 9 here). It argued:

> Two main types of on-site visits/inspections are required. One would be a *short notice on-site information visit* and the other would be *short notice on-site inspections*. There would be no need for a separate type of routine visits/inspections.[11]

It went on to specify that:

> *Short notice on-site information visits* could cover what is referred to as 'validation/information visits/inspections' in the [UK] paper. A selection of the most relevant facilities/activities from those declared for *short notice on-site information visits* should be made, on the basis of elaborated modalities, in order to achieve an appropriate limitation in the number of such visits.

However, the paper argued further that:

> If information is received indicating that a facility/activity in a State Party has not been declared, although it would seem to fulfil the declaration criteria, or if there are other questions arising from declarations, there should be a mechanism for clarification and consultations ...

This thinking would appear to foreshadow the elements of the rolling text (reviewed earlier in Chapter 6) dealing with items that should have been declared and with clarification procedures and clarification visits.

It is interesting that in answering a question over whether American concerns about protecting its industry and biodefence, and non-aligned concerns, had led to a less than adequate regime in the Protocol, Ambassador Tóth pointed specifically, in May 2000, to the clarification visits mechanism: 'My feeling is that the emerging visits regime in the protocol is probably second-to-none and is quite comparable to other arrangements ... '.[12] After making a comparison with the CWC, he went on:

> I would like to call attention to the category of clarification visits, which has no comparable equivalent in the Chemical Weapons Convention. These visits are a really flexible tool used to address certain concerns at the lowest possible level of controversy, without resorting to more controversial investigations ...

He then noted how this idea could be traced back to other agreements such as the IAEA's Additional Protocol.

At the time that these follow-on analyses of visits were being made, consideration was also being given to the triggers required for declarations. The 11 July 1995 paper of the Friend of the Chair on Compliance Measures had, for example, listed military microbiological programmes/facilities, high containment facilities, work with listed pathogens and toxins, aerobiology/aerosol dissemination, production microbiology and genetic manipulation and had discussed some other possibilities and exemptions.[13] In November 1995, at the third session of the AHG, France and Germany presented a paper which fleshed out many of the details, in order to provide a fuller basis for further discussion.[14] The France/Germany paper listed military research and development programmes/facilities for biological defence, facilities containing areas protected according to the standard for maximum (BL4) containment laboratories, facilities containing areas protected according to the standard BL3 (or equivalent) if they possess microbiology production capability and work with agents contained in a annexed list or agents with characteristics corresponding to a second annexed list, production of vaccines for the protection of humans and past offensive or defensive biological research and development programmes. An indication of what might need to be provided in the declaration (the declaration format) was also given. The practical investigation of the implications of using such triggers and the consequent analysis of how they might need to be refined is evident in the Netherlands working paper reporting on a questionnaire survey of a large number of its potentially relevant BWC-related facilities.[15]

In this context Ireland submitted a working paper, to the fourth session of the Ad Hoc Group in July 1996, on the Common Position of the European Union relating to the preparation for the Fourth Review Conference of the BTWC. This stated, in part, that:

> 2. Member States will accordingly seek maximum progress on verification measures in the context of the Ad Hoc Group and at the Review Conference. In particular, at the Review Conference they will seek:
> – endorsement of the main results achieved by that time ...
> – a decision to intensify the work of the Ad Hoc Group in order to complete the negotiations on a BTWC verification protocol as soon as possible, before a further Special Conference of BTWC States Parties to take place no later than the middle of 1998 ... [16]

It is possible to sense a certain impatience in the succeeding sentence which suggested that the work of the AHG should be substantially increased in 1997 and 1998 'irrespective of other priorities in the international disarmament agenda'.

On the following day in July 1996 the European Union submitted a detailed working paper on triggers for declarations[17] and another on short-notice non-challenge visits.[18] The latter paper noted:

> Non-challenge visits would help to build transparency and could clarify concerns which might otherwise lead to false judgements being made. *A system of non-challenge visits would enable the future BTWC organisation to verify declarations and to resolve uncertainties about declarations.* (emphasis added)

The paper went on to discuss questions of intrusiveness. It stressed the advantages of such non-confrontational visits and noted that costs could be kept low because the number needed each year to achieve the desired effects would not be large: 'The total number of non-challenge visits could be in the range of a minimum (e.g. 20) and up to a maximum (e.g. 50) per year ... '. The paper also discussed criteria that might be applied to the selection of facilities to be visited by the organization from the agreed quota. But it also pointed out that a separate category of visits outside of the quota would be required to clarify ambiguities.

Practical investigations

It is clear from the working papers submitted to the AHG that a number of States Parties besides the Netherlands began to investigate what the practical consequences of the triggers and visits under discussion might be for their own states and concerns. In September 1997 Pearson[19] was able to analyse surveys carried out by:

Canada   (BWC/AD HOC GROUP/WP.6) November 1995;
Netherlands   (BWC/AD HOC GROUP/WP.10) November 1995;
United Kingdom   (BWC/AD HOC GROUP/WP.81) July 1996;
Italy   (BWC/AD HOC GROUP/WP.146) March 1997;
Denmark, Finland, Iceland, Norway and Sweden (BWC/AD HOC GROUP/WP.173) July 1997.

The first survey by Canada demonstrated that military microbiology as a 'stand-alone' trigger and another trigger combining any relevant activity with work with listed agents would be effective in requiring declarations from a reasonable number of facilities. Pearson concluded, firstly, that:

> The conclusions reached by Canada in its survey reported in November 1995 that triggers could be military microbiology, as a stand alone trigger, and the other proposed triggers (e.g. production microbiology) in combination with listed agents and toxins, have turned out to be largely confirmed by the subsequent surveys so far reported by other States Parties ...

This is to say that it proved possible to refine the triggers in a sensible manner.

Secondly, Pearson turned his attention to the number of declarations that would be required:

> The broad conclusion that emerges is that the number of facilities in each country that would need to be declared under triggers chosen to capture those facilities of most relevance to the Convention would be relatively limited with the numbers of the order of 10s in each country ...

The surveys had been carried out in developed countries and such triggers would be unlikely to trigger a greater number of declarations in developing countries. The total number of declarations would clearly not be unmanageable if these kinds of triggers applied.

In a related paper, Pearson subsequently considered the size of the organization likely to be set up to oversee the operation of the Protocol.[20]

He argued that if there were an average of 10–50 declarations per State Party, and 140 Parties, the number of annual declarations would lie between 1400 and 7000. A reasonable estimate might be in the order of 4000 per year. The CWC is the arms control agreement most comparable to the BTWC so it is possible to estimate what a lean and mean Organization for the Prohibition of Biological Weapons (OPBW) might look like by subtracting the destruction of chemicals aspects from the Organization for the Prohibition of Chemical Weapons (OPCW). This led Pearson to the conclusion that: 'the BTWC Organisation would need about 200 posts and an annual budget of under $30 M: it would be well under half the size of the OPCW with a budget of less than half that of the OPCW'. Such an organization would be able to effectively carry out about 100 visits and investigations in total in any one year.

Employing assumptions of the same order as Pearson, and using a visit length of 2–4 days (suggested as adequate, for example, by an early Canadian practice non-challenge visit to a defence research establishment[21]), Chevrier[22] was able to present a spreadsheet model of the future OPBW to delegations of the AHG in June 1998. That such a detailed analysis could be put forward by a non-governmental organization (the Federation of American Scientists) perhaps illustrates the extent to which, by the start of 1998, the States Parties had developed and published their views. But what of the real visits? If industry and biodefence were to be adequately included in the intended verification mechanism, could visits be carried out in such a way as to conform to the mandated requirements, particularly that of protecting commercial proprietary information (CPI) and national security information?

Practice visits

A number of practical trials of non-challenge visits have been carried out and reported on to the AHG (Table 7.2). The relevant working papers were reported to the AHG over a three-year period by Brazil and the UK,[23] Australia,[24] the UK,[25] five Nordic counries,[26] Austria,[27] Switzerland[28] and Iran.[29] The series of reports therefore came from a wide spectrum of States Parties; Japan and Germany were also represented at the Austrian trial, and there was an Austrian observer at the Swiss trial.

All the trials followed a pattern based on that expected to be decided on by the AHG. A facility that had made a declaration was visited for a short period of days by a small number of inspectors. Exact details of the objectives and aspects to be concentrated on varied, but the visits

Table 7.2 Practice non-challenge visits

---

1. Report of a Joint UK/Brazil Practice Non-Challenge Visit (WP. 76, July 1996).
2. Trial Inspection of a Biological Production Facility (WP. 77, July 1996).
3. Report of a visit to a Pharmaceutucal Research Facility (WP. 258, January 1998).
4. Report of a Trial Random Visit to a Biopharmaceutical Production Facility (WP. 298, August 1998).
5. Report on an International Trial Random Visit conducted in Austria, 10–11 August 1998 (WP. 310, September 1998).
6. Report of a National Trial Visit to a Vaccine and Serum Production Facility (WP. 345, January 1999).
7. Report on a Trial Inspection based on a Random Visit to a Vaccine Production Facility (WP. 371, June 1999).

---

typically involved a briefing, a short discussion of the briefing, a tour of the facility, then the visit proper and, lastly, a final reporting/review session. Though the details again varied, the visiting inspectors typically concentrated their attention on visual inspections, auditing and interviews and the visited facility used techniques of managed access when deemed appropriate. Of particular interest are the *precision* of the attempt to check the validity of the declaration and the implications there were for CPI during the visit.

Brazil/UK

This report[23] begins by noting that while the UK had conducted four practice challenge inspections, no practical work had so far been done on non-challenge visits. Among the objectives of the exercise were:

> To examine the practicalities and issues involved in non-challenge visits, including the role of declarations; [and]

> To test the utility of VEREX on-site measures ...

The visit was carried out at the Instituto Butantan in São Paulo, a site which produced vaccines and sera. The role-playing exercise took two-and-a-half days. In regard to the activities undertaken, particularly in regard to the role of the declaration, the report states:

> The IT [inspection team] did not, however, attempt to track down each and every item of equipment or to verify the declaration's quantitative statements. Instead the details were used to aid visits to key

parts of the site, and to provide a basis for detailed questions about, for example, the origins, installation and use of specific equipment.

There were few problems of confidentiality during this exercise as the institution was a public asset. However, there was some sensitivity about a new purification process which was being developed at the time.

Australia

Following the discussions of the potential utility of non-challenge visits at the AHG session in November/December 1995, Australia decided to carry out a practice visit and this was reported to the fourth session of the AHG in mid-1996. The trial was carried out at a biotechnology company and among its objectives were to:

Investigate the feasibility of verifying a declaration through a routine inspection;
[and]
Assess the impact of a routine inspection on the activities of a commercial facility, given the legitimate concerns which have been expressed about ... commercially sensitive information ... [24]

The site covered approximately 2.4 hectares, employed 130 personnel, produced an animal vaccine and planned to manufacture a human therapeutic product in the near future.

The report concluded that the company was operating a legitimate commercial facility. Again, no attempt was made to check all the details of the declaration:

All of the equipment and activities observed during the inspection were consistent with the details provided ... and with the additional information received. ... Using a random selective access approach, the inspection team was also able to check the production information provided ...

The report states that an inspection of this type would provide a high level of assurance and that the company did not foresee any difficulties with receiving inspections based on the principles that had been followed in the trial. Furthermore, the company stated that it received much more intrusive inspections under Australian licensing rules and that it was 'expecting to be subject to intrusive inspections under the US Food and Drug Administration inspection process' regarding its plans to manufacture a human therapeutic product. Growing international inspection systems for reasons other than arms control have been suggested to be an important, perhaps neglected, background context to the development of the BTWC Protocol.[30]

The UK

Given the implications for the pharmaceutical industry, the United Kingdom undertook a second practice visit in order to explore the issues more thoroughly. This time the visit was to a large, multidiscipline, industrial site of the type considered likely to be declared under the Protocol.

Regarding the value of the visit for providing transparency, the report was cautious about the value of a single visit to a complex site, but it also concluded that:

> the real benefits to transparency may only arise over a much longer timeframe – probably over 5 to 10 years – in which visiting teams become better versed in the type and nature of sites, and what they could expect to see at particular categories of facility ... [25]

In regard to CPI, the report noted:

> Tight control of information made it difficult for the VT [visiting team] to acquire the data it needed. However, given the wealth of open literature about the facility's activities coupled with the comprehensive briefing, the control needed to protect CPI did not make the VT's task impossible ...

Table 7.3   Reasons why CPI control works*

---

1. The procedures governing the visit made it clear that all on-site activities were subject to managed access.
2. The VT [Visiting Team] size was limited to three people and it was not allowed to sub-divide.
3. Preparation and pre-briefing of company personnel helped ensure that those involved were better equipped to handle VT requests.
4. Strict documentation control ensured that no CPI-sensitive documents were inadvertently handed over.
5. The visit's limited duration kept potential exposure to CPI to a minimum.
6. Re-packaging information in summary form to exclude CPI enabled the company to discuss key areas of its activities.

Note: *From Chapter 7, reference 25.

The paper is particularly interesting for the six reasons it gives for why the company never came close to losing control of its CPI. These reasons are shown in Table 7.3.

The five Nordic countries

This two-day international trial was carried out at a biopharmaceutical production facility. The facility was a medium-sized, privately-owned, fermenter-based facility in Norway. Part of the main purpose of the exercise was to determine if it was possible to: 'obtain sufficient information concerning the consistency of declarations, while taking due consideration of the need to protect Commercial Proprietary Information (CPI)'.[26] The report states that there were no language problems since English was used without any need for interpretation or translation services. Moreover, the facility was accustomed to inspections of various kinds and had fairly well-organized documentation available.

The conclusions of the report included the following items:

> The facility visited considered that the visit had only limited and acceptable resource implications ...

> ... the facility visited considered that the visit did not in any way interfere with or disrupt the daily production.

> The facility was confident that CPI was adequately protected during the visit ...

From the inspectors' siide the report concluded that: 'All questions relating to the facility's declaration were fully clarified. The Visiting Team found that the facility could account for all its declared activities and how production was conducted ... '. Though it was not easy to be sure of equipment usage during periods of non-production, the report also concluded that this would be possible by reviewing adequate records and interviewing staff.

Later practice visits

Similar results were reported from two following international trials, the Austrian report stating clearly that there was no risk of losing CPI during the visit[27] and the Swiss paper concluding: 'Finally, it should be emphasised that this trial inspection demonstrated that visits offer major benefits in obtaining a clear idea of the profile and activities in a plant that cannot be provided by a declaration alone.'[28] An Iranian trial concluded that:

> The random visit is considered to be a necessary measure within an effective compliance Protocol. The visiting team, with the cooperation of the visited State Party shall be able to validate the accuracy of the declarations without interruption of the normal work of the facility.[29]

By early 1999, therefore, there would appear to have been a widely shared opinion amongst States Parties that this seemingly crucial aspect of the Protocol could be operated efficiently and effectively. What is more this opinion was based on a considerable body of *empirical data* and not on conjecture. So whilst it might have been expected that there would be a number of difficult issues to resolve as the negotiations moved on from Ambassador Tóth's second phase (inclusion of detailed provisions into the rolling text) to his third (detailed negotiations on the key elements within the final framework), this issue of visits would not be one of them. However, it was not to be, and the cause of the problem came from a perhaps unexpected source.

The process of erosion

Reporting in *Disarmament Diplomacy* in December 1999, Henrietta Wilson noted, under the heading 'Visits', that: 'During the Sixteenth Session it became clear that the issue of visits was causing political problems within the Western Group ... '.[31] These problems had continued during the recently completed 17th session of the AHG and were related to the provisions for randomly-selected visits. As Wilson recorded:

> The Western Group favours developing an intrusive system of measures to monitor compliance. The majority interpret this as requiring strong provisions for randomly-selected visits, although it is understood that this majority has not necessarily included the US, Japan and to a lesser extent Germany ...

The reluctance, she suggested, was linked to the fact that all three had major industries on which the largest burden of visits would fall. The US also had the largest biodefence establishment which would also necessarily be included.

Germany

During the 15th session of the AHG in June/July 1999 the German delegation had introduced a new concept called transparency visits.[32] The basic idea was explained at a joint German–American meeting. It was: 'to leave the information provided by the visited facility to the discretion of the visited state party and the facility ... The concept, includes no elements of intrusiveness like sampling, accounting, and so forth ... '.[33] At the 16th session in September/October 1999 Germany introduced a working paper about how this concept was tried out at two practice visits. According to the concept, the purpose of these visits was:

To enhance transparency of declared facilities and activities;

To promote accuracy of declarations; and

To ensure that the Technical Secretriat [of the organisation] acquires and retains a comprehensive and up-to-date understanding of the different types of facilities and activities declared globally.[34]

At the 19th session in early 2000 Spain reported a similar trial of a transparency visit.[35]

It will be noted that the objectives of transparency visits as just detailed do not include any sense of verification of the declaration in a rigorous way. Indeed, the conduct of such visits is stated as including:

A facility briefing ...
A facility tour;
A question period; and
The drafting of a *factual account*.[34] (emphasis added)

What is particularly noticeable is the absence of interviewing and auditing. In regard to auditing, for example, the report of the Australian trial states: 'A random selective access approach to auditing was developed, to provide confidence in the accuracy of the information provided ... relating to production of the animal vaccine.'[24]

As a result of this measure the report concluded that:

The inspection team was able to gain assurance that any lower than expected monthly production figures were not indicative of diversion of material (or use of the equipment) for undeclared purposes in violation of the BWC, and that the records inspected were consistent with the information provided by the company ...

According to the report in *Disarmament Diplomacy*, Germany had been prepared to move along with the development of a common European position favouring a stronger approach. The same was apparently not true of the United States.

The United States

According to the *Disarmament Diplomacy* account, the UK attempted to bridge the gap between the US and other delegations in the Western Group at the 16th session: 'The majority felt that Britain's suggested "transparency visits" (a proposed alternative to randomly-selected visits) were too weak, although the US felt they were too strong ... '.[31]

Partly in response to this disagreement it appears that some members of the Western Group publicly went along with a NAM (Non-Aligned Movement) working paper that clearly contained elements unacceptable to most of the Western Group. With the Western Group in open disarray, its leadership role, and particularly that of its leading state, the US, was obviously diminished in the AHG.

The US difficulties, however, long predated this stage in the negotiations. As Jonathan Tucker reported in early 1998, for the first three years of the negotiations a deadlock amongst the relevant agencies in Washington prevented the United States from developing a coherent negotiating position in Geneva.[36] According to Tucker, its officials there were kept 'on the sidelines'. Despite the huge size of the US delegation, other States Parties, such as South Africa and the UK, were producing much more material in working papers.

Only in January 1998, at a high-level meeting, did the political heads of the three key agencies – the Secretary of Defense, the Secretary of State and the Secretary of Commerce – hammer out a package of compromise proposals. This led to the release of a Fact Sheet by the White House on 27 January 1998.[37] However, the problems did not disappear. Tucker wrote: 'Nevertheless, the new U.S. proposals are quite vague and many critical details will have to be worked out in the inter-agency process, which is likely to remain contentious ... '. In particular, he noted that the high-level compromise had not changed the views in the Pentagon that the BTWC was 'essentially unverifiable'.

Against that background, the disarray and lack of leadership amongst and by the critically important Western Group is understandable. Moreover, the difficulties were unlikely to end if the high-level compromise allowed for more inter-agency contention in Washington. Not surprisingly, therefore, Jenni Rissanen, reporting on the 18th session of the AHG in January and February 2000, stated in a section on 'Compliance Measures' that the US had circulated a paper on transparency visits at the very end of the session: 'It is understood that the US position is that *transparency visits should not be considered as a way of ensuring that declarations are accurate and complete*, and, that the mandate of the transparency visit should be defined accordingly ... '[38] (emphasis added). In accordance with this position, it was also understood that the United States considered: 'visits should consist of only a tour and a briefing at the facility and should take place at the discretion of the visited State Party ... '. With the paper being circulated at the end of the session, reactions were expected later. Reporting on the 20th session in July 2000 Rissanen stated that:

> The United States delegation has opposed the concept of random visits. ... It has received little support for its position, even in the Western Group where the EU considers visits as essential for an effective Protocol, and is becoming increasingly isolated ... [39]

What then *was* the United States in favour of in a Protocol? Clearly, the US position, as set out in its paper of February 2000,[40] suggests the weakest possible version of a visit (Table 7.4). The reasons why this position, so at odds with its allies, had come about are explored in the next chapter.

Table 7.4 Elements of US views on transparency visits*

Purpose
' ... The United States does not agree that validation of declarations can or should be done through such visits ... '

Mandate
' ... There should be no suggestion in the mandate that the purpose of the visit is to validate the declaration ... '

Conduct
' ... The United States cannot support provisions that suggest that the facility is expected to provide more access than afforded in a general tour of the facility ... '

Record
'The document prepared by the team at the conclusion of the visit should simply be a factual account of the team's activities. The provisions in this section should not suggest that the team draw conclusions or make findings.'

Note: *From Chapter 7, reference 40.

8
The Role of US Industry

Some of the official US thinking on the BTWC Protocol was elucidated in September 2000 in testimony by Ambassador Donald Mahley, State Department Special Negotiator for Chemical and Biological Arms Control. In his view, although there were benefits to be had from a protocol and it was not technically impossible to achieve, he explained:

> First of all, *this is not an issue of verification*. As you know, the United States has substantive requirements for attributing effective verification to a treaty. It involves being able to make a judgement of high confidence in detecting a violation before it can become a militarily significant threat...[1] (emphasis added)

Ambassador Mahley elaborated this point by reminding the audience that a small biological weapons programme could become a threat and how a legitimate programme could be used to cover illicit activity in a way that made differentiation imprecise. He continued: 'The United States has never, therefore, judged that the Protocol would produce what is to us an effectively verifiable BWC...'. As we saw in the early chapters of this book, much depends on how the word 'verification' is defined. According to this definition of effective verification it is impossible but others, using a different definition of adequate verification, might not agree. The continuation of Mahley's testimony would appear to open up the possibility of compromise:

> There is, however, real value in increasing the transparency associated with biological activity. What we have sought in the negotiations is greater transparency into the dual-capable activities and facilities that could be misdirected for BW purposes...

With some flexibility on either side it would thus appear to have been possible to reach a compromise position with the European Union. But the question is, what degree of flexibility did the US negotiators actually have? We have already seen reference by knowledgeable commentators[2] to difficulties in the inter-agency process in Washington. Another player that might have been expected to help, given the record of the US chemical industry in relation to the CWC, was the US pharmaceutical/biotechnology industry.

Alternative US viewpoints

It is not, of course, that there is a lack of debate or presentation of alternative views in the United States. The Federation of American Scientists (FAS) has long had a Working Group on BW Verification and it has presented a series of papers on compliance measures,[3-5] and particularly on visits.[6-8] For the FAS, the purpose of visits is: 'To reassure each State Party that other States Parties have accurately declared the dual-use biological capabilities within their jurisdiction or control according to the requirements of the Protocol.'[7] And for that purpose, the mandate for the visits should be: 'To confirm that declarations are consistent with the requirements of the *protocol*...'. To achieve this the conduct of the visit should certainly allow the protection of confidential information through the application of managed access. In short, this position is much closer to the position of the European Union than to that of the United States.

The pharmaceutical/biotechnology industry

The diverse biotechnology industry is well represented in Washington, but it is clear that in regard to the BTWC Protocol negotiations the representatives of the Pharmaceutical Research and Manufacturers Association (PhRMA) have taken the leading role on behalf of the whole group in dealing with government.[9] Moreover, these representatives have had considerable access. As reported in Congressional testimony in September 2000 by Susan Koch, Deputy Assistant Secretary for Threat Reduction Policy: 'BWC measures will for the most part focus on a different universe of facilities [than the CWC]. We therefore have worked hard to ensure that facilities that are likely to be affected are fully appraised of negotiating developments...'.[1] Furthermore, the pharmaceutical manufacturers were well appraised of all the CWC negotiations, regularly attending the monthly meetings of the US Chemical

Manufacturers Association CW Committee which met from the mid-1980s through to the mid-1990s.[10] We can assume, therefore, that the *Statement of Principle on the Biological Weapons Convention* approved by the PhRMA Board on 16 May 1996,[11] and backed up by detailed documentation[12] and discussion by their representatives[13] over the following years, is a carefully considered account of their views. The statement makes it clear that PhRMA supports the goals of the BTWC and points out that both classical microbiology and the new biotechnologies will enable many new health products to be developed. It continues:

> Their development should continue, while appropriate restrictions on the potential misuse of the technologies to create weapons is enforced in a manner which does not expose American industry to the loss of its legitimate competitive trade secrets and other confidential business information.[11]

That seems a reasonable opinion for the industry to hold, and it has to be said that there was widespread understanding of the need for the protection of CPI from the debate on the CWC,[14] and some detailed consideration had been given, even outside of the industry, to how such information might best be protected within a strengthened BTWC.[15]

The interesting point is what PhRMA, as representative of the industry as a whole, considered to be 'appropriate restrictions'. The headings for their ideas, as set out in December 1996,[12] are given in Table 8.1. Now some of these points are quite unexceptional. It is hardly likely, for example, that inspectors not acceptable to States Parties would be employed by the organization (item 9 in Table 8.1). Similarly, of course, managed access would have to be available to protect CPI in any on-site activity (item 7). Other points in this list might be highly contested by some experts. Why, for example, should Challenge Inspections in the Chemical Weapons Convention item 6 be governed by a 'Red Light' process (in which there has to be a vote to *stop* a well-founded challenge) whilst a weaker 'Green Light' process (in which there has to be a vote to agree to it *going ahead*) is used in the Biological and Toxin Weapons Convention? Does this mean that the proliferation of biological weapons is a less significant threat than that of chemical weapons? And what does this mean in regard to toxins – two of which are on the Schedule 1 of the Chemical Weapons Convention? Other points seem contradictory. What, for example, is the point of making the failed Confidence-Building Measures mandatory (item 1) if there is no effective mechanism for ensuring their accuracy (items 3 and 5)?

Table 8.1 PhRMA's views on appropriate restrictions*

1. PhRMA supports requiring current confidence building measures becoming mandatory, but what is declared should not be expanded.
2. PhRMA does not believe that there is any characteristic or combination of characteristics which discriminate a legitimate industrial facility from a potential violator of the 1972 BWC.
3. On-site inspections must be limited to challenge inspections.
4. Chemical Weapons Convention inspections are fundamantally different from Biological Weapons Convention inspections.
5. Other types of inspections have been proposed, none of which are supported by PhRMA.
6. Allegations which may result in a Challenge Inspection must be reviewed using the 'Green Light' Process before proceeding.
7. Managed Access must be employed during any on-site inspection.
8. The inspected facility must have the final determination of what is proprietary and therefore what information will be shared with the inspection team.
9. Inspection teams must be qualified and individual inspectors must be acceptable to the inspected State Party.

Note: *From Chapter 8, reference 12.

Table 8.2 PhRMA's objections to visits*

Routine Inspections
'PhRMA believes that routine inspections at facilities declared under the BWC have a low likelihood of detection or deterrence. The primary reasons for this are the ability to remove virtually all traces of any development, manufacturing or storage of biological warfare agents within the period of notification that an inspection will take place. Clean-in-place (CIP) systems can remove virtually all traces in about 1 hour...'

Other Non-Challenge Inspections
'Inspections that are shorter in notice, more intrusive, and more specific than routine visits, yet are not challenge inspections, have a low likelihood of detection or deterrence for the same reasons as routine inspections.
Routine inspections, and any inspections other than challenge, have the potential to inflict more harm to the site than benefit, due to the potential loss of confidential busines information, inspection cost, and adverse publicity...'

Note: *From Chapter 8, reference 12.

These issues have been widely debated and we will return to that general debate later in the chapter. Of primary interest here is the detailed reasoning behind PhRMA's rejection of any type of on-site activity apart from Challenge Inspections (which, given their 'Green Light' procedure, would be most unlikely ever to occur). PhRMA's detailed reasoning on visits is set out in Table 8.2. What is particularly striking is its narrow scope and technical attributes. There is no sense here of the purpose of visits being to check declarations through visual inspection, interview and audit. Instead, the 'primary reason' for rejecting visits is that the site could potentially be cleaned to remove traces of micro-organisms. Sampling and analysis were discussed in the VEREX process, but it is clearly not seen as being central to the developing concepts under discussion by the AHG in Geneva.

Surprisingly, this misunderstanding of the role of visits and the measures to be used persists in a detailed analysis given by a PhRMA representative in 1998:

> Using just a manual flushing system, a vaccine manufacturer could clear an entire production pathway in less than eight hours. More daunting for an inspectorate trying to detect cheating, many pharmaceutical plants have modern clean-in-place technology, which gives them the ability to purge an entire system in an hour...[13]

This passage is part of a rejection, not of randomly-selected visits, but of other kinds of visits (such as clarification visits). So it is clear that PhRMA has argued for a two-pillar system: CBMs and Challenge Inspection.

It is possible, of course, that the rather theoretical stance adopted by PhRMA was connected with the lack of any practice visits carried out, and reported to the AHG, by the United States. Certainly, as we saw in the last chapter, empirical evidence from the practice visits that *were* reported suggests that PhRMA's concerns over loss of CPI, costs, and loss of reputation (Table 8.2, last paragraph) were much exaggerated. Some members of the US industry obviously felt that to be the case. The leading US journal *Science* carried a 'Policy Forum' article in late 1998 by two senior members of a company selected to be amongst those to be considered as suppliers of new defensive vaccines. In their view: 'As representatives of an industry engaged in defensive programs, we consider such declarations and visits to be non-threatening and manageable...'.[16] Moreover, outside of the United States, industry found some of the arguments in favour of visits persuasive.[17] In particular, the reasoning behind a clarification process (which might end in a visit) at a lower level than Challenge Inspection was not dismissed.[18]

Despite this, it was being reported in 1999 that there was in public circulation a letter from William Daly, Secretary of Commerce, to Madeleine Albright, Secretary of State, which read, in part: 'I still believe we should continue to oppose random and routine visits, including "transparency visits" ...I seriously question a negotiating strategy of attempting to mollify the most hard-line members of the Western Group...'.[19] The letter was dated 24 May 1999 and the available extract ended tellingly: 'We have repeatedly assured U.S. industry that we oppose random and routine on-site activities.' Thus the reasons for the American position described in the last chapter, the consequent disarray in the Western Group and the lack of leadership in the AHG are much clearer. Whilst Secretary Daly provided other arguments for this position than just the protection of US industry, that must surely have played a significant role.

Even in May 2000 it was clear that PhRMA had not changed its position on the crucial issue of visits. A joint statement by PhRMA and FAS noted their agreement on certain points in the developing Protocol, but also stated:[20]

> We...disagree on the value of non-challenge visits, which include proposed tranparency and declaration clarification visits. FAS believes that these visits are essential for an effective protocol; industry however does not believe their value overrides the risk to confidential business information and facility reputations.[20]

Also in early 2000, it became clear through a series of statements that PhRMA's position had been taken up by a number of the industry's trade organizations in other countries. The European Federation of Pharmaceutical Industries and Associations (EFPIA) was concerned that: 'there may have been up to now, insufficient consultation between States Parties within the European Union and with the pharmaceutical and biopharmaceutical companies within those countries'.[21] The Federation included the national pharmaceutical industry associations in 17 European countries, as well as almost 50 individual pharmaceutical companies. Its concerns had a familiar ring including, for example, items such as the potential loss of proprietary information through site visits and investigations, risk of adverse publicity and the costs of completing declarations and preparing for on-site activities.

The Forum for European Bioindustry Coordination, PhRMA and the Japan Bioindustry Association produced a joint position paper on the Protocol. This paper included the following points: 'Our industries support simple declarations of relevant activities in order to promote transparency and build confidence that their facilities engage in legitimate enterprises...'.[22] This perhaps signalled a shift from PhRMA's earlier position that only the flawed CBMs should be made mandatory. There was also a reasonable request that the triggers for declarations should be clear and precise enough to pick out what was of greatest relevance. Unfortunately, the paper then went on to argue:

> In the event of questions and/or ambiguities about declarations, clarification procedures between the International Secretariat and the State Party concerned are regarded as appropriate *but should not necessitate any on-site activities.* (emphasis added)

It continued:

> Since the nature of microbiology is such that [it] is often easy to remove traces of any development, manufacture or storage of a biological-warfare agent, *any routine on-site activity is not a useful concept under the Protocol.* (emphasis added)

So there would be no mechanism for ensuring the accuracy of declarations, again for the same inappropriate reason.

Circulating in Geneva was another paper setting out the position of the 'Global Industry'. This paper acknowledged that private industry could not be exempt from the Protocol and again the idea of simple declarations in order to promote transparency was accepted. However, it added:

> It is also prepared to accept 'familiarisation' visits, provided they are voluntary and under the full control of the company inspected. Such visits can also have an educational role for international inspectors. *They must not aim at resolving questions about declarations...* (emphasis added)

This paper appeared to be written on behalf of PhRMA and the EFPIA. Essentially, it would appear that PhRMA had not changed its position overmuch and the other associations had been assimilated into the PhRMA stance. It is perhaps not remarkable then, since it had what it wanted nationally and internationally, that PhRMA reportedly did not wish to pursue the issue further. The chairman of Congressional subcommittee hearings on 'The Biological Weapons Convention: Status and Implications' opened the 13 September 2000 session by commenting: 'regrettably, we are not joined this morning by a representative from the Pharmaceutical Research and Manufacturers Association of America (PhRMA), who declined our invitation to participate...'.[24] He went on to stress PhRMA's responsibilities and looked forward to its future participation.

The contrast between industry involvement in the CWC and in the BTWC Protocol negotiations was emphasized in a critical editorial at the end of the year 2000: 'Regrettably, negotiation of the protocol has not had the depth of industry–government cooperation in the technical analysis and design of verification measures that so benefitted the CWC...'.[25] Instead, the editorial continued: '...to the detriment of both government and industry, dialogue has often been superficial and at times even polarised...'. Some NGOs were less restrained. One stated '[P]harmaceutical industry torpedoes biowarfare treaty'[26] and one author[27] saw biologists in general as having 'blood on their hands' if biological warfare ever broke out, because of their widespread indifference to their responsibilities. Indeed, for a major industry that had received a battering (including on the price of its shares) over GM food, the industry seemed curiously insensitive to the overall threat to its public image, despite warning signs such as the development aid charity Oxfam launching a major campaign against the way operation of its patents denied medicines to people suffering from AIDS in the developing world.[28]

As the year 2000 drew to a close, and the Review Conference of late 2001 appeared clearly upon the horizon, two questions needed answering. Could a Protocol be produced in time and what kind of Protocol would it be? For any progress to be made, the Chairman of the Ad Hoc Group had to achieve sufficient consensus about key differences to put a 'Chairman's text' on the table. We shall turn to that in the next chapter.

9
The Chairman's Text

During the 22nd Session of the Ad Hoc Group (AHG) meeting in Geneva a number of delegations called on the Chairman to provide a complete composite text in order that a full picture of what he thought possible – given the remaining differences between States Parties – was available to the delegations. During and immediately after this February 2001 session, the Chairman provided delegations with written elements of almost all of the Protocol and continued his intensive bilateral discussions with delegations. Then, at a meeting on 29 March in Geneva on 'Facing the challenge of disease in the 21st century', Ambassador Tóth stated that a composite text would be available to delegations the following day.[1] This, in essence, signalled that he felt he could and should produce a composite text to bridge the remaining differences and that the negotiations of the AHG had effectively reached a conclusion.

The composite Protocol text

The complete Chairman's text[2] was a document of 210 pages which was recognizably of the same basic structure as the last version of the rolling text produced by the 22nd session of the Ad Hoc Group in February.[3] However, there was a certain rewording of the Articles and a use of Arabic rather than Roman numerals for the Articles. The structure of the articles in the composite Protocol text and the final version of the rolling text are compared in Table 9.1. An overall analysis of the two texts[1] strongly suggested that an attempt had been made by the Chairman to find positions which gave reasonable weight to the differences between States Parties in his compromise proposals and that little new had been introduced where agreement had already been reached. This analysis also concluded that, overall, the composite Protocol text would, if agreed by States Parties,

Table 9.1 Comparison of the composite Protocol text and the final version of the rolling text*

Composite Protocol text (CRP.8)	Previously in rolling text (AHG/55-1 & 55-2)
Preamble	Preamble
Article 1 General Provisions	Article I General Provisions
Article 2 Definitions	Article II Definitions
Article 3 Lists and Criteria, Equipment and Thresholds	Article III A, B, C Lists and Criteria, Equipment and Thresholds
Article 4 Declarations	Article III D I Declarations
Article 5 Measures to ensure submission of declarations	Article III D III Measures to ensure submission of declarations
Article 6 Follow-up after submission of declarations	Article III D II Follow-up after submission of declarations
Article 7 Measures to strengthen implementation of Article III of the Convention	Article III F Measures to strengthen implementation of Article III (of the Convention)
Article 8 Consultation, Clarification and Cooperation	Article III E Consultation, Clarification and Cooperation
Article 9 Investigations	Article III G Investigations
Article 10 Additional provisions on declarations, visits and investigations	Article III H Additional provisions on declarations, visits and investigations
Article 11 Confidentiality provisions	Article IV Confidentiality provisions
Article 12 Measures to redress a situation and to ensure compliance	Article V Measures to redress a situation and to ensure compliance
Article 13 Assistance and protection against bacteriological (biological) weapons	Article VI Assistance and protection against bacteriological (biological) weapons
Article 14 Scientific and technological exchange for peaceful purposes and technical co-operation	Article VII Scientific and technological exchange for peaceful purposes and technical co-operation
Article 15 Confidence-building measures	Article VIII Confidence-building measures
Article 16 The Organization	Article IX The Organization
Article 17 National implementation measures	Article X National implementation measures
Article 18 Relationship of the Protocol to the Convention	Article XI Relationship of the Protocol to the Convention
Article 19 Settlement of disputes	Article XII Settlement of disputes
Article 20 Review of the Protocol	Article XIII Review of the Protocol
Article 21 Amendments	Article XIV Amendments
Article 22 Duration and Withdrawal	Article XV Duration and Withdrawal

Table 9.1 Continued

Composite Protocol text (CRP.8)	Previously in rolling text (AHG/55-1 & 55-2)
Article 23 Status of the Annexes and Appendices	Article XVI Status of the Annexes and Appendices
Article 24 Signature	Article XVII Signature
Article 25 Ratification	Article XVIII Ratification
Article 26 Accession	Article XIX Accession
Article 27 Entry into Force	Article XX Entry into Force
Article 28 Reservations	Article XXI Reservations
Article 29 Depositary	Article XXII Depositary
Article 30 Authentic Texts	Article XXIII Authentic Texts

Note: *From Chapter 9, reference 1.

represent an effective strengthening of the Biological and Toxin Weapons Convention. That broader issue will be further considered at the end of the chapter, but it is necessary to look first at the differences remaining in February 2001 over the key Articles of concern to us, and at how the Chairman sought to resolve them.

These disagreements over the rolling text are, of course, clear from the sections, particularly whole paragraphs, which remained in square brackets. The key articles, from the analysis of interest here, are those among the first nine of the composite text which attempt to strengthen *verification* of the BTWC.

The Preamble, Article 1 General Provisions and Article 2 Definitions

The Preamble of the composite text does not have legal force; rather, it sets out the rationale for what is to follow. The last but one of the 16 substantive paragraphs is of particular interest since it reads:

> *Convinced* that the most effective way to promote a world free of biological and toxin weapons is through strengthening the provisions of the Convention by the measures contained in the Protocol, and through promoting universal adherence to the Convention and this Protocol; further convinced that this will contribute to delivering significant benefits in terms of international security and development.

This paragraph, which combined two largely agreed paragraphs from the final version of the rolling text, clearly states the central reason for the Protocol – as the most effective way of promoting a world free of biological weapons – and the associated benefits in terms of development that it could bring.

Article 1 General Provisions begins with a new opening paragraph which draws upon some of the material in two paragraphs which remained in overall square brackets in the rolling text. This opening paragraph states the specific purpose of the negotiators of the Protocol:

> 1. The purpose of this Protocol shall be to strengthen the effectiveness, and to improve the implementation, of the Convention through the measures set out herein. Each State Party to this Protocol, reaffirming its obligations under the Convention, undertakes to fulfil the provisions contained herein.

The final, seventh, paragraph of Article 1 of the composite text clarifies completely the relationship between the measures in the Protocol and the Convention:

> 7. The definition of terms and objective criteria, which are an integral part of this Protocol, shall be used solely for the application of the specific measures set out in this Protocol.

This new paragraph therefore removes any doubt – nothing in the Protocol measures can in any way be seen as modifying the Convention itself. This view is reinforced by looking at the key definitions given in Article 2 Definitions. The definition of 'bacteriological (biological) and toxin weapons' and of 'purposes not prohibited by the Convention' are drawn directly from Article I of the Convention. Other definitions, which might have been understood as modifying the Convention (and which were therefore in square brackets in the rolling text), are omitted from the composite Protocol text. One new definition of 'biological materials' in the composite text defines them as:

> Liquid, dry or paste-like products containing any of the agents or toxins listed in Annex A, which are intended for the assessment of the means and methods of defence against bacteriological (biological) and toxin weapons, excluding culture collections of microbial organisms, at facilities declared in accordance with Article 4 (6).

The definition relates to increasing transparency in national biological defence programmes and/or facilities, and to the long argument over threshold levels, as we shall see below. However, it does this within the confines of the Protocol measures and does not affect the General Purpose Criterion of Article I of the Convention.

The remainder of the 24 definitions in Article 2 are either drawn directly – or by taking compromises between different options – from the rolling text, or by the addition of useful uncontroversial new definitions where this is appropriate (e.g. for Conference, Director-General and Organisation).

Article 3 Lists and Criteria, Equipment and Thresholds

Article 3 of the composite Protocol text consists of three sections:

A. List of Agents and Toxins;
B. List of Equipment; and
C. Annual and Current Transparency Threshold Levels.

The contents of these sections are closely related to those of Annex A of the final version of the rolling text.

The first section, A. List of Agents and Toxins, begins with a paragraph which is based on the paragraph which began Annex A of the rolling text. This makes clear that the list is for use with the declaration trigger for work with listed agents and toxins as well as for the declaration formats for national defence programmes and for declared facilities. The second paragraph states:

> 2. The list is not exhaustive. It does not exclude the relevance for the Protocol either of unlisted microbial or of other biological agents or toxins, which potentially can be used as weapons or as vectors used deliberately to spread disease.

There can thus be no doubt that the list of agents and toxins set out in the Annex on Lists (Annex A) is *illustrative* of the General Purpose Criterion, not a definition of what it covers. The list of agents and toxins set out in Annex A of the composite text is very similar to that in the rolling text, although there are some minor changes. Under the heading 'Human and zoonotic pathogens' are listed 15 viruses, ten bacteria and one protozoan species. Six animal pathogens and eight plant pathogens are also listed, as are 11 toxins. The third and fourth paragraphs of Article 3A then lay down the procedure for review and modification of this agreed list of agents. The criteria to be used are as those agreed previously and set out in Annex A of the rolling text.

Section B. List of Equipment has three paragraphs. These indicate which declaration triggers and declaration formats apply to the list of equipment, provide for the use of the list of equipment during a facility investigation, and then set out how the list may be reviewed and amended. The list of equipment given in the Annex on Lists (Annex A) is essentially equivalent to that already agreed in the rolling text. It covers items such as aerosol chambers, fermenters, freeze-driers, microencapsulation equipment, automatic DNA synthesizers, automatic peptide synthesizers, plant inoculation cabinets/chambers providing quarantine and cabinets/chambers designed or used for rearing insects.

Section C. Annual and Current Transparency Threshold Levels of the composite Protocol text is developed from the hotly contested Article III C. Thresholds of the rolling text. A footnote (number 20) to the title of this part of the rolling text recorded the long-held concerns of some parties about attempts to define threshold limits to the possession of biological agents and toxins. This footnote argues, on the one hand, that such attempts could undermine Article I of the Convention and that: 'Peaceful quantities of an agent cannot be defined independently of the particular circumstances of the use, which means that fixed thresholds cannot be used...'. It continued:

There would be a risk of a threshold for work for defence purposes being used to conceal offensive activities. The application of threshold limits could provide inaccurate impressions of the scale of activities at a facility because the self-replicating nature of microorganisms means that an agent amount at or below a threshold could be exceeded within a matter of hours...

Finally, the footnote added: '... even small quantities of biological agents and toxins could, depending upon their intended purpose, violate the object and purpose of the Convention'. Against this argument the footnote sets the opposing case that the 'establishment of threshold quantities of biological agents and toxins is essential for effective verification' and that such limits 'do not contradict in any way the mandate of the Group' nor 'affect the scope of Article I of the Convention'. This debate, of course, had run for a long time – even from the days of the VEREX process.[1]

The composite Protocol text provides a solution by emphasizing, in the first of its nine paragraphs of this section, that the aim is to enhance transparency:

In order to *enhance transparency*, each State Party shall provide in the annual declaration of facilities declared in accordance with Article 4(6)

[Biodefence] quantitative data on annual and current transparency threshold levels relating to the presence and quantity of biological materials as defined in Article 2(5). (emphasis added)

Then, at the end of the paragraph, use is made of the definition of biological material added to Article 2 in the composite Protocol text. The additional information is to be provided in declaration formats for biodefence facilities in Appendix C.

Article 4 Declarations

A central issue for the negotiators was to determine *what* was to be declared. This involved deciding on the triggers for declarations. The triggers in the final version of the rolling text (in Article III D. Declarations) are shown in Table 9.2. Even at the level of the titles it can be seen that a large measure of disagreement remained within the Ad Hoc Group.

Table 9.2   Declaration triggers in the final version of the rolling text*

Initial Declarations

- (A)   Offensive Biological and Toxin Programmes and/or Activities Conducted Prior to Entry into Force of the Protocol for each State Party
- (B)   Defensive Biological and Toxin Programmes and/or Activities Conducted Prior to Entry into Force of the Protocol for each State Party

Annual Declarations

- (C)   Defensive Biological and Toxin Programmes and/or Activities Conducted During the Previous Year
- (D)   Vaccine Production Facilities
- (E)   Maximum Biological Containment [(BL-4-WHO [and OIE] Classification)] Facilities
- [(F)   High Biological Containment [(BL-3-WHO [and OIE] Classification)] Facilities ...]
- [(G)   Plant Pathogen Containment ...]
- (H)   Work with Listed Agents and Toxins
- [(I)   Other Production Facilities ...]
- [(J)   Other Facilities ...]
- [(K)   Transfers ...]
- [(L)   Declarations on the Implementation of Article X of the Convention and Article VII of the Protocol ...]

[Notifications]

- [(M)   National Legislation and Regulations ...]
- [(N)   Outbreaks of Disease ...]
- [(O)   Current Exceeding of Threshold ...]

Note: *From Chapter 9, reference 3.

Like the rolling text, the composite Protocol text for Article 4 is divided into three sections:

A. Submission of Declarations;
B. Initial Declarations; and
C. Annual Declarations.

Section A consists of two paragraphs which first set out the requirement for States Parties to declare all activities and facilities of the types listed in the Article, and for the appropriate declaration forms in the Appendices to be submitted within 180 days after entry into force of the Protocol – for initial declarations – and no later than 30 April each year for annual declarations. The cases of declarations (and visits or investigations) where more than one State Party, or a State not party to the Protocol, is involved (for example, by having a facility on its territory belonging to a State Party) are dealt with in the composite Protocol text in the separate Article 10.

The triggers for initial and annual declarations are then set out in the two following sections. These triggers are summarized in Table 9.3. It is immediately evident, in comparing the triggers in the composite Protocol text (Table 9.3) with those of the rolling text (Table 9.2), that the list of triggers has been greatly shortened in order to focus on key issues concerned with compliance and that the list has been simplified by amalgamation of some of the remaining items into more coherent groups.

Table 9.3   Declaration triggers in the composite Protocol text*

B. Initial Declarations
Offensive biological and toxin programmes and/or activities conducted prior to entry into force of the Protocol for each State Party.
National biological defence programme(s) and/or activities against bacteriological (biological) and toxin weapons conducted prior to entry into force of the Protocol for each State Party.

C. Annual Declarations
National biological defence programme(s) and/or activities against bacteriological (biological) and toxin weapons conducted during the previous year.
Maximum biological containment
High biological containment
Plant pathogen containment
Work with listed agents and/or toxins
Production facilities

Note: *From Chapter 9, reference 2.

The philosophy behind the selection of declaration triggers and the precise aim of those involved was clearly delineated by one of the negotiators, at a NATO Advanced Studies Instititute in late March 2001. He pointed out first:[4]

> The philosophy used to select declaration of programs and facilities is based on the following assessments. Declarations, whilst being cost effective, must provide a maximum security benefit by obliging a potential proliferator to declare scientific and technical facilities which are most likely to be used to conduct such biological programs...[4]

He continued:
'This means that, due to the duality of most facilities and activities, *criteria of relevance for declarations may be based on the ease with which they can be turned from legitimate activities to hostile ones ...*' (emphasis added). The point was reinforced strongly in the following paragraph:

> It is important to note as well that declarations aim at giving information on *capabilities* of State Parties and of companies under their jurisdiction or control. In that sense, the fact that a facility is used or not has no real importance for declaration obligations... (emphasis added)

The problem, of course, is that the ease with which a facility or activity can be turned to hostile use is not a totally objective measure. There is a genuine grey area where people may honestly disagree, as well as some aspects that are hard to avoid including in any sensible set of triggers. To see how the composite Protocol text has sought to deal with this problem, a closer look at the individual measures is necessary, but it should first be noted that the formats for declarations in the associated Appendices (Table 9.4) are very well developed in the composite Protocol text. States Parties will not be able to provide material in the form that they individually believe to be appropriate. Instead they will have to provide data in formats which take up 45 pages of text and have considerable – but well-defined – detailed questions requiring answers.

Section B requires two initial declarations. The first of these involves a summary of *offensive biological weapons programmes/activities* conducted in the period between 1 January 1946 and the entry into force of the Convention for that State Party. Each State Party also has to provide, in the manner specified in Appendix A, details of facilities that produced microbial or other biological agents or toxins which were weaponised or

Table 9.4 Appendices on declarations required by Article 4 of the composite Protocol text*

Appendix A
Declaration of Offensive and/or Defensive Biological and Toxin Programmes and/or Activities Conducted Prior to Entry into Force of the Convention/ Protocol for each State Party

Appendix B
Declaration of Current National Biological Defence Programmes and/or Activities

Appendix C
Declaration Format for Facilities Declared in Accordance with Article 4 (6)

Appendix D
Declaration Format for Facilities Declared in Accordance with Article 4 (8) to (14)

Appendix E
Listing of Facilities in Accordance with Article 4 (7)

Appendix F
Listing of Facilities in Accordance with Article 4 (15)

*Appendix G***
Facilities Existing on the Territory of a State Party but Falling Under the Jurisdiction or Control of Another State Party/State

---

Notes: *From Chapter 9, reference 2.
 **Associated with Article 10, not 4.

stockpiled – and any use of such weapons – in the period 10 years prior to entry into force of the Convention for that State Party. Any information that subsequently comes to light has also to be declared within a specified time period. The second set of declarations is concerned with any *defensive biological weapons programmes and/or activities* conducted during the ten years prior to the entry into force of the Protocol for each State Party. Part B of Appendix A provides for this information to be provided in a relatively summarised format.

It has to be emphasized that the information provided in these initial declarations is there to show goodwill and transparency, but there is no intention for it to be verified in detail. The date of 1 January 1946 was chosen as a compromise. Some states would have liked the date to be 1925 (Geneva Protocol and catching Japanese activies in China) or 1975 (BTWC itself) The compromise date is the same as that decided in the 1991 review, in Confidence-Building Measure F, and therefore makes some sense. However, it is difficult to believe that all archive material (even if it still exists) has been thoroughly reviewed in every state. The ten-year period for which more detailed information is required is surely sensible in this situation.

Section C, on annual declarations, begins with a trigger concerned with *national biological defence programmes and/or activities* (Table 9.3). This requires first a summary of the general objectives and main elements of the programmes/activities and a summary of the research and development carried out. The major problem that had to be considered – evident from the heavily bracketed paragraphs in this part of the last rolling text – concerned the facilities that had to be declared.

The background to this problem essentially had three elements.[5] Firstly, not many States Parties (perhaps some 15 per cent of the 143 States Parties to the BTWC) operated a national biological defence programme. Secondly, these programmes were very diverse, ranging from thousands of people involved to tens, and costing from $1–2 billion to very little. Thirdly, it was widely expected that the number of States Parties operating such programmes would grow substantially over the coming decades. How, then, was a reasonable balance to be struck between the interests of such divergent parties whilst ensuring that no major loopholes were left through which large-scale illegality could remain unmonitored in the future? Clearly, a state with a very large programme would favour the declaration of a small number of major facilities, but this would risk the remainder being potentially open for misuse. A state with a small programme might prefer the declaration of a very small set number of facilities with a simple listing of the rest. But again, if those lists were not subject to any follow-up procedure (of the kind used for declared facilities) then again they could potentially be open to misuse. Since a biodefence facility is obviously one of the places where misuse might most easily occur, an effective solution on this trigger was crucial for the future success of the Protocol. This trigger catches not only military and government facilities but also civil facilities carrying out work for a government on its national biological defence programme.

The requirements for facilities declared in this category (Article 4(6)) are shown in Table 9.5. Now it could be argued that under Article 4(6)(c)(i) a State Party with a very large programme could carry out innocuous work at 10 facilities having 15 persons involved and then not be subject to monitoring of what it did elsewhere. However, it should be noted that the earlier requirement for a summary of the whole programme would certainly indicate that other facilities were involved and, if these were of any significance in terms of levels of total funding or personnel, it would surely be likely that questions would arise that could be taken up through other articles of the Protocol. For a programme

Table 9.5 Annual declarations of biodefence facilities*

Article 4. Paragraph 6 ... (c)
(i) All facilities conducting research and development on pathogenicity, virulence, aerobiology or toxinology at any site** at which 15 or more technical and scientific person years of effort or 15 or more technical and scientific personnel were engaged on such research and development as part of the national biological defence programmes(s) and/or activities;
(ii) If fewer than 10 facilities are declared in accordance with ... (i), a State Party shall declare the largest facilities, measured in terms of whichever criterion (technical and scientific person years of effort, number of technical and scientific personnel employed or level of financial resources expended) it selects, representing 80 per cent of the national biological defence programmes(s) and/or activities devoted to research and development on pathogenicity, virulence, aerobiology or toxinology.

Article 4. Paragraph 7
If no facilities are declared in accordance [with the above] each State Party shall...list and provide general information on all of its facilities, at which more than two technical and scientific person years of effort, or two technical and scientific personnel were employed, conducting research and development involving experimental work in the areas identified [above]. Where a State Party has three or more facilities subject to listing in accordance with this paragraph, it shall declare the largest facility in terms of whichever criterion [as above] it selects, and list the remainder. Listed facilities shall not be subject to randomly-selected transparency visits in accordance with Article 6 (3)(b).

Notes: *From Chapter 9, reference 2.
**A site is defined in Article 2 (see Table 9.6).

in which there were not ten facilities of the level required to trigger declaration under Article 4(6)(c)(i), the next requirement, under 6(c)(ii), would ensure that a large part of the programme was subject to declaration because of the 80 per cent total component of the programme that must be represented. Under paragraph 7, the composite Protocol text clearly provides for some insight into even very small programmes and requires declaration from any which are above a mimimal level and doing experimental work. Overall, it would not be difficult to argue that significant concessions had been made to states with large programmes, particularly the United States, in this section of the composite Protocol text. If, as seems probable, the United States would declare ten facilities under Article 4(6)(c)(i), it would not have to declare in any detail the other elements of its programme and would therefore be relieved of a considerable burden.

The next trigger in Section C, of facilities with *maximum biological containment*, has never been controversial, but such facilities are not widespread and none exist in the large majority of countries.[4] On the other hand, there are many facilities with high biological containment in the developed world. To require the declaration of such facilities, using high biological containment as a 'stand-alone' trigger, would clearly bring into the system a large number of facilities with no particular relevance to the Convention. For this reason, it has been argued that High Biological Containment (BL3) should not be used as a stand-alone trigger in the Protocol.[6] This appears to have been the position taken by the Chairman. Facilities with *high biological containment* are only to be declared if, additionally, there is production of vaccines (under Article 4(12)) or certain other forms of production (under Article 4(13,14,15) or:

> *Insertion of any nucleic acid sequence(s) into, or other intentional modification of the nucleic acid of, an agent listed in Annex A or an organism producing a toxin listed in Annex A,* for the purpose of creating a novel or genetically modified agent, organism or toxin; or to enhance the production of a toxin or its toxic sub-units... (emphasis added)

or:

> *Insertion of a nucleic acid sequence from any agent, or coding for any toxin listed in Annex A, or coding for a toxic sub-unit of such a toxin, into an organism* for the purpose of creating a novel or genetically modified organism with increased disease causing or toxic properties characteristic of one or more agents or toxins listed in Annex A, or to enhance the production of any such toxin or toxic sub-units... (emphasis added)

These requirements, which are needed in combination with high biological containment, would appear, effectively, to restrict the declarations triggered to facilities of real relevance to the Convention. In the composite Protocol text there is an additional requirement – that the working area under continuous high biological containment must exceed $100\,m^2$ for declaration to be necessary This again removes smaller, less relevant, facilities from the declaration requirement.

The *plant pathogen containment* trigger which follows on the list was bracketed in the final version of the rolling text, but is retained in the composite Protocol text, again though with the requirement that the area under a continuous system of plant pathogen containment must exceed $100\,m^2$.

The next trigger for declarations is *work with listed agents and/or toxins.* Facilities have to be declared if they have conducted any of a series of specified activities with listed agents or toxins during the previous calendar year. These activities are, first, production or recovery of any of the agents using certain specified levels of apparatus. Then there are the two related to genetic manipulation already quoted above (under high biological containment) and, finally, intentional aerosolization of any agent or toxin listed under specified conditions. It seems unlikely that many industrial facilities would be caught by this trigger, due to the way the detailed requirements of the trigger are set. On the other hand, the limited nature of the list of agents does not seem to matter as such facilities deal with many pathogenic organisms and varying the organisms does not appear to change what facilities are caught.[7]

The final trigger for declarations – *production facilities* – is, of course,of real interest to industry. Each State Party is required to make declarations under a series of sub-headings. First it has to declare each facility which, during the previous calendar year:

> with primary production containment or high biological containment produced with the use of fermenters and/or bioreactors, embryonated eggs or other means, with or without recovery by concentration or isolation, micro-organisms or substances causing a specific and protective immune response as an ingredient of:
>
> (a) Any vaccine for humans that is for the general public or for armed forces, or which was licensed, registered or otherwise approved by a component of the government of the State Party for distribution or sale;
>
> (b) Any vaccine for animals that is available to the general public, or which was licensed, registered or otherwise approved by a component of the government of the State Party for distribution or sale.

This is equivalent to the 'Vaccine Production Facilities' trigger which long figured in various versions of the rolling text. Many of the key words in the composite Protocol text are defined in Article 2 (Table 9.6) which adds to the impression that this trigger has been carefully drawn to catch what is of real concern.

The succeeding paragraph in the listing, under production facilities, is probably the next most important to industry after that on vaccine production facilities. The paragraph states that each party shall declare: 'each facility, which during the previous calendar year, produced and recovered any micro-organism (other than for food or beverages for humans or as a waste or by-product) or microbially produced diagnostic

Table 9.6 Some relevant definitions from Article 2*

Facility means:
   (a) For the purpose of declarations in accordance with Article 4, and follow-up after submission of declarations in accordance with Article 6:
      –Any room or suite of rooms, laboratory(ies), building(s), structure(s) or parts of a building(s) or other structures which is or are used to conduct activity(ies) as specified in Article 4. Such a facility may have an identifiable boundary and/or single operational control;
   (b) For the purpose of facility investigations in accordance with Article 9:
      –The buildings, parts of buildings or other structures within the final perimeter.

Primary production containment means:
   –Features in any system of equipment for the production of microbial or other biological agents or toxins, that are designed to separate the production process from the environment thereby preventing release that could compromise the health of workers or cause harm to the product or the environment.

Production, for the purpose of declarations, means:
   –The cultivation of replicative biological agents by any means, or the synthesis, biosynthesis or extraction of non-replicative biological agents including toxins.

Site means:
   –The location and the integration of one or more facilities to be declared in accordance with Article 4 (6) (c) within a geographically and/or physically defined area which may have an identifiable boundary and which cannot be smaller than a building.

Vaccine means:
   –Any preparation, including live-attenuated, killed or otherwise modified micro-organisms or components obtained from organisms, including inactivated toxins and nucleic acids, which when introduced by any route into a human being or animal, induces in it a specific immune response for prophylaxis or protection against infections disease(s) or intoxination, and which is safe for human beings and/or animals.

Note: *From Chapter 9, reference 2.

reagent for public sale'. It then specifies a series of additional quantitative requirements such as fermenter sizes and quantities of growth media which also have to be exceeded in order to trigger a declaration. In the analogous paragraph of the rolling text there was a mention not only of micro-organisms but also of the production of 'other substances'. However, 'other substances' was in square brackets and is not in the composite Protocol text. This omission would exempt from consideration facilities theoretically very capable of misuse[7] in countries with major industries and again might be viewed as a concession to these countries – particularly the United States. The argument that this represents a significant weakening of the Protocol is contradicted to an extent by the final trigger for production facilities (see below).

The penultimate trigger under production facilities requires declarations for each facility which: '...produced and recovered any biocontrol agent ... or any plant inoculant ... using one of the following' and again there follows a series of quantitative requirements that need to be exceeded before a declaration is triggered. In Article 2 a biocontrol agent is defined as: 'A living organism or biologically active substance originated from such an organism, used for the prevention, elimination or reduction of plant diseases, pests or unwanted plants.' A plant inoculant is defined as: 'Any formulation containing a pure or predetermined mixture of micro-organisms that alter the properties of plants or crops...'. This trigger is probably not, at present, of major significance to industry, particularly as the quantitative limits are set at quite a high level. However, the relevant industry is growing and this trigger could increase in importance.

The final paragraph of the set under production facilities represents an interesting innovation which, to some extent, corrects the deficiency noted above and opens up the possibility of further development in the future. The paragraph requires that each State Party:

> list and provide information on all of its facilities unless otherwise declared under this Article which, during the previous calendar year, produced for public sale *microbially produced substances* (other than for food or beverages for humans, or as a waste or by-product), whether or not chemically modified, using one of the following...

Again there is a series of quantitative requirements that must also be exceeded. These are followed by the statement:

> The first Review Conference shall decide whether such facilities should become subject to randomly-selected transparency visits, taking into account the experience gained from the implementation of randomly-selected transparency visits, and the fulfilment of the objectives of the Protocol.

This ends the text of Article 4. In summary, it seems reasonable to argue that in the composite Protocol text the Chairman has arrived at a sensible balance between the interests of the various States Parties as evidenced by the remaining differences (square-bracketed text) in the last version of the rolling text. The numbers of facilities likely to be declared were not going to be very different from previous estimates because nothing radically new had been brought into the text by the Chairman.

Article 5 Measures to Ensure Submission of Declarations

This short article represents a useful departure from previous practice as employed in the Chemical Weapons Convention (CWC). It provides for an increasingly severe set of penalties that can be applied to States Parties which do not provide their declarations according to the agreed timetables. This development can clearly be viewed as being to an extent provoked by delays in the submission of CWC declarations, particularly by the United States. The penalties begin quite severely with a denial of access to declarations from other States Parties and escalate over a short period through a series of increasingly serious measures to exclusion from membership of the Executive Council and denial of a vote in the Conference of States Parties. These appear to be tough penalties likely to encourage the submission of declarations on time.

Article 6 Follow-up after Submission of Declarations

Article 6 is divided into four sections:

A. The role of the Technical Secretariat;
B. Randomly-selected transparency visits;
C. Voluntary assistance visits; and
D. Declaration clarification procedures.

Each section will be briefly considered in turn.

Section A deals with the *role of the Technical Secretariat*. In order to promote fulfilment of the declarations obligations of States Parties under the Protocol, it is required to:

(a) Process and make a technical analysis of the declarations;
(b) Conduct a limited number per year of randomly-selected transparency visits to facilities declared in accordance with Article 4 ...
(c) If, in its analysis ... it identified any ambiguity, uncertainty, anomaly or omission related solely to the content of the declaration, seek clarification from the State Party, in accordance with the procedures set out [in Section D].
(d) Provide technical assistance to States Parties to help them compile individual facility and national declarations ... including, if requested, a voluntary assistance visit, in accordance with the procedures set out [in Section C].

A State Party which has questions concerning the declaration of another State Party may seek clarification either according to Article 6 Section D or through Article 8 on Consultation, Clarification and Cooperation. Ten paragraphs in Section A deal with the allocation of the different types of visit, the selection of facilities for randomly-selected transparency visits, limitations on the numbers of these visits and on voluntary clarification visits, the review of these provisions by the first and subsequent Review Conferences and with the annual programme of visits and its review by the Executive Council. The key features of the visit system in these paragraphs are that: there is an overall limit of 120 visits in any calendar year worldwide, the number of randomly-selected transparency visits must be between 50 per cent and 75 per cent of the total; the number of voluntary assistance visits must be between 5 per cent and 25 per cent of the total; any clarification visits are deducted alternately from the total number of randomly-selected transparency visits and the total number of voluntary assistance visits. Provision is made for the Review Conferences to revise these arrangements in the light of experience. It is probable that the voluntary assistance visits and clarification visits will be predominantly required early in the life of the Protocol as States Parties learn what has to be done. Later on it can be expected that there will be less need for such visits. Some built-in flexibility is therefore sensible and necessary.[4]

Article 6 states that randomly-selected transparency visits shall be spread among a representative range of facilities in terms of their scientific and technical characteristics, and that the timing of a visit to any particular facility shall not be predictable.

Another set of provisions places limits on the impact of the randomly-selected transparency visits on States Parties such that no State Party will receive more than seven randomly-selected transparency visits in any one year; each State Party that declares facilities will receive at least two randomly-selected transparency visits in any five-year period; no individual facility will receive more than three randomly-selected transparency visits in any five-year period. Taking these limits into account, the probability of a State Party receiving a visit will be proportional to the number of declared facilities. Additionally, no State Party will receive more than five voluntary (that is, requested by it) clarification visits in any five-year period. The composite Protocol text thus sets out a straightforward visit system – equitably spread across States Parties and different types of facilities and visits – for the effective follow-up of declarations.

Section B deals with *randomly-selected transparency visits*. The objectives stated for such visits are:

(a) Increasing confidence in the consistency of declarations with the activities of the facility and encouraging submission of complete and consistent declarations;
(b) Enhancing transparency of facilities subject to the provisions of this section;
(c) Helping the Technical Secretariat ... to acquire and retain a comprehensive and up-to-date understanding of the facilities and activities declared globally.

Such visits can also be extended to provide technical advice or information.

It is clear, therefore, that the purpose of these visits has resulted from a complex compromise. Whilst not there to exactly *check the accuracy of a declaration* in the sense of ticking items off on a list, the visit aims to *'increase confidence'* in the *'consistency of the declarations with the activities of the facility'*. In keeping with this, the name of 'transparency visits' seems appropriate. The size of the visiting team is limited to four members of the full-time Technical Secretariat, and the visit should not have a duration of longer than two days.

The section goes into considerable detail on the organization of such visits with sub-sections dealing with equipment, administrative arrangements, notification of the State Party, the mandate, visited State Party representatives, rights and obligations, initial briefing, tour of the facility, the visit plan, debriefing, possible co-operative activities and reporting. It may be noted, for example, that in the sub-section on rights and obligations the composite Protocol text states that the visited State Party shall: 'Provide access to the visiting team within the facility to be visited ... sufficient to fulfil its mandate...'. But, illustrating the balance between rights and obligations, it continues: 'The nature and extent of all access inside the facility, and to the information it contains, shall be at the discretion of the visited State Party.' What then is the visiting team able to do within these constraints?

The sub-section headed 'Visit plan' states that the visiting team, after its briefing and tour, shall prepare a plan indicating whether it wishes to carry out a range of activities. These are set out as follows:

(a) Review and discuss with facility personnel the declaration and the information contained in the briefing and tour provided by the visited facility.

(b) Discuss, with the consent of the visited State Party, specific factual points, related to the visit mandate, on the activities of the declared facility as described in the facility declaration, briefing and tour, with facility personnel who are able to address these factual points...

(c) Review, with the consent of the State Party, documentation relevant to the mandate in order to facilitate further understanding of the visiting team of the declared activities...

(d) Visit, and revisit if necessary, to ensure fulfilment of the mandate, parts of the facility involved in the declared activities...

A final sub-paragraph (e) allows for the visited State Party to offer additional access or to grant the visiting team the opportunity to carry out other on-site activities that it or the team may suggest. This last point is important to note because it is clear from the experience of the CWC[8] and practice visits[9] that adoption of a helpful attitude by a facility with nothing to hide is likely to result in a short and trouble-free visit. It follows that a visited facility/State Party which takes a difficult and obstructive attitude is at least likely to raise questions in the minds of a visiting team.

Opportunities for being difficult and obstructive are necessarily built into the arrangements for randomly-selected visits because of the need for a balance of rights and obligations. For example, in regard to the final report on the visit, the text states that:

The visiting team shall submit the final report to the Director-General and the visited State Party not later than seven days after the receipt of any comments from the visited State Party. *The Director-General shall, as a rule, provide copies of the final report, on the request of any State Party, unless otherwise indicated by the visited State Party.* (emphasis added)

A State Party would be within its rights to refuse any other State Party(ies) access to the report – but this would surely carry costs for the visited State Party.

Section C sets out the details of the system for *voluntary assistance visits*. These are obviously an important component of the fulfilment of the overall mandate of the Ad Hoc Group but much more important for our central concern with compliance measures is *Section D* which deals with *declaration clarification procedures*. Concerns over the declaration of any facility of a State Party can, as previously noted, be dealt with under this section of Article 6 or through the provisions of Article 8. This applies also in the case of a clarification request relating to a facility which is believed to meet the criteria for declaration, but which has not been declared. In this case the State Party whose facility is in question (the requested State Party) has to notify the Director-General of which article it decides to use for its response. The important point is that facilities which appear to meet the criteria for declaration but have not been declared are subject to question. In general, the procedures under Article 6 would appear to be of a less severe nature than those under Article 8 and thus perhaps the option of choice.

Section D of Article 6 has sub-sections dealing with requests for clarification, consultations including a consultative meeting, initiation of a voluntary clarification visit and post-consultative meeting procedures. Notably, if the process does not resolve the issue, the Executive Council has to consider information provided by the Director-General on the implementation of the clarification procedures. The Executive Council then has a range of options open to it including:

(a) That no further action is justified;
(b) To recommend further consultations with the requested State Party ...
(c) By a decision to be taken in accordance with Article 16 [the Organization], to initiate a clarification visit ...
(f) Determine whether the clarification process initiated by a State Party has been abused, and if so, whether the requesting State Party should be held to account for such abuse. If so determined, the Executive Council shall decide on appropriate measures.

This last provision gives all States Parties protection from unwarranted use of this section of Article 6. The procedures for carrying out a clarification visit are set out in the remaining part of the section. A final report of such a visit can lead to the Executive Council requiring the visited State Party to: 'take any necessary measures such as revision of, or addition to, the declaration concerned or submission of a new declaration within a specified time limit'. It has been pointed out that this clarification system has some elements of deterrence.[4] If a proliferator tries to use a declared facility, that facility may be visited but an undeclared facility may also be subject to clarification and the illegal activity thereby exposed. Clearly, a State Party could refuse any visit to its territory, but a refusal is likely to raise further questions and the possibility of more rigorous forms of enquiry.

Article 8 Consultation, Clarification and Cooperation

Article 8 allows States Parties, without prejudice to their rights under Article V of the Convention, or their rights to request an investigation, to consult through a variety of mechanisms:

> on any matter which may be raised relating to the object and purpose *of the Convention*, or the implementation of the provisions of this Protocol, and clarify and resolve any matter which may cause concern about possible non-compliance with the obligations of this Protocol or the Convention...

The article therefore deals with a much wider range of issues than the compliance measures within the Protocol, but it is also clearly possible for issues concerning declarations to be dealt with under this article and indeed possible that a voluntary clarification visit in regard to a declaration could come about in this way. Unresolved concerns on any issue raised under the article could eventually be handled by the Executive Council or the Conference of States Parties.

Article 9 Investigations

The ultimate compliance measures in the composite Protocol text are contained in Article 9 on investigations. Though it seems improbable that investigations will occur with any frequency they are an essential measure in the Protocol should all else fail to resolve a substantial concern over non-compliance. Article 9 is a weighty element in the composite Protocol text, having nine sections (Table 9.7).

Table 9.7 Sections of Article 9 investigations*

A. Types of Investigations
B. Outbreaks of Disease
C. Consultation, Clarification and Cooperation
D. Initiation of Investigations
E. Information to be Submitted with a Request for an Investigation to Address a Concern of Non-Compliance with the Convention
F. Follow-up after Submission of an Investigation Request and Executive Council Decision-Making
G. Access and Measures to Guard against Abuse During the Conduct of Investigations
H. Final Report
I. Review and Consideration of the Final Report

Note: *From Chapter 9, reference 2.

Section A describes the two types of investigation:

(a) Investigations to be conducted in geographical areas where release of, or exposure of humans, animals or plants to, microbial or other biological agents and/or toxins has given rise to a concern about possible non-compliance under Article I of the Convention or use of bacteriological (biological) and/or toxin weapons, hereinafter referred to as *'field investigations'*.

(b) Investigations of alleged breaches of obligations under Article I of the Convention, to be conducted inside the perimeter around a particular facility at which there is a substantive basis for a concern that it is involved in activities prohibited by Article I of the Convention, hereinafter referred to as *'facility investigations'*. (emphasis added)

The crucial issue is the degree of automaticity with which requests to the Executive Council for investigations are allowed to proceed. The composite Protocol text allows for five possibilities which may be summarized as follows:

1. A request for a field investigation of alleged use of biological weapons on the territory (or places under the control) of the requesting State Party shall proceed unless a three-quarters majority of members present and voting decide otherwise.
2. A request for a field investigation of alleged use of biological weapons on the territory (or places under the control) of another State Party shall proceed unless a simple majority of members present and voting decide otherwise.
3. A request for a field investigation on the territory (or places under the control) of a requesting State Party where there is concern that an outbreak of disease is related to prohibited activities shall go ahead unless two-thirds of members present and voting decide otherwise.
4. A request for a field investigation on the territory (or places under the control) of another State Party when there is a concern that an outbreak of disease is related to prohibited activities shall only go ahead if approved by a simple majority of members present and voting.
5. A request for a facility investigation should only go ahead if approved by a simple majority of members present and voting.

These cases represent a sliding scale of 'red light' through to 'green light' procedures. The important point is that the investigations go ahead if the Executive Council so decides.

An assessment of the composite Protocol text

It is easy to argue that the negotiators could have done better and that the composite Protocol text could have been stronger in many respects.[10] However, the composite text is a compromise between states with varying interests and as such, no parties – including those wanting the strongest possible compliance measures – were going to achieve all their aims. But how well did the negotiators do in the end?

The BTWC and the BTWC Protocol regime

The first point of comparison is with the Biological and Toxin Weapons Convention itself.[1] What more would a Protocol based on the composite text bring to the BTWC regime? The starting point of any comparison must be to note that the Protocol regime brings much else besides a set of enhanced compliance measures. It would bring an organization where none exists today and that would be the necessary foundation for the care and development of the regime. It would also bring an elaborated set of specific measures and a Cooperation Committee and Department of the Technical Secretariat for international co-operation where none exists today. The Protocol would also entail the establishment of national authorities and penal legislation, provisions for assistance and transfer procedures. Together these represent a massive advance over the Convention alone.

In terms of compliance measures, mandatory declarations replace patchy and variable Confidence-Building Measures. Analysis of declarations and follow-up with visits and clarification procedures are entirely new, as are voluntary assistance visits. The processes of consultation through to investigations replace the practically unused Article V and Article VI measures of the Convention. Field investigations add to the possibility of UN Secretary-General-initiated investigations and facility investigations are quite new.

In short, it is difficult not to see the BTWC Protocol regime as a major advance on the BTWC alone brought about – if it can be brought to a successful conclusion – by a decade of work by the international community.

The BTWC Protocol regime and the CWC

How well, though, does the envisaged BTWC Protocol regime stand in relation to the most comparable modern arms control agreement – the Chemical Weapons Convention? It has to be understood first that the CWC is being implemented to the general satisfaction of the international community. As the Director-General noted in May 2000: 'Today, the Chemical Weapons Convention is a modern international treaty matching the challenges of the time. It has a sound scientific basis and is implemented with political care and in a balanced manner...'.[11] Though the destruction of chemical weapons and chemical weapons-producing facilities has no parallel in the BTWC Protocol regime, it is clear that in all other regards the two regimes bring the same general approach to the same type of dual-use problem.[12]

In relation to the potential BTWC Protocol regime, it can be seen that the CWC lacks certain features of the newer regime. It lacks measures to ensure submission of declarations, declaration clarification procedures, provisions for voluntary assistance visits, and looking beyond compliance measures, it lacks the detailed elaboration of specific measures for international co-operation and a Cooperation Committee. This should not be a surprise since it was to be expected that the international community would learn from its experience since the negotiation of the CWC in the early 1990s.

How well would the BTWC Protocol regime work?

It is all very well to compare the potential BTWC Protocol regime with other agreements, but the real question is, how well will it do the job it needs to do? In the view taken here the overall job is to reinforce the norm of non-use of biological weapons. This is done firstly by building trust and confidence amongst States Parties, then by providing some elements of deterrence and potential detection for States Parties which sign up, and a means of focusing attention and applying measures against those that do not sign up (particularly, of course, if they violate the norm of non-use of biological weapons).

How well, then, would the BTWC Protocol regime function in deterring non-compliance by a State Party? One way to measure this is to ask questions about the intensity of the safety net developed by the international community in different international prohibition regimes. As Ambassador Tóth has argued: 'IAEA is spending annually nearly $100 million on nuclear-related verification, OPCW is spending 60 million Euros annually on the activities undertaken by the organisation and CTBTO, the test ban organisation, is spending about $60 million just on verification-related activities'.[13] He went on to point out that these are not just numbers, but monetary amounts that translate directly into the strength of the relevant safety nets – particularly into on-site visits to check what is happening on the ground.

What then of the BTWC Protocol regime? For the CWC, it is as well to remember that in a country such as the UK 545 plants were declared at over 150 sites. Most estimates suggest that the number of facilities declared by countries like the UK under the BTWC Protocol regime will be smaller by a factor of ten. Furthermore, under the CWC the frequency of visits varies for different types of facilities, but under the BTWC Protocol regime it will be the same for all types of facilities. It can be reasonably argued, therefore, that the intensity of the safety net will be greater under the Protocol. Even so, some may argue that the compromises adopted by the Chairman to achieve the composite Protocol text have so weakened the compliance measures that they may give a false sense of reassurance if agreed. But would a potential proliferator wish to sign up to the Protocol envisaged? Are the measures such that a state wishing to undertake a militarily-significant offensive biological weapons programme feels safe to sign up in the face of these measures? It seems most unlikely that an unequivocal 'yes' would be the answer to that question.

If the Protocol can be agreed in its present form, and if it can be put into practice relatively rapidly by the States Parties, a significant step will have been taken to assure the international community that modern biology will be used only for beneficial, peaceful purposes and *not* for warfare as with so many previous scientific and technological advances.

10
The United States and the BTWC Protocol

This book began by noting President's Nixon crucial role in abandoning the US offensive biological weapons programme and how this led on to the successful conclusion of the Biological and Toxin Weapons Convention in 1972. In Chapter 2 reference was also made to the vital part President George Bush senior played in the negotiation of the Chemical Weapons Convention. Unfortunately for the BTWC Protocol, it appears that the United States has abandoned that leadership role. Reference has been made in this book, for example, to the opposition of relevant sectors of US industry to critical aspects of a strong Protocol, to the inability of the American government to formulate an effective position, to lack of real input into the Protocol negotiations and to the debilitating consequences of US inability to resolve differences with its allies on this issue. Where then did the United States stand when the Chairman formally introduced his composite Protocol text to the Ad Hoc Group at the start of the 23rd Session in late April 2001?

In a report on 25 April, the *International Herald Tribune* stated: 'The Bush administration is reviewing the U.S. position on an inspection program, and diplomats here say no progress in the Geneva talks was likely until that was finished.'[1] Of course, the United States is not solely to blame for the difficulties encountered in the negotiations, but its positive leadership is certainly a necessary condition for a very rapid and successful conclusion. Writing in the March 2001 edition of the *CBW Conventions Bulletin*, the editors stressed the critical nature of the decisions being made for hopes of completing the Protocol, as agreed, by the end of the year. They added: 'The first and potentially most important decision is to be made in the United States, where the new administration of President George W. Bush has launched what is reported to be a broad review of US policy toward the BWC Protocol.'[2] The editors were not sanguine about the outcome of this review.

They argued that the people from earlier administrations re-entering office had a 'well-known skepticism towards multilateral arms control agreements such as the BWC' and they suggested that American participants in the review would weigh success in the negotiations against potential costs to US biodefence and anti-terrorism programmes and to the US pharmaceutical and biotechnology industries. The editors argued that it was not clear whether any value was seen, by those involved, in the norm-setting function of the Convention itself and they suggested that in regard to the Protocol, 'members of the US delegation have made no secret in Geneva of their desire for a change in the mandate for the negotiation'. A change in a mandate is always possible, but given the acrimony likely on a breakdown of current efforts to agree a Protocol, that may not be a realizable hope.

Influential American commentators have certainly tried to look beyond such a breakdown and to ask what might be done if a Protocol cannot be agreed.[3,4] However, our concern here is with the more immediate issue of the Protocol itself. The editors of the *CBW Conventions Bulletin* were in no doubt about what was required of the United States.[2] They suggested that if other major countries such as Iran, Russia and China were prepared to make some compromises in their positions (on export controls, definitions and thresholds, and declared information respectively), and if the western states moderated their position on Article X, Ambassador Tóth might be able to fashion an agreement which could command support in the AHG as a whole. Under such circumstances, they argued:

the decision would again be Washington's to make: whether to take the lead with such a text, as an earlier Bush Administration has done for the CWC, thus strengthening the regime against bioweapons at state and sub-state levels, or to be responsible for the failure of the Protocol negotiations in 2001.

But is the United States capable of taking on such a leadership role or does it even wish to do so?

Fashioning US policy?

A major problem in the United States, as in other key states, is the desperate lack of public awareness of the Protocol negotiations and of how a Protocol could help deal with the dangerous problem of future proliferation of biological weapons.[5] Whilst there are, of course, honourable exceptions such as the Pugwash Movement,[6] it has to be said that biologists and medical professionals have generally not faced up to their ethical responsibilities[7] in this area and thus the general public has not had the information and support it needs to form a sound judgement of what is required. The lack of political will to reach an international agreement on the Protocol rather inevitably follows from this lack of awareness and informed support.

Unfortunately, the difficulties of the United States go far beyond a lack of informed public support. At what may, at first sight, appear to be a trivial level, the United States Institute of Peace (USIP) reported in October 2000 that senior foreign diplomats perceived US negotiators as being 'legalistic and blunt'. It reported that: 'many around the world perceive the United States as dictatorial at times, as in "What's mine is mine. What's yours is negotiable". They would like to see the role of the hegemon played with more grace and humility.'[8] It is fair to report that such views of the US representatives are widespread in Geneva and that is not conducive to fellow negotiators trying to do all they can to ease the US position. More seriously, the US Institute of Peace notes: 'There are special concerns about U.S. unilateralism and indifference to local circumstances and the domestic requirements of other countries.' We shall have cause to return to the issue of unilateralism later, but clearly the perception of US indifference to the concerns of others is likely to be compounded and augmented by the perception that the US representatives are blunt, arrogant and lacking in grace and humility.

A USIP Special Report, *Adapting to the New National Security Environment*, shows how these perceptions of US representatives link to an outmoded structure of bureaucracy (dating back to 1947) for dealing with major security issues. Among the recommendations of this special report – based on the work of a bipartisan 'Commission on National Security in the 21st Century' – some of the steps worth considering were:

Re-establish the importance of strategic policy planning capabilities;

Strengthen the duties, accountability, and standards of our diplomats and other foreign affairs officials;

Improve the quality and resources of our civilian agencies involved in international affairs so they are better prepared for interagency cooperation and enlarge the array of possible instruments of policy ...[9]

Certainly in Geneva it was common, during the Protocol negotiations, to encounter the view that a major cause of the lack of US leadership was an inability to resolve differences in the inter-agency debate in Washington. Worse, it seemed to many observers that for US representatives the debate in Washington was the real focus of their attention and not the negotiation of the Protocol in Geneva.

Such difficulties in Washigton do not, of course, just bring *minor* problems abroad. The document has a major section on 'Coalition building' which reads in part: 'The United States is in a league of its own among the world's nations. ... We are the most potent change agent in the world, yet there is so much in the world that we are incapable of coping with, especially alone ... '. It goes on to ask how Washington can best go about building coalitions to deal with such problems – not, one would have thought, by adopting positions that antagonize its allies. As one British commentator noted in a wide-ranging debate with a staff member of the US Senate Committee on Foreign Relations:

> What is frustrating for Europeans is the schizophrenic attitude America adopts: on the one hand, the 52 bilateral and multilateral treaties you mention have brought the United States a multitude of benefits; on the other hand, America sometimes seems all too ready to threaten such gains by wilfully disregarding the rules that it helped to establish.[10]

Nowhere is this illustrated better than in arms control.

The US move towards establishing a National Missile Defence (NMD) system by the fastest possible route, and without due regard to the concerns raised, is widely viewed as potentially very destabilizing. As the Director-General of the Department of Disarmament and Arms Control at the Ministry of Foreign Affairs in Beijing put it, in early 2000:

> The real motive of the US Government is to make use of the country's unrivalled economic and technological might to grab the strategic high ground for the 21st century in both the scientific and military fields, so as to break the existing global strategic balance, seek absolute security for itself and realise its ambition for world domination.[11]

If it becomes clear that the United States really is on a course of '*unrestrained selfish hegemony*'[12] then there is likely to be a very strong and prolonged reaction as other countries seek to preserve their sovereignty and autonomy. This possibility and the long-term consequences of such an action/reaction process make many outside of the United States very concerned about its policies.

One commentator asked what the rest of the world should do, with the new Bush Administration seemingly driving a juggernaut with an uncertain level of control:

> Powered beyond most people's comprehension, the US juggernaut looks set to mow down anything perceived to be in its way: collective security arrangements, environmental and arms treaties, relations with Russia and China, non-proliferation efforts ... [13]

The article looked to the great risks in the future:

> It is not only individual treaties, such as Kyoto and the CTBT that are under attack: the United States' cavalier attitude risks undermining the system of treaty-based international laws and norms that has been built up over centuries. We face global problems, but the United States seems determined to prevent global responses ...

The view that the United States has moved to a position of considering unilateral action based on its technological, intelligence[14] and military superiority in the later 1990s is widely shared.[10,11,12,13,14]

Another European-based commentator graphically summarized the current situation, at the start of the twenty-first century: 'The US imperceptibly has been shifting its focus from the need to foster global and regional consensus against proliferation, to the desire to keep all political and military options open and, indeed, broaden their scope ... '.[14] So the uncertainty in Geneva about US policy towards the Chairman's composite Protocol text did not come without a context. Indeed, it came against a background of general despair about the American attitude to multilateral negotiations as a whole and arms control agreements in particular.

The reception of the Chairman's text

When the AHG reassembled for its 23rd Session in late April 2001, a number of participants took the floor to comment on the composite Protocol text. The representative of Sweden, speaking on behalf of the European Union and associated states, welcomed the text:

> The EU believes that through your initiative, Mr. Chairman, the Ad Hoc Group will be able to find solutions to the remaining open

questions in order to conclude the negotiations before the deadline in November set out by the Fourth Review Conference and agreed upon by all States Parties.[15]

Ambassador de Valle Pereira of Brazil similarly stated that: 'the Brazilian delegation is of the view that we have here a balanced text that can serve as a satisfactory basis for further work ... '.[16] That is to say that the Chairman's text should replace the rolling text as the basis for discussion and a rapid conclusion could thus become possible. Other parties were less certain on these points, but none spoke to reject it as an important contribution.

Ambassador Soutar of the United Kingdom (one of the three Depositary States of the BTWC) spoke in strong support of moving forward on the basis of the Chairman's text:

> Yesterday some delegations seemed to be contemplating a debate on the status of your text. That is a debate in which I do not intend to take part. To repeat only one element of the EU statement of 23rd April, the United Kingdom is firmly of the view that this text is now the platform for the further political decisions that will be required in the course of this year.[17]

This is not to say that the UK was *entirely* happy with the text, which it clearly felt should be strengthened in a number of places.

The United States did not make a statement during the first week of the session, once again demonstrating the lack of leadership that had characterized its general approach to the whole negotiation. A report did, however, appear in the influential *Chemical and Engineering News* (*C & EN*) journal. This stated that: 'the Bush Administration has rejected the latest draft of a verification protocol intended to strengthen the Biological Weapons Convention ... '.[18] The report continued:

> But stunned by ally reaction to U.S. withdrawal from the Kyoto protocol on global warming, U.S. officials are searching for a diplomatic way of announcing the rejection, possibly – but not likely – at a multilateral negotiation session next week...

A more straightforward view was that: 'Whether Bush officials will keep their position quiet at the April session, in the unlikely hope that China, Iran, or other countries will do the dirty work for them, remains to be seen.'[19] One observer of the AHG suggested that the room was full of mesmerized rabbits with one snake. Everyone was waiting to see what the United States would do.

As the *C & EN* story was not publicly denied by the US, it appeared at least likely that opponents of the Protocol – including PhRMA – might have got their way. Yet the pharmaceutical industry itself was still reeling from the impact of world opinion and the forced withdrawal of its AIDS drug case in South Africa. Furthermore, there were signs that the media were beginning to home in on the question of future biological weapons and what should be done to prevent the awful prospect of proliferation of these weapons.[20] The battle for the BTWC Protocol seemed far from over in the Spring of 2001.

Renewed debate in the United States

At the end of the 23rd Session of the AHG in mid-May 2001, the Procedural Report noted that the Chairman had conducted extensive formal and informal discussions on his composite text and that:

> The discussions were aimed at *an exploration of future solutions of a limited number of specific issues*, as identified by the Chairman, in the following areas: Definitions; Declarations; Follow-up After Submission of Declarations; Measures to Strengthen the Implementation of Article III of the Convention; Investigations; Legal Issues... [21] (emphasis added)

The report noted that the AHG would continue its work at the next session so as to submit its report. It could therefore be concluded that the AHG might well be able to finish work on this limited number of specific issues in time for the November/December Fifth Review Conference as intended. At this point an unusually full and revealing debate broke out in the United States, with hearings in the House of Representatives,[22] a special issue of *Arms Control Today*,[23] and a major report from the Henry L. Stimson Center[24] in addition to newspaper coverage.

In this debate the Chairman's text was certainly not without support. Ambassador Leonard, who negotiated the original Convention on behalf of the United States, for example, told the Congressional hearings:

> With regard to the basic question, would the completion of this negotiation and bringing into force a protocol along the lines of the one that has been submitted by the Chairman of the ad hoc group,

would that be in the national interest? Would that enhance our security? I want to say that I think very clearly it would.[22]

Also, in the *Arms Control Today* collection of papers Marie Chevrier argued, as a political scientist who had carefully monitored the negotiations in Geneva throughout the work of the Ad Hoc Group,[25] that it was 'A necessary compromise'.

What were alarming from a European standpoint, however, were the US-centric views put forward in this debate. One scientist who had served on the US delegation in Geneva from 1991 to 1999 stated: 'Unlike any other state party to the convention, the United States has conducted a series of scientifically controlled mock inspections designed to test the measures (alone and in combination) under consideration in the protocol negotiations ... '.[26] He contended that these trials, carried out in the mid-1990s, were suppressed by 'a single staffer on the National Security Council', and were not therefore available to show other delegations the impracticability of their proposals. However, the trials appear to have been based on the limited view that: 'in order to achieve "verifiability", the measure in the protocol must be able to identify violations with a 50 percent probability or greater – and be able to do so before weapons were deployed or used ... '. Moreover, the trials carried out by other States Parties as the negotiations evolved, and publicly reported to the AHG, appear to have been totally ignored. It is also curious, if the matter had been so settled in the mid-1990s, that trials of on-site measures in relation to the BTWC Protocol were still being carried out in the United States in 2001.[27]

The ongoing interest in trial visits and inspections in the United States seemed strongly out of place viewed from the perspective of Geneva, where the negotiations had entered their final phase, and after all manner of adjustments had already been made in an effort to accommodate the United States. A particular example of a US approach to issues which had been the subject of negotiation years earlier in Geneva was the report, *House of Cards: the Pivotal Importance of a Technically Sound BWC Monitoring Protocol*.[24] This reported on some brainstorming sessions and a one-day trial visit by a group of biotechnologists, many of whom 'had given this subject little or no consideration' prior to taking part. The report, again using a limited view of verification, states:

After reviewing summaries of the draft inspection terms in the BWC rolling text, the industry group gave the negotiators a 'D' for their efforts. The inspection terms must provide ways to differentiate between the good guys and the bad guys, not leave question marks hanging over all facilities...[24]

The study concluded that a great deal of work was still required and cautioned – after almost a decade of multilateral investigations and negotiations – against a 'premature conclusion of a protocol'.

The 24th Session of the Ad Hoc Group in July 2001

Meanwhile a resolution was passed in the European Parliament on 14 June calling upon all BTWC States Parties: 'to show maximum flexibility and readiness to compromise so that the short deadline may be met and a Protocol may be adopted before the fifth BTWC Review Conference in November–December 2001'.[28] In London the Government, in answer to a question from Lord Judd, stated on 23 July:

> HMG will continue to press for a successful outcome to the negotiations on a Protocol to the Biological and Toxin Weapons Convention. At the next session of the Ad Hoc Group the UK Delegation will be working actively with the Chairman and other delegations involved to seek agreement on a Protocol text that is acceptable to all...[29]

The answer continued, significantly given what was to happen shortly in Geneva: 'Given the leading role that HMG has played in these negotiations, it would be a matter for regret if any countries were eventually unable to join consensus. HMG will, however, work hard to avoid such an outcome.' They and others, unfortunately, were not to succeed in this objective.

The AHG meeting began well enough on 23–24 July, with some 50 of the approximately 55 participating states – including all the major players save for the United States – making plenary statements supporting the Chairman's text as the basis for the necessary political decisions needed to adopt the Protocol prior to the Fifth Review Conference.[30] Then, in Bonn as if to set the scene for the US pronouncement in Geneva, the world community of 186 nations – minus the US – adopted the Kyoto Protocol on 23 July.[31] In Geneva there was uncertainty over what the United States would say, but against this background, and convincing press reports,[32,33] every reason to fear the worst. The worst was indeed what the US provided when it spoke on 25 July.

US Ambassador Mahley's statement (see Appendix 2 for the full version) was set out in seven major sections:

Introduction;
Objectives;
The Paradigm;
Biodefence Issues;
On-Site Activity Utility;
Constitutional and Ratification Issues;
Export Controls;
Disturbing Negotiation Positions;
Conclusion.[34]

The statement's final conclusion was that the Chairman's text was not an adequate basis for completing the Protocol, that it could not be made an adequate basis by further negotiation and, furthermore, that the whole conceptual framework on which the negotiations had been conducted would have to be changed. This statement has been subjected to detailed analysis and shown to be groundless on all counts.[30]

In analysing the US statement in regard to the key question, here, of verification, it is important to recall the mandate given to the Ad Hoc Group. As we saw in Chapter 3 this called for:

the establishment of a coherent regime to enhance the effectiveness and improve compliance with the Convention. This regime would include, *inter alia*, potential verification measures, as well as agreed procedures and mechanisms for their efficient implementation ... [35]

Specifically, the AHG was to consider: 'A system of measures to promote compliance with the Convention, including, as appropriate, measures identified, examined and evaluated in the VEREX report ... '. Now it is clear that if a system of measures was sufficiently comprehensive and intrusive it would be capable of detecting violations of the Convention with reasonable certainty. This was not the intention of the mandate. The mandate was to enhance the effectiveness of, and improve compliance with, the Convention. If a system of measures was designed according to less intrusive criteria, it would still be possible for States Parties to have increased assurance of improved compliance with the Convention and, indirectly, for the greater transparency involved to deter possible evasions.

This was well understood by the people involved in the VEREX and AHG processes. For example, Edward Lacy (now, in 2001, the US Principal

Deputy Assistant Secretary of State for Verification and Compliance) stated in 1994:

> the international process of strengthening the BWC must...go forward. The nations of the world should proceed expeditiously to craft a *transparency or verification* regime for the BWC, but they should do so in full recognition that without perfect intelligence – an all-but-impossible goal – even the most intrusive of verification regimes will not be foolproof...[36] (emphasis added)

A United Kingdom Foreign Office official also wrote in 1996:

> A compliance regime should be seen primarily as a *deterrent*. The prospect of a inspection team turning up at short notice to investigate and ask questions does make life difficult for clandestine production....A BTWC compliance protocol consisting of declarations of relevant activities and challenge inspections will provide a useful tool for investigating and clarifying potential *compliance concerns*. It will not provide all the answers, but represents a qualitative improvement on the current situation...[37] (emphasis added)

There is no doubt that many States Parties would have liked the Protocol to retain a stronger compliance regime of the type under discussion in the early stages of the negotiations. However, despite the watering down of their proposals – often by the United States – they still felt the Chairman's Protocol text contained enough for them to give it their support.[30]

It is alarming, to say the least, to find that the section of the US statement of 25 July headed 'Objectives' begins in this way: 'One central objective of a Protocol is to *uncover illicit activity...*'.[34] This is irrelevant since it was never in the purview of the mandate. Indeed, it is reminiscent of the US statement that gave Myrdal such concern when the BTWC was being negotiated (Chapter 1). The American statement, however, goes much further in arguing, for example in the introduction, that: 'The draft Protocol will not improve our ability to verify BWC compliance. It will not enhance our confidence in compliance and will do little to deter those countries seeking to develop biological weapons...'.[34] This is clearly nonsensical as a comparison of the Convention alone and the Convention plus the Protocol makes perfectly clear. The mandatory declarations, declaration follow-up procedures, non-compliance concern consultations/investigations and field and facility investigations in the Protocol are part of an effective strengthening of the Convention according to the mandate.[38]

The US statement then rejects the conceptual basis on which the negotiations have been carried out over the last six years. In the section headed 'The Paradigm' it states:

> These negotiations have worked from the outset on the model of regimes that have gone before. The most frequently cited paradigm for our work has been the Chemical Weapons Convention. Indeed, many of the arguments and justifications for the scope and nature of activities envisaged under the draft Protocol have used the CWC as the example of comparison.
>
> This [comparison] is, unfortunately, seriously flawed...

Ambassador Mahley's statement goes on to argue, quite incorrectly, that the universe of relevant facilities for the CWC can be defined whereas that for the BTWC cannot (see Chapter 2), and it is therefore suggested that whereas the CWC is acceptable the BTWC Protocol regime is not. Careful analysis shows that the intensity of verification in the proposed Protocol will be superior to that of the CWC.[30] Moreover, the US argument omits to address the obvious overlap between the two regimes in regard to mid-spectrum agents[39] and the fact that the genomics revolution is merging chemistry with biology at an ever-increasing rate.[40]

More serious than all the illogicalities of the United States statement is the contradiction between it and the official US position throughout the negotiations. It is clear that the mandate of the Ad Hoc Group (AHG) was, to a large extent, a reflection of American proposals. It is also clear that minimal US input in the form of working papers to the negotiations reflected particular American concerns, not a sustained critique of the paradigm and that the United States had (for example, in Working Paper 296 of July 1998) joined its allies in calling for a Protocol designed to meet the mandate in the very way that the Chairman's text eventually did.

When the world's leading state reneges on its commitments in this manner, there must necessarily be a huge impact on its standing, and on the trust that other states will place in its word. Indeed, given the US track record during the 1990s and early years of the new century, rejection of the Protocol is likely to *increase* mistrust of its intentions. So while the US statement claims that America will come forward with new proposals to replace the Protocol, in the unlikely event that it *can* find anything new to offer, the reception to its ideas is not going to be a sympathetic one. Furthermore, the US view that its actions will not damage the norm established by the Convention itself is hardly convincing, given that it is abandoning almost a decade of effort by many states – including all its major allies.

Numerous hypotheses were being advanced in mid-2001 to explain US behaviour. Some suggested that perhaps, since it had removed the Soviet and Iraqi biological weapons threats without having to get tied up in multilateral agreements which might restrict its freedom of action in the future, it felt no need to agree a Protocol. More darkly, some observers wondered if the real cause of concern in the US was that its biological defence programme was involved in too many black (secret) programmes that would be very difficult to explain. A more benign hypothesis was that while there had always been a broad consensus against the Protocol at the US lower inter-agency level, the political actors until recently would have been prepared to accept a Protocol. However, even they were never convinced that biological warfare was a sufficient threat to put it at the top of the political agenda and the resistance to agreement amongst some other states in Geneva, therefore, was enough to block progress in the absence of a strong US lead of the kind given to conclude the CWC. What changed in 2001 was the arrival of the new US administration, with high-level appointees who were ideologically in sympathy with the opposition to arms control agreements in general. Thus the inter-agency view was able to become the official US policy.

Whatever the reasons, the AHG was left with a difficult task in its 24th meeting, after the US statement on 25 July. Essentially, after a period of some confusion, it was decided that an attempt should be made to produce a Procedural Report which could then be taken up by the Review Conference in November/December. The intended Procedural Report was to cover four main issues:

– The work of the AHG to the 23rd session;
– the events of the 24th session;
– the mandate of the AHG; and
– the future work of the group.[41]

The AHG continued to work right through to the early hours of 18 August in an effort to produce the required consensus report, but this proved impossible, it appears, because of disagreements over how to describe what had happened at the 24th Session (was the US to be 'named' in some way for causing the breakdown?), and how precisely the future work of the group was to be set out.[41,42]

With this outcome the future of the Protocol remains very uncertain. While the mandate of the AHG remains intact and the matter could be taken up again by the First Committee in the United Nations General Assembly session in October and again at the Review Conference in November, the acrimony generated at the 24th Session of the AHG could be seen as quite likely to prevent any constructive progress. Even more seriously, it is clearly possible that at the review the acrimony will get in the way of any constructive progress in regard to the Convention as a whole, as well as preventing progress on the Protocol. Thus it is entirely possible that the decades of neglect of the BTWC will continue after the Review Conference.[43] Moreover, if there is no agreement on a consensus Final Document at the Review Conference, there is a concern that there will be no mechanism available to set a date for the Sixth Five-Year Review Conference. The whole treaty regime appears to be in jeopardy.

Futures?

One outcome of the US rejection of the Chairman's Protocol text might be seen as beneficial to the future prevention of biological warfare. The mass media at last began to take an interest in the issue and saw it as part of a general pattern of US opposition to multilateral methods in international relations. As *The Independent* of London headlined it: 'Now Bush rejects germ warfare treaty'.[44] A little reflection, however, was sufficient to bring the observer back to earth. While the US was busy rejecting the Protocol, it was reported that the Secretary of Defense testified to Congress that America believed 13 nations were seeking to acquire an offensive biological weapons capability.[45] Serious sources were suggesting that the Soviet offensive programme might still be in operation in Russia,[46] or that its fragmentation might have led to further proliferation.[47] Rumours of other major countries beginning to apply modern biotechnology to biological warfare were also not difficult to find.[48]

More to the point, by digging a little deeper it was possible to find the military contemplating how biological warfare might evolve. As the author of a US study of the 'Implications and effects of advanced biological and biological/chemical weapons at the operational planning level' stated: 'I do not agree with ... arguments against the development of biochem weapons for deterrence or offensive action ... biochem technology could develop stable, usable weapons for tactical employment ...'.[49] The ever-present danger of misperceptions of intentions leading to the initiation of new offensive programmes[50,51] should not be ignored in a situation where there remain so few means of clarifying what states are doing. Furthermore, while US officials from the top down continue to make great play about the dangers to the civilian population of bioterrorism, the immense difficulties of protecting the civilian population of the United States are obvious in any sensible assessment. As former Senator Nunn reportedly told Congress at the time of the US rejection of the Protocol: 'U.S. governments, from federal to village, are woefully unprepared to deal with biological warfare...'.[52] Yet States Parties to the Protocol would have been required to enact the kind of national legislation which, amongst other policies, would have helped to diminish the possibililty of bioterrorism. Whilst much less public debates were taking place in other major countries, quiet preparations were underway to deal with the possible deliberate use of disease against civilians.[53]

The deeply unfortunate fact of the matter is that failure of US leadership in the BTWC Protocol negotiations is likely to increase the chance that biological weapons will be used in the early decades of the twenty-first century. The consequences that could follow, as the fully-fledged genomics revolution is applied to this uniquely terrible kind of warfare, are not something a biologist would wish to contemplate. A Protocol to the BTWC could, at reasonable cost, have brought benefits to all States Parties.[54] The failure of US leadership has denied the world a timely Protocol to the BTWC.

11
Epilogue

The manuscript for the previous chapters of this book went to the publishers in late August 2001. There was agreement that a short note would be added in early December to cover the outcome of the Fifth Review Conference of the BTWC and thus to round off the story of the development of the regime from the 1991 Third Review Conference. It was not expected, however, that much public attention would be paid to the issue during the autumn of 2001. That assumption proved to be incorrect when terrorism in the United States brought the misuse of biological agents to the centre of world attention.

Even before the dramatic attacks with hijacked airliners in the United States on 11 September, revelations about the US biodefence programme had raised some very difficult questions. On 4 September a report in the *New York Times*[1] detailed three projects planned or carried out by various parts of the US government. The Pentagon had drawn up plans to genetically engineer anthrax in order to test whether such a bug, which had been produced earlier by Russian scientists, could be countered by the standard US anthrax vaccine.[2] Two other projects had been completed earlier.

In the second project a 'germ factory' was assembled in the Nevada desert from commercially available parts in order to test whether this could be done by a terrorist group or rogue state. The factory carried out test runs of production with harmless organisms. In the third project, named 'Clear Vision', the CIA 'built and tested a model of a Soviet-designed germ bomb that agency officials feared was being sold on the international market'. The CIA's device lacked a fuse and certain other elements that were required for a working bomb. The agency had attempted to buy such a bomb but when that attempt failed it decided to build the bomb to test how well it functioned.

The White House, it was reported, only learned about the project after it was under way. A joint assessment by several departments had concluded that the project did not violate the treaty, but a fresh dispute had broken out when it was completed. The *New York Times* reported that: 'A State Department official argued for a strict reading of the treaty: the ban on acquiring or developing "weapons" barred states from building even a partial model of a germ bomb no matter what the rationale.'[1] Mary Elizabeth Hoinkes who, between 1994 and 1999, had been general counsel of the Arms Control and Disarmament Agency in the United States, disputed the official view that such work was not a violation of the Biological and Toxin Weapons Convention.[3] She was described as a leading expert on the Convention and clearly did not accept the official view that it was acceptable to build parts of a bomb as long as the purpose was 'protective' and not hostile. Ms Hoinkes was quoted as saying: 'You see a room full of people manufacturing bombs and they say "I'm only doing this for defensive purposes and I have no intention of even doing it for real because my heart is pure".' She obviously did not accept the distinction, believing that Article I of the BTWC clearly prohibits such work. Another well-known expert, Spurgen M. Keeny, agreed. In his view, '[i]n the eyes of the world, it's going to look like we've been clandestinely violating the treaty'. Others felt that any violation was marginal and that these developments were foolish rather than illegal.

In any event, such issues were submerged in the public debate which followed the awful events of 11 September and the deaths due to anthrax in the United States.[4] Some hoped, however, that the shock would produce a change of course in the Bush Administration's foreign policy. A major article in the influential journal *Arms Control Today* argued:

> The tragic events of 'Black Tuesday' should be a wake-up call about the dangers of a unilateralist foreign policy. The best course for a safer, more secure United States lies in the President returning to multilateral treaties and other forms of action taken in concert with the rest of the world.[5]

However, Avis Bohlen, US Assistant Secretary for Arms Control, made it clear to the First Committee of the United Nations General Assembly on 10 October that the United States had not changed its view on the BTWC Protocol.[6] Other states made clear their regrets over the failure of the negotiations but exhibited considerable uncertainty as to what to do next.[7]

In the run-up to the November Review Conference President Bush proposed a series of measures to strengthen the Convention.

He proposed that all Parties:

- Enact strict national criminal legislation against prohibited BW activities with strong extradition requirements;
- Establish an effective United Nations procedure for investigating suspicious outbreaks [of disease] or allegations of biological weapons use;
- Establish procedures for addressing BWC compliance concerns;
- Commit to improving international disease control and to enhance mechanisms for sending expert response teams to cope with outbreaks;
- Establish sound national oversight mechanisms for the security and genetic engineering of pathogenic microorganisms;
- Devise a solid framework for bioscientists in the form of a code of ethical conduct that would have universal recognition; and
- Promote responsible conduct in the study, use, modification, and shipment of pathogenic organisms.[8]

The president added that he had directed his administration to consult on these proposals, and that the administration looked forward to hearing other new ideas. The president's proposals were certainly interesting and the pointed suggestions about the responsibilities of scientists were strongly reinforced by the Chair of the Department of Defense task force on bioterrorism in a lecture in London as the Review Conference approached.[9,10]

The Review Conference opened on 19 November 2001 with a massive task on its hands[11] despite the somewhat more encouraging position apparently coming from the United States, and the genuine sympathy for the country in view of the events of the autumn. The statement from the United States representative John R. Bolton, Under Secretary of State for Arms Control and International Security, on the first day revived the sense of shock from the summer. He stated: 'The United States has repeatedly made clear why the arms control approaches of the past will not resolve our current problems. This is why we rejected the flawed mechanism of the draft Protocol ... '[12] He went on to accuse a number of States Parties of violating the Convention and added that he could have named others. Observers of the three-week-long meeting reported that there remained major differences and that proceedings were difficult.[13]

The Review Conference proceedings fell into three phases. In the first week general statements were made and proposals were put forward in regard to what should be said vis-à-vis each article of the Convention in the Review Conference's Final Declaration. In the second week these proposals were discussed by a Committee of the Whole (Conference). Finally, in the third week, a Drafting Committee, assisted by numerous facilitators on particular topics, set about trying to agree the Final Declaration.

Despite the difficulties, the last day of the conference, 7 December, saw the drafters reaching Article XII of the 15 articles in the Convention. In discussing this article – 'Review Conferences' – the delegations had to deal with two points: the future of the Review Conferences, and what to report regarding the work of the Ad Hoc Group since this had been put on the agenda for consideration under Article XII by the Fourth Review Conference in 1996. Given what had happened during the summer, and Mr Bolton's opening statement, these looked like difficult issues, but there were obvious possible compromises if diplomats wished to achieve them (for example, see reference 11). It would have been possible to make progress on some of the ideas put forward by the United States and by other States without pushing the issue of the differences over the Ad Hoc Group to a final conclusion.

At this point the United States introduced a paper: 'insisting that the Conference "terminates" the mandate of the Ad Hoc Group...'. It then became impossible to agree anything other than suspension of the work of the Review Conference and an arrangement to meet again in a year's time (November 2002). Whether the United States intended to produce this result or whether it had badly misjudged the likely reaction to a bargaining proposal is unclear, but it was obvious that many delegations had expected that a compromise would be achieved and were bitter about the outcome.

The net result of the United States' actions was to leave the BTWC in a state of suspended animation – a low point even in the chequered history of this regime.[15] And this at a time when the World Health Organization thought the danger of biological weapons sufficient to issue the second edition[16] of its report, *Public Health Responses to Biological and Chemical Weapons*, thirty years after the first edition which had been so influential in the original negotiation of the Convention.

If the United States' destruction of the Review Conference was unintentional it again calls into question the capabilities of its diplomacy. On the other hand, if the destruction was intentional it exposes a fatal contradiction: if the United States can only strengthen the prohibition against biological weapons effectively through this multilateral instrument, it cannot do so by insisting that only what *it* wants is acceptable. As 2001 drew to a close, the failure of US leadership in strengthening the BTWC, for whatever reason, left the international community much more exposed to the potential development and use of biological weapons than it need have been.

Appendix 1 The 1972 Biological and Toxin Weapons Convention

CONVENTION ON THE PROHIBITION OF THE DEVELOPMENT, PRODUCTION AND STOCKPILING OF BACTERIOLOGICAL (BIOLOGICAL) AND TOXIN WEAPONS AND ON THEIR DESTRUCTION

Signed at London, Moscow and Washington on 10 April 1972
Entered into force on 26 March 1975
Depositaries: UK, US and Soviet governments
The States Parties to this Convention,

Determined to act with a view to achieving effective progress towards general and complete disarmament, including the prohibition and elimination of all types of weapons of mass destruction, and that the prohibition of the development, production and stockpiling of chemical and bacteriological (biological) weapons and their elimination, through effective measures, will facilitate the achievement of general and complete disarmament under strict and effective international control,

Recognizing the important significance the Protocol for the Prohibition of the Use in War of Asphyxiating, Poisonous or Other Gases, and of Bacteriological methods of Warfare, signed at Geneva on June 17, 1925, and conscious also of the contribution which the said Protocol has already made, and continues to make, to mitigating the horrors of war,

Reaffirming their adherence to the principles and objectives of that Protocol and calling upon all States to comply strictly with them,

Recalling that the General Assembly of the United Nations has repeatedly condemned all actions contrary to the principles and objectives the Geneva Protocol of June 17, 1925,

Desiring to contribute to the strengthening of confidence between peoples and the general improvement of the international atmosphere,

Desiring also to contribute to the realization of the purposes and principles of the Charter of the United Nations,

Convinced of the importance and urgency of eliminating from the arsenals of States, through effective measures, such dangerous weapons of mass destruction as those using chemical or bacteriological (biological) agents,

Recognizing that an agreement on the prohibition of bacteriological (biological) and toxin weapons represents a first possible step towards the achievement of agreement on effective measures also for the problem of the development, production and stockpiling of chemical weapons, and determined to continue negotiations to that end,

Determined, for the sake of all mankind, to exclude completely the possibility of bacteriological (biological) agents and toxins being used as weapons,

Convinced that such use would be repugnant to the conscience of mankind and that no effort should be spared to minimize this risk,

Have agreed as follows:

Article I
Each State Party to this Convention undertakes never in any circumstances to develop, produce, stockpile or otherwise acquire or retain:

1. Microbial or other biological agents, or toxins whatever their origin

or method of production, of types and in quantities that have no justification for prophylactic, protective or other peaceful purposes;

2. Weapons, equipment or means of delivery designed to use such agents or toxins for hostile purposes or in armed conflict.

Article II
Each State Party to this Convention undertakes to destroy, or to divert to peaceful purposes, as soon as possible but not later than nine months after the entry into force of the Convention, all agents, toxins, weapons, equipment and means of delivery specified in article I of the Convention, which are in its possession or under its jurisdiction or control. In implementing the provisions of this article all necessary safety precautions shall be observed to protect populations and the environment.

Article III
Each State Party to this Convention undertakes not to transfer to any recipient whatsoever, directly or indirectly, and not in any way to assist, encourage, or induce any State, group of States or international organizations to manufacture or otherwise acquire any of the agents, toxins, weapons, equipment or means of delivery specified in article I of the Convention.

Article IV
Each State Party to this Convention shall, in accordance with its constitutional processes, take any necessary measures to prohibit and prevent the development, production, stockpiling, acquisition or retention of the agents, toxins, weapons, equipment and means of delivery specified in article I of the Convention, within the territory of such State, under its jurisdiction or under its control anywhere.

Article V
The States Parties to this Convention undertake to consult one another and to cooperate in solving any problems which may arise in relation to the objective of, or in the application of the provisions of, the Convention. Consultation and cooperation pursuant to this article may also be undertaken through appropriate international procedures within the framework of the United Nations and in accordance with its Charter.

Article VI
1. Any State Party to this Convention which finds that any other State Party is acting in breach of obligations deriving from the provisions of the Convention may lodge a complaint with the Security Council of the United Nations. Such a complaint should include all possible evidence confirming its validity, as well as a request for its consideration by the Security Council.

2. Each State Party to this Convention undertakes to cooperate in carrying out any investigation which the Security Council may initiate, in accordance with the provisions of the Charter of the United Nations, on the basis of the complaint received by the Council. The Security Council shall inform the States Parties to the Convention of the results of the investigation.

Article VII
Each State Party to this Convention undertakes to provide or support assistance, in accordance with the United Nations Charter, to any Party to the Convention which so requests, if the Security Council decides that such Party has been exposed to danger as a result of violation of the Convention.

Article VIII
Nothing in this Convention shall be interpreted as in any way limiting or

detracting from the obligations assumed by any State under the Protocol for the Prohibition of the Use in War of Asphyxiating, Poisonous or Other Gases, and of Bacteriological Methods of Warfare signed at Geneva on June 17, 1925.

Article IX

Each State Party to this Convention affirms the recognized objective of effective prohibition of chemical weapons and, to this end, undertakes to continue negotiations in good faith with a view to reaching early agreement on effective measures for the prohibition of their development, production and stockpiling and for their destruction, and on appropriate measures concerning equipment and means of delivery specifically designed for the production or use of chemical agents for weapons purposes.

Article X

1. The States Parties to this Convention undertake to facilitate, and have the right to participate in, the fullest possible exchange of equipment, materials and scientific and technological information for the use of bacteriological (biological) agents and toxins for peaceful purposes. Parties to the Convention in a position to do so shall also cooperate in contributing individually or together with other States or international organizations to the further development and application of scientific discoveries in the field of bacteriology (biology) for prevention of disease, or for other peaceful purposes.

2. This Convention shall be implemented in a manner designed to avoid hampering the economic or technological development of States Parties to the Convention or international cooperation in the field of peaceful bacteriological (biological) activities, including the international exchange of bacteriological (biological) agents and toxins and equipment for the processing, use or production of bacteriological (biological) agents and toxins for peaceful purposes in accordance with the provisions of the Convention.

Article XI

Any State Party may propose amendments to this Convention. Amendments shall enter into force for each State Party accepting the amendments upon their acceptance by a majority of the States Parties to the Convention and thereafter for each remaining State Party on the date of acceptance by it.

Article XII

Five years after the entry into force of this Convention, or earlier if it is requested by a majority of Parties to the Convention by submitting a proposal to this effect to the Depositary Governments, a conference of States Parties to the Convention shall be held at Geneva, Switzerland, to review the operation of the Convention, with a view to assuring that the purposes of the preamble and the provisions of the Convention, including the provisions concerning negotiations on chemical weapons, are being realized. Such review shall take into account any new scientific and technological developments relevant to the Convention.

Article XIII

1. This Convention shall be of unlimited duration.

2. Each State Party to this Convention shall in exercising its national sovereignty have the right to withdraw from the Convention if it decides that extraordinary events, related to the subject matter of the Convention, have jeopardized the supreme interests of its country. It shall give notice of such withdrawal to all other States

Parties to the Convention and to the United Nations Security Council three months in advance. Such notice shall include a statement of the extraordinary events it regards as having jeopardized its supreme interests.

Article XIV

1. This Convention shall be open to all States for signature. Any State which does not sign the Convention before its entry into force in accordance with paragraph (3) of this Article may accede to it at any time.

2. This Convention shall be subject to ratification by signatory States. Instruments of ratification and instruments of accession shall be deposited with the Governments of the United States of America, the United Kingdom of Great Britain and Northern Ireland and the Union of Soviet Socialist Republics, which are hereby designated the Depositary Governments.

3. This Convention shall enter into force after the deposit of instruments of ratification by twenty-two Governments, including the Governments designated as Depositaries of the Convention.

4. For States whose instruments of ratification or accession are deposited subsequent to the entry into force of this Convention, it shall enter into force on the date of the deposit of their instruments of ratification or accession.

5. The Depositary Governments shall promptly inform all signatory and acceding States of the date of each signature, the date of deposit of each instrument of ratification or of accession and the date of the entry into force of this Convention, and of the receipt of other notices.

6. This Convention shall be registered by the Depositary Governments pursuant to Article 102 of the Charter of the United Nations.

Article XV

This Convention, the English, Russian, French, Spanish and Chinese texts of which are equally authentic, shall be deposited in the archives of the Depositary Governments. Duly certified copies of the Convention shall be transmitted by the Depositary Governments to the Governments of the signatory and acceding States.

Appendix 2

Geneva, Switzerland
July 25, 2001

Mr. Chairman, Colleagues:

I take the floor today after twenty-three sessions of the Ad Hoc Group, spanning some six and a half years of negotiation trying to develop a legally-binding document to enhance confidence in compliance with the Biological Weapons Convention. The relevance of our objective has not diminished over those years. Everyone should understand the importance the United States places on the Biological Weapons Convention and the global ban on biological weapons it establishes.

No nation is more committed than the United States to combating the BW threat. This is a threat we face not only at home but also abroad. Our forces and our friends and allies may well be the victims of this weapon of terror and blackmail. We must counter this complex and dangerous threat with a full range of effective instruments – nonproliferation, export controls, domestic preparedness, and counterproliferation. We are firmly committed to combat the spread of biological weapons.

After years of arduous negotiation, with the sterling work of numerous friends of the chair to facilitate discussions about specific issues, this group had gone as far as that technique would permit in resolving individual issues and questions along the model set forth in the original rolling text in 1997. You, Mr. Chairman, then undertook the challenging and onerous task of proposing a set of mutual compromises, based on that rolling text, as a potential way to bring the negotiations to closure in a short period. The United States congratulates you on the effort you have made to resolve very contentious issues.

The United States has subjected the 'Composite Text' proposal to detailed scrutiny. As every veteran of these negotiations will recall, the United States has had serious issues with both individual proposals and the general approach to some issues throughout these negotiations. Those concerns and requirements have not changed – indeed, they remain one of the consistent criteria against which the United States has evaluated this text.

In addition to the text, we have looked at the overall issue of biological weapons threat. Our approach for doing so is comprehensive, and includes new, affirmative ideas for strengthening the Biological Weapons Convention. We believe we can strengthen the Biological Weapons Convention through multilateral arrangements. To be valuable, however, we believe any approach must focus on effective innovative measures.

The review conducted in Washington has encompassed more than the substantive content of individual issues. We recognize that in any negotiation no individual country can dictate the outcome on all elements of the final text. We also recognize that the proposals in the 'Composite Text' frequently do reflect values and views the United States has inserted into the negotiation. However, as indicated in the Twenty-Third session and for years before that, the United States still has very serious substantive difficulties with the textual proposals in these negotiations. We have recognized the substantive and political values many of the participants here attach to a successful completion of the Protocol, and that the demonstrated ability to achieve a consensus result, even if it cannot satisfy every signatory's preferred outcomes, is perceived as a potential benefit in itself. The United States view, therefore, has been considered at the most senior levels of our government. We continue to have problems and certainly are not going to mislead anyone on this point.

After extensive deliberation, the United States has concluded that the current approach to a Protocol to the Biological Weapons Convention, an approach most directly embodied in CRP.8, known as the 'Composite Text,' is not, in our view, capable of achieving the mandate set forth for the Ad Hoc Group, strengthening confidence in compliance with the Biological Weapons Convention. One overarching concern is the inherent difficulty of crafting a mechanism suitable to address the unique biological weapons threat. The traditional approach that has worked well for many other types of weapons is not a workable structure for biological weapons. We believe the objective of the mandate was and is important to international security, we will therefore be unable to support the current text, even with changes, as an appropriate outcome of the Ad Hoc Group efforts.

The draft Protocol will not improve our ability to verify BWC compliance. It will not enhance our confidence in compliance and will do little to deter those countries seeking to develop biological weapons. In our assessment, the draft Protocol would put national security and confidential business information at risk.

The United States intends to develop other ideas and different approaches that we believe could help to achieve our common objective of effectively strengthening the Biological Weapons Convention. We intend to explore those ideas and other alternative approaches during the next several months with the goal of reaching a consensus on a new approach for our shared objective.

There is no basis for a claim that the United States does not support multilateral instruments for dealing with weapons of mass destruction and missile threats. We strongly support the Australia Group, and will be working actively to strengthen it at its next meeting in Paris October 1–4. Indeed, we support all multilateral arms control, nonproliferation, and export control regimes that are currently in force, such as – the NPT, the CWC, the BWC, MTCR, NSG, IAEA, Zangger Committee, and the Wassenar arrangement.

Let me outline some of the reasons for reaching the conclusion I have just announced about this Protocol. As I noted earlier, many of these will not be new or surprising. They reflect positions the United States has advanced repeatedly throughout these negotiations.

Objectives

One central objective of a Protocol is to uncover illicit activity. Traditionally, this has meant seeking regular on-site inspections of locations potentially able to conduct such activity, the shorter-notice and the more intrusive, the better. Always, there is a balance between pursuing illicit actions and protecting legitimate national security and proprietary information unrelated to illicit activity.

In the draft Protocol, there is an inherent dilemma associated with the question of on-site activities. The provisions for on-site activity do not offer great promise of providing useful, accurate, and complete information to the international community. However, when we examined the prospects of the most intrusive and extensive on-site activities physically possible – which we believed were likely not acceptable to most other countries – we discovered that the results of such intrusiveness would still not provide useful, accurate, or complete information.

One objective is to agree on a declaration base that would provide reasonable inventories of activity in a country relevant to the underlying Biological Weapons Convention. Our assessment of the range of facilities potentially relevant to the Convention indicates that they number, at least in the case of the United States, in the thousands, if not the tens of thousands. In addition, their number and locations change on an irregular but frequent basis. Thus, we had no hope that any attempt at a comprehensive declaration inventory would be accurate, timely, or enduringly comprehensive.

In short, after extensive analysis, we were forced to conclude that the mechanisms envisioned for the Protocol would not achieve their objectives, that no modification of them would allow them to achieve their objectives, and that trying to do more would simply raise the risk to legitimate United States activities.

This is not a new perspective. We have voiced it since the initial negotiating sessions in 1995. The United States has worked with other countries to try to find the way to create an appropriate balance in the draft Protocol. However, despite the efforts of many, we are forced to conclude that an appropriate balance cannot be struck that would make the draft Protocol defensible as an instrument whose utility outweighs its risk.

The paradigm

Another key objective for a Protocol to strengthen the Biological Weapons Convention would be to deter or complicate the ability of a rogue state to conduct an illicit offensive biological weapons program. These negotiations have worked from the outset on the model of regimes that have gone before. The most frequently cited paradigm for our work has been the Chemical Weapons Convention. Indeed, many of the arguments and justifications for the scope and nature of activities envisioned under the draft Protocol have used the CWC as the example of comparison.

This is, unfortunately, seriously flawed. When developing the ban on chemical weapons, the question of dual-capability was in the forefront. It was, and is, a legitimate question with respect to the CWC, since the immediate precursors of chemical agents require production facilities capable of making chemical agents, but have legitimate commercial applications. The same kind of dual-capability issue exists in biology to an even greater extent.

In chemical manufacturing, although the precursors have legitimate application, the economics of their production dictates making them in a limited number of facilities. Such facilities, because of the toxicity and corrosiveness of the precursors, have recognizable infrastructure requirements.

When setting up the CWC, we were able to require universal declaration for such facilities, and then establish an international regime that would visit each such facility on a regular and repeated basis. If there were such a recognizable facility that were not declared, the very lack of declaration would be sufficient to raise questions about its role and function.

The Ad Hoc Group quickly recognized that no such cataloging was possible with respect to biology to biological facilities. Almost any facility that does biological work of any magnitude possesses the capability, under some parameters, of being diverted to biological weapons work. Trying to catalog them all would be tantamount to impossible. Likewise, visiting even those selected – almost arbitrarily – for declaration on the same universal and regular basis as the CWC would require an international organization of the size and possession of rare skills among its employees that no one in the Ad Hoc Group was willing to contemplate.

What we are left with, then, is a regime that contemplates – at best – declaration of an almost randomly-selected set of facilities from among those actually relevant to a potential proliferator. To compound the difficulty, among that random sample of facilities, regular on-site activity would take place at only a random sample of even that sub-set. And, given the distribution of biological activity around the world, despite the best efforts at finding a 'smoothing function' to distribute on-site activity, the overwhelming bulk of such activity would take place on the territory of those States Parties least likely to be proliferation candidates.

In the considered judgment of the United States, the small scope of applications of this kind of twice-removed randomness, coupled with a required emphasis on the wrong targets from among the susceptible population, simply does not provide anything remotely resembling a deterrent function on a proliferator, even a non-state actor. We therefore conclude that the conceptual approach used in the current negotiating effort fails to address the objective we have sought throughout the negotiations. This approach, although relevant in the references to non-biological areas used throughout the negotiations, simply does not apply to biology. If we are to find an appropriate solution to the problem, we need to think 'outside the box'. It will require new and innovative paradigms to deal with the magnitude of biological activity that can be a threat, the explosively changing technology in the biological fields, and the varied potential objectives of a biological weapons program. We simply cannot try to patch or modify the models we have used elsewhere.

Biodefense issues

Defense against biological weapons is of great concern to the United States. As we have stated repeatedly, any Protocol needed to ensure that the ability to protect against those who would violate the norm of abolishing biological weapons was not impaired. The United States has the most extensive biodefense program described by any participant in these negotiations. The United States therefore has more national security equities directly at risk through this Protocol than any other participant. At the same time, the potential downside of undercutting biodefense efforts is not limited to the United States. We share the results of our efforts with other countries in assisting them to protect themselves against potential biological weapons attack. Our concerns, then, are not limited to self-protection. They are concerns that should be relevant to many of the countries in this room.

We recognize that finding a balance of protection and disclosure has been especially difficult in the biodefense arena. The proposal in the 'Composite Text' is far from what some countries have suggested, and even incorporates a number of elements the United States has demanded. However, there are still provisions in the current proposals we believe would be inimical to legitimate national security efforts.

More importantly, as we have analyzed the options, we came to the conclusion that the same inherent flaw I described earlier is present in the approach to biodefense. Between declarations on biodefense and other categories, such as working with listed agents, the current proposals do not provide sufficient protection. At the same time, the exclusions in declarations would permit a potential proliferator to conceal significant efforts in legitimately undeclared facilities. Conversely, if we try to make the declarations comprehensive enough to capture all biodefense activity, the level of risk to legitimate and sensitive national security information becomes truly unbearable.

On-site activity utility

Earlier I noted the dysfunction of concentrating on-site activity in places that would be largely irrelevant to possible biological weapons concerns. This alone detracts seriously from any value for the objectives of the Ad Hoc Group. However, there is a second liability of on-site activity as envisioned in the 'Composite Text'.

The activities outlined to take place on a regular basis, transparency visits, actually risk damage to innocent declared facilities, despite the fact that they would have almost no chance of discovering anything useful to the BWC if they took place at a less-than-innocent facility. This risk is a two-edged sword: proprietary or national security information may be at risk, and/or the activity may serve to misdirect world attention into non-productive channels.

A number of safeguards have been inserted into procedures to protect information not relevant to the BWC. Those safeguards are insufficient to eliminate unacceptable risks to proprietary or national security information. The nature of proprietary information in the biological field is very diverse. It ranges from overall capacities, which reveal market size and profit potential, to routine physical production configurations that provide efficiency and output advantages. Protecting such a diverse and innocent-seeming range of information would require facilities to exercise the protections incorporated in the draft Protocol language extensively and, even then, they would have no firm assurance proprietary information could not be inferred from what was seen by inspectors.

At the same time, the very exercise of the protections incorporated in the draft language could misdirect the attentions of the international community. Countries, or competitors, with economic or political agendas of disruption could raise unfounded allegations. Such allegations would be refutable only with economic or national security costs, and refutation after the fact would likely already have resulted in commercial damage to private firms. The United States, with its visibility in the world, is perhaps more sensitive to such a situation than some. Our concern, however, is not for the United States alone. We simply cannot agree to make ourselves and other countries subject to such risks when we can find no corresponding benefit in impeding proliferation efforts around the globe.

Constitutional and ratification issues

Throughout this negotiation, we have made all our colleagues aware of the constraints we face in achieving ratification of an international agreement. This is, to the United States, a crucial component of any outcome. We do not believe in negotiating, nor signing, agreements that do not support their stated objectives. At the same time, the United States operates in a specific Constitutional framework. It requires the executive branch of our government, to submit the results of any negotiation to the United States Senate for advice and consent to ratification. In good faith throughout these deliberations, we have brought to the attention of the Ad Hoc Group the issues where we believed there were explicit requirements to allow the United States to achieve ratification. We have operated on the assumption – which we still believe is valid – that creating an instrument that would preclude United States participation was not in the best interests of this negotiation or of the Biological Weapons Convention.

We also have explicitly recognized that some of the conditions necessary to satisfy these requirements would theoretically allow abuse. For our own part, the United States does not use such devices in an abusive fashion. We also believe that if others were to do so, the nature of their use would be obvious to any objective observer, and the international community could draw appropriate conclusions. Thus, we do not believe the potential abuse argument outweighs our own responsibility to create an instrument to which we believe we could become an active party.

There are elements of the 'Composite Text' draft that violate the requirements with respect to this issue. I do not intend to try to detail them today – they are familiar to all in this room who have sat through the numerous Ad Hoc Group sessions where we have detailed both the appropriate solution and the rationale for it.

However, the result is a text that, even if the United States were convinced had substantive merit in achieving its stated objectives to strengthen the Biological Weapons Convention, would not be one we could predict with reasonable probability the United States would become a party to. This is, in our view, a futile effort. We deeply regret if the nature of these specific requirements was not made clear throughout the negotiations, but it was certainly not for lack of effort on the part of the United States delegation.

Export controls

The nations involved in this negotiation should be commended for their ability to attack a subject with as many divergent national views such as global control of biotechnology. I have referred several times to the central objective of the United States in undertaking this work: to assist in the global effort to stem, or at least inhibit, proliferation of biological weapons. We believe that remains an essential goal for international security.

Some of the participants in this negotiation, however, have approached the situation with a different mix of national priorities. They view the issue as much from the perspective of technological development as from direct security enhancement measures. While the United States agrees with the concept that global technological development in biotechnology helps create a more secure environment, we view this as a subordinate element to the compliance–enhancement aspects of any Protocol to the Biological Weapons Convention.

The Convention is, after all, a disarmament treaty, not a trade treaty. There are competent organizations throughout the world whose principal function is to fight disease, enhance trade, and promote development. The United States supports those organizations, and applauds their successes in their own areas of competence.

Other delegations appear to disagree fundamentally with our assessment. Just this week, we have heard that '...Confidential Proprietary Information (CPI) is the concern of only a few advanced countries, where National Security Information is the concerns (sic) of all States Parties.... (T)herefore, my delegation expects the deletion of the references to CPI in the final text'. In addition, we hear that 'any parallel export control regimes have to be dissolved after the Protocol enters into force (for States Parties to the future Protocol)'.

We have explained at length why ignoring the protection of legitimately sensitive information, both for proprietary and national security reasons, is an essential element of focusing any instrument on the disarmament objectives we should be seeking rather than trade enablements, which should be the purview of other organizations. We also take seriously the threat of biological weapons proliferation. A Protocol should be, if it were properly focused and implemented, another instrument in the set of tools countering proliferation of weapons of mass destruction. Never has the argument been made successfully that it could have become the single answer to the proliferation problem. To insist that other effective tools be forfeited in order to establish a Protocol is an indication of the wide gap between demands and possible solutions still existing in these negotiations.

We do not believe the Ad Hoc Group product, or the international organization – affectionately known as the OPBW – envisioned by the current draft Protocol, is an appropriate substitute for those other organizations. In fact, we fear that the inevitable competition of alternative international organizations with overlapping mandates could actually impede some of the effectiveness of those other already existing organizations.

Likewise, we are perplexed by the arguments of some participants in these negotiations that commitments in the areas of trade and development are necessary 'prices' to pay for the security-enhancing compliance measures envisioned in other elements of the draft Protocol. Global political situations would indicate that the very countries trying hardest to argue for compensation to agree to security enhancement are those most likely to have a biological weapons threat to their own security. The logic of their position is not apparent.

From the beginning, the Protocol the Ad Hoc Group has sought has been an additional tool to address the biological weapons threat. We all recognize that the threat is both real and growing. Other efforts already exist to address the threat, including the BWC itself. While they have not eliminated the problem, they nonetheless have been useful in retarding the threat.

The United States believes very strongly in employing all available means to enhance international security. One of the things we will not allow is any degradation of those tools we already have to fight a serious challenge to security. Throughout these negotiations, some participants have attempted to do just that. Such an effort is flatly unacceptable to the United States.

It is the responsibility of all of us, since we are already parties to the Biological Weapons Convention, to inhibit or prevent biological weapons being in the hands of any state or party whatsoever, by both national and international means. We take that national responsibility very seriously. To the degree we can enhance our efforts through cooperation with other states parties, we will continue to do so. Efforts to constrain, impede, or eliminate such efforts will be unacceptable to the United States now and at any time in the foreseeable future. Those who think there is any flexibility on this point in the United States are sadly mistaken, and should abandon any such pursuits.

Disturbing negotiating positions

Some participants in these negotiations have also sought outcomes that are, frankly, disturbing to the United States. We do not understand, even after repeated explanations, the rationale for such efforts. We can only urge that states reexamine their basis for such positions.

The mandate of the Ad Hoc Group clearly states that any Protocol must not abridge, diminish, or otherwise weaken the Biological Weapons Convention. The United States has tried to keep that principle in mind whenever we have proposed measures or other elements for the draft Protocol.

We must wonder, though, when we are asked to consider provisions that would constrict the potential scope of the prohibitions in the Convention by fixing the meaning of terms in the Convention itself. We have heard repeatedly about the flexibility needed to keep up with explosively changing technology. It seems to us that efforts in contrary directions cannot be in the interests of the object and purpose of the Convention.

Likewise, we have long held that seeing the actual effects of a biological weapons program would be one of the less ambiguous issues in evaluating potential threat. While less ambiguous, such effects are not unambiguous. It therefore seemed to us that being able to examine such effects, including disease outbreaks, was an important capability for any Protocol regime. Attempts to restrict such investigations do not seem in the best interests of all parties.

Conclusion

I apologize for the length of this intervention. As I stated at the outset, the United States understands and appreciates the amount of effort, and the amount of compromise, that have marked the negotiations to this point. We agree with the assessment that it was time to move from the rolling text to a composite text in an effort to formulate compromise solutions to outstanding issues. We have analyzed those efforts from both a political and substantive perspective, recognizing the sincere desire of most of the participants to reach an outcome that would have a product ready for consideration and signature by States Parties.

The United States does believe that many, if not all, of the difficulties I have outlined today are things the participants in this room have heard, repeatedly, over the last six years. These are not new ideas the United States has just now formulated – they are long-standing concerns. At the same time, we recognize that no country in a multilateral negotiation achieves all of its desired positions, and that some of the compromises reflected in the composite text are difficult for others to accept.

Others in this room have the same objectives as the United States for a Protocol – enhancing international security. The various expressions of support for the composite text we have heard clearly indicate that others have evaluated the draft Protocol and have concluded that, however imperfect, it does satisfy those objectives. Regrettably, the United States has come to a different conclusion.

We have spent the effort to examine the text in detail, and at the senior-most levels. We have also examined the principles on which the text is based. We have looked for a set of specific changes that could alter our fundamental conclusions. These intensive reviews have led us to conclude that this effort simply does not yield an outcome to which we would be prepared to agree. I have outlined above some of the reasons why we have reached this conclusion. Because the difficulties with this text are both serious and, in many cases inherent in the very approach used in the text, more drafting and modification of this text would, in our view, still not yield a result we could accept.

Some have argued both publicly and privately that not having this Protocol will weaken the BWC itself. The United States categorically rejects that supposition. Let me re-emphasize that the U.S. fully supports the global ban on biological weapons embodied in the BWC, and remains committed to finding effective ways to strengthen the overall regime against the BW threat, including multilateral ones. The United States will, therefore, work hard to improve – not lessen – global efforts to counter both the BW threat and the potential impact such weapons could have on civilization. And we would reply to those who cry that not having this Protocol weakens the global norm against BW that there absolutely is no reason that kind of reaction need occur. It will happen only if we convince ourselves that it is happening, and we would urge others to join with us in ensuring such a reaction does not take place.

Thank you Mr. Chairman and colleagues.

*US Department of State's Office of International Information Programs (usinfo.state.gov).

References

Introduction

1. President Nixon (1972) Letter to the Senate: Convention on the Prohibition of the Development, Production and Stockpiling of Bacteriological (Biological) and Toxin Weapons and on their Destruction, 10 August. *Documents on Disarmament*. United States Arms Control and Disarmament Agency, Washington, DC, 553–4.
2. Pearson, G. S. (1999) The essentials of biological threat assessment. In R. A. Zilinskas (ed.), *Biological Warfare: Modern Offense and Defense*. Boulder: Lynne Rienner.
3. Alibek, K. and Handelman, S. (1999) *Biohazard*. New York: Random House.
4. Mangold, T. and Goldberg, J. (1999) *Plague Wars*. London: Macmillan.
5. Dando, M. R. (1994) *Biological Warfare in the 21st Century*. London: Brassey's.
6. Nathanson, V., Darvell, M. and Dando, M. R. (1999) *Biotechnology, Weapons and Humanity*. London: Harwood Academic Publishers (for the British Medical Association).
7. Background Document (2001) *Hearings on the Biological Weapons Convention*. Sub-Committee on National Security, Veterans Affairs and International Relations, House of Representatives, Washington, DC, 10 July.

1 The problem of biological warfare

1. Porter, R. (1997) From Pasteur to penicillin. In R. Porter (ed.), *The Greatest Benefit to Mankind: a Medical History of Humanity from Antiquity to the Present*. London. Harper Collins.
2. War Office (1908) *Royal Army Medical Corps Training*. London: HMSO.
3. Weatherall, D. (1995) *Science and the Quiet Art: Medical Research and Patient Care*. Oxford: Oxford University Press.
4. Dando, M. R. (1999) The impact of the development of modern biology and medicine on the evolution of offensive biological warfare programmes in the twentieth century. *Defense Analysis*, 15 (1), 43–62.
5. Dando, M. R. (1994) *Biological Warfare in the 21st Century*. London: Brassey's.
6. Office of Technology Assessment (1993) *Proliferation of Weapons of Mass Destruction: Assessing the Risks*, OTA-ISC-559, August. Office of Technology Assessment, United States Congress, Washington DC.
7. van Courtland Moon, J. (1993) Controlling chemical and biological weapons through World War II. In R. D. Burns (ed.), *Encyclopedia of Arms Control and Disarmament*, Volume III. New York: Charles Scribner's Sons.
8. Boserup, A. (1973) *The Problem of Chemical and Biological Warfare: Volume III: CBW and the Law of War*. Stockholm: Almqvist and Wiksell (for SIPRI).
9. Dando, M. R. (1999) The development of international legal constraints on biological warfare in the 20th century. In M. Koskenniemi, Takama, K. T. and

Augustine, L. G. (eds), *The Finnish Yearbook of International Law*, Volume VIII (1997). The Hague: Martinus Nijhoff.

10. Goldblat, J. (1971) *The Problem of Chemical and Biological Warfare: Volume IV: CB Disarmament Negotiations 1920–1970*. Stockholm: Almqvist and Wiksell (for SIPRI).

11. Perry Robinson, J. (1971) Appendix 3. The CB weapons controls of the Western European Union Armaments Control Agency. In A. Boserup, M. Meyrowitz and K. Ipsen K. (eds), *The Problem of Chemical and Biological Warfare: Volume V: the Prevention of CBW*. Stockholm: Almqvist and Wiksell (for SIPRI).

12. Wynen Thomas, A. V. and Thomas, A. J. (1968) *Development of International Legal Limitations on the Use of Chemical and Biological Weapons*. Volume II: Basic Report (Book 1, Part 2). Prepared for the US Arms Control and Disarmament Agency under Contract No. ACDA/GC-128.

13. Myrdal, A. (1980) *The Game of Disarmament: How the United States and Russia Run the Arms Race*. Nottingham: Spokesman.

14. Dando, M. R. (2000) *New Biological Weapons: Threat, Proliferation and Control*. Boulder: Lynne Rienner.

15. Mangold, T. and Goldberg, J. (1999) *Plague Wars: a True Story of Biological Warfare*. London: Macmillan.

16. Meselson, M. (1999) 'The problem of biological weapons'. Paper presented at the 18th Stated Meeting of the American Academy of Arts and Sciences, Cambridge, Mass., 13 January.

17. United States (1970) Statement by the United States Representative (Leonard) to the Conference of the Committee on Disarmament: Chemical and biological weapons, 21 April. *Documents on Disarmament* United States Arms Control and Disarmament Agency, Washington, DC, 170–4.

18. Secretariat (1980) *Background Paper Relating to the Convention on the Prohibition of the Development, Production and Stockpiling of Bacteriological (Biological) and Toxin Weapons and on their Destruction*. BWC/CONF.I/4, 20 February, Geneva: United Nations.

19. Sims, N. (1971) Biological disarmament: Britain's new posture. *New Scientist*, 2 December, 18–20.

20. Sims, N. (1988) *The Diplomacy of Biological Disarmament: Vicissitudes of a Treaty in Force, 1975–85*. London: Macmillan.

21. United Kingdom (1969) Statement by the British Representative (Mulley) to the Eighteen Nation Disarmament Committee: Chemical and Biological Warfare, 10 July. *Documents on Disarmament*. United States Arms Control and Disarmament Agency, Washington, DC, 318–24.

22. United States (1971) Statement by the United States Representative (Martin) to the First Committee of the General Assembly: Draft Convention on Biological and Toxin Weapons, 29 November. *Documents on Disarmament*. United States Arms Control and Disarmament Agency, Washington, DC, 793–6.

23. ter Haar, B. (1991) *The Future of Biological Weapons*. The Washington Papers 151. New York: Praeger.

24. Canada (1970) Canadian Working Paper Submitted to the Conference of the Committee on Disarmament: Verification of Prohibitions of Development, Production, Stockpiling, and Use of Chemical and Biological Weapons, 21 April. *Documents on Disarmament*. United States Arms Control and Disarmament Agency, Washington, DC, 375–9.

25. Yugoslavia (1970) Yugoslav Working Paper Submitted to the Conference of the Committee on Disarmament: Elements for a System of Control of the Complete Prohibition of Chemical and Biological Weapons, 6 August. *Documents on Disarmament.* United States Arms Control and Disarmament Agency, Washington, DC, 382–5.

26. France (1971) Statement by Foreign Minister Schumann to the General Assembly [Extract], 28 September. *Documents on Disarmament.* Arms Control and Disarmament Agency, Washington, DC, 590–2.

27. France (1970) Statement by the French Representative to the First Committee of the General Assembly [Extract], 9 November. *Documents on Disarmament.* Arms Control and Disarmament Agency, Washington, DC, 563–8.

28. France (1971) Statement by the French Representative (Mattei) to the First Committee of the General Assembly [Extract], 29 November. *Documents on Disarmament.* Arms Control and Disarmament Agency, Washington, DC, 786–93.

29. Japan (1969) Statement by the Japanese Representative (Asakai): Prohibition of Chemical and Biological Weapons, 14 August. *Documents on Disarmament.* Arms Control and Disarmament Agency, Washington, DC, 408–12.

30. Operations Research Group (1961) *Arms Control of CBR Weapons, I Military Aspects.* Operations Group Study No. 23, US Army Chemical Corps, Army Chemical Center, Maryland, 9 February.

31. Spertzel, R. O., Wannemacher, R.W. and Linden, C.D. (1994) *Biological Weapons Proliferation: Technical Report.* US Army Medical Institute for Infectious Diseases, Fort Detrick, Maryland.

32. SIPRI (1973) *The Problem of Chemical and Biological Warfare: Volume VI Technical Aspects of Early Warning and Verification.* Stockholm: Almqvist and Wiksell.

33. Wright, S. (1997) Cuba case tests treaty. *Bulletin of the Atomic Scientists,* November/December, 18–19.

34. Soutar, S. I. (1997) *Letter to All States Parties to the Biological and Toxin Weapons Convention.* United Kingdom Permanent Representation to the Conference on Disarmament, 15 December, Geneva,

35. United States (1970) *Working Paper on Toxins.* Conference of the Committee on Disarmament, CCD/286, 21 April, Geneva.

36. United States (1992) *Biologically Derived Toxins: Quantities for Legitimate Use.* Ad Hoc Group of Governmental Experts to Identify and Examine Potential Verification Measures from a Scientific and Technical Standpoint. BWC/CONF.III/VEREX/WP.88, 4 December, Geneva.

37. Carus, W. S. (1999) Unlawful acquisition and use of biological agents. In J. Lederberg (ed.), *Biological Weapons: Limiting the Threat.* Cambridge, Mass.: The MIT Press.

38. Ember, L. R. (1999) Bioterrorism: Combating the threat. *C & EN,* 5 July, 8–17.

39. Ferguson, J. R. (1999) Biological weapons and U.S. Law. In J. Lederberg (ed.), *Biological Weapons: Limiting the Threat.* Cambridge, Mass.: The MIT Press.

40. Meselson, M. (1997) *Background Notes on Biological Weapons.* Mimeo, Department of Molecular and Cellular Biology, Harvard University, 20 August.

41. Zilinskas, R. A. (1986) Verification of the Biological Weapons Convention. In E. Geissler (ed.), *Biological and Toxin Weapons Today.* Oxford: Oxford University Press (for SIPRI).

42. Office of Technology Assessment (1993) *Technologies Underlying Weapons of Mass Destruction: Background Paper*. OTA-BP-ISC-115, Office of Technology Assessment, United States Congress, Washington DC.

43. Armed Forces Medical Intelligence Center (undated) *Signatures for Biological Warfare Facilities*. 93C1-01/940614.

44. MacEachin, D. J. (1998) Routine and challenge: Two pillars of verification. *CBW Conventions Bulletin*, 39, 1–3.

45. Alibek, K. and Handelman, S. (1999) *Biohazard*. New York: Random House.

46. Rimmington, A. (1996) From military to industrial complex? The conversion of biological weapons' facilities in the Russian Federation. *Contemporary Security Policy*, 17 (1), 80–112.

47. Leitenberg, M. (1996) *Biological Weapons Arms Control*. Project on Rethinking Arms Control, Paper No. 16, School of Public Affairs, University of Maryland at College Park.

48. Tucker, J. B. (1993) Lessons of Iraq's biological warfare programme. *Arms Control*, 14 (3), 229–71.

2 The Chemical Weapons Convention and the worldwide chemical industry

1. Karkoszka, A. (1977) *Strategic Disarmament: Verification and National Security*. London: Taylor and Francis Ltd. (for SIPRI).

2. Krass, A. (1985) *Verification: How Much is Enough?* London: Taylor and Francis Ltd. (for SIPRI).

3. Stern, J. E. (1993) All's well that ends well? Verification and the CWC. In J. B. Poole and R. Guthrie (eds), *Verification, 1993*. London: Brassey's.

4. Myrdal, A. (1980) *The Game of Disarmament: How the United States and Russia Run the Arms Race*. Nottingham: Spokesman.

5. Bailey, K. C. (1992) Global proliferation of chemical weapons: Policy problems and alternatives. In J. G. Tower et al. (eds), *Verification: the Key to Arms Control in the 1990s*. Washington DC: Brassey's (US) Inc.

6. Breckon, M. L. (1991) *Letter dated 22 May 1991 from the Acting Representative of the United States of America Addressed to the President of the Conference on Disarmament Transmitting a Statement Issued by the President of the United States of America Concerning the United States Initiative for Completing the Negotiations on a Chemical Weapons Convention, in a White House Fact Sheet on the Initiative*. CD/1077, 23 May.

7. Kenyon, I. R. (2000) *Controlling Chemical Weapons*. ISIS Briefing No. 75, International Security Information Service, London, January.

8. Perry Robinson, J., Stock, T. and Sutherland, R. G. (1993) The Chemical Weapons Convention: the success of chemical disarmament negotiations. *SIPRI Yearbook*, 705–56.

9. Guthrie, R. (1993) The Chemical Weapons Convention: a guide. In J. B. Poole and R. Guthrie (eds), *Verification, 1993*. London: Brassey's.

10. Smithson, A. E. (ed.) (1993) *The Chemical Weapons Convention Handbook*. Washington DC: The Henry L. Stimson Center.

11. Organization for the Prohibition of Chemical Weapons (1999) *Chemical Disarmament: Basic Facts*. The Hague: OPCW.

12. Dando, M. R. (1998) An arms control regime for the 21st century. In T. Woodhouse, R. Bruce and M. R. Dando (eds), *Peacekeeping and Peacemaking: Towards Effective Intervention in Post-Cold War Conflicts.* London: Macmillan.

13. Sidell, F. R., Urbanetti, J. S. Smith, W. J. and Hurst, C. G. (1997) Vesicants. In F. R. Sidell, E. T. Takafuji and D. Franz (eds), *Medical Aspects of Chemical and Biological Warfare.* Office of the Surgeon General, Department of the Army, United States.

14. Sidell, F. R. (1997) Nerve agents. In F. R. Sidell, E. T. Takafuji and D. Franz (eds), *Medical Aspects of Chemical and Biological Warfare.* Office of the Surgeon General, Department of the Army, United States.

15. United States (1991) *A Report on the Destruction of 3-Quinuclidynyl Benzilate (BZ).* CD/1074, CD/CW/WP.336. Geneva: United Nations, 20 March.

16. Pearson, G. S. (1995) Chemical and Biological Defence: an Essential Security Requirement. *Proceedings 8th International Symposium on Protection Against Chemical and Biological Warfare Agents.* Stockholm, Sweden, 11–16 June.

17. Office of Technology Assessment (1993) *Technologies Underlying Weapons of Mass Destruction.* Office of Technology Assessment, United States Congress, Washington DC. OTA-BP-ISC-115, December.

18. Mathews, R. J. (1993) Verification of the chemical industry under the Chemical Weapons Convention. In J. B. Poole and R. Guthrie (eds), *Verification, 1993.* London: Brassey's.

19. Layman, P. L. (1999) BASF still tops global Top 50. *C & EN,* 26 July, 23–5.

20. Storck, W. J. (1999) World chemical outlook: United States. *C & EN,* 13 December, 15–17.

21. General News (1999) CIA predicts world growth. *Manufacturing Chemist,* 70 (3), p. 8.

22. Service, R. F. (1998) Chemical industry rushes toward greener pastures. *Science,* 282, 23 October, 608–10.

23. Carpenter, W. D. (1986) Government regulation of chemical manufacturing in the USA as a basis for surveillance of compliance with the projected Chemical Weapons Convention. In *The Chemical Industry and the Projected Chemical Weapons Convention,* Volume II. Proceedings of a SIPRI/Pugwash Conference. Oxford: Oxford University Press (for SIPRI).

24. Palmer, E. A. (1994) For businesses, a high price for chemical weapons ban. *Defense & Foreign Policy,* 17 September, 2584–7.

25. Webber, F. L. (1997) CMA celebrates 125th anniversary. *C & EN,* 2 June, 12–17.

26. Webber, F. L. (1996) The US chemical industry stake in the Chemical Weapons Convention. *Chemical Weapons Convention Bulletin,* 34 (December), 1–2.

27. Perry Robinson, J. (1998) *The CWC Verification Regime: Implications for the Biotechnology and Pharmaceutical Industry.* Briefing Paper No. 11, Department of Peace Studies, University of Bradford. Available at <http://www.brad.ac.uk/acad/sbtwc>

28. Franz, D. (1997) Defense against toxin weapons. In F. R. Sidell, E. T. Takafuji and D. Franz (eds), *Medical Aspects of Chemical and Biological Warfare.* Office of the Surgeon General, Department of the Army, United States.

29. Cooper, G. H. (1986) Verification of the non-production of chemical weapons: the United Kingdom approach. In *The Chemical Industry and the Projected Chemical Weapons Convention,* Volume II. Proceedings of a SIPRI/Pugwash Conference. Oxford: Oxford University Press Oxford (for SIPRI).

30. Chairman of the Open-ended Consultations (1989) *National Trial Inspections: Final Report by the Chairman of the Open-ended Consultations*. Ad Hoc Committee on Chemical Weapons, Conference on Disarmament. CD/CW/WP.248/Rev.1, 23 June.
31. Germany and United Kingdom (1991) *Report on Two Joint Chemical Weapons Practice Challenge Inspections*. Conference on Disarmament, CD/1056/CD/CW/WP.330, 8 February.
32. United States (1991) *Report on the Fourth United States Trial Inspection Exercise*. Conference on Disarmament, CD/1107/CD/CW/WP.366, 23 August.
33. Kenyon, I. R. (1988) *Non-Compliance Concern Investigations: Initiation Procedures*. Briefing Paper No. 15, Department of Peace Studies, University of Bradford. Available at <http://www.brad.ac.uk/acad/sbtwc>
34. Leklem, E. J. (1997) Senate gives advice and consent: U.S. becomes original CWC party. *Arms Control Today*, April, 32–6.
35. Levy, L. A. (1999) The CWC: A unique OSI framework. *Disarmament Forum*, 3, 17–26.

3 Developing the BTWC, 1975–1995

1. Sims, N. A. (2000) '25 Years of the Biological and Toxin Weapons Convention: Assessing Risks and Opportunities'. Paper presented to a Commemorative Seminar, Palais des Nations, Geneva, 27 March.
2. Sims, N. A. (1988) *The Diplomacy of Biological Disarmament: Vicissitudes of a Treaty in Force 1975–85*. New York: St Martin's Press.
3. Dando, M. R. (1994) *Biological Warfare in the 21st Century: Biotechnology and the Proliferation of Biological Weapons*. London: Brassey's.
4. United Nations (1980) *Final Document*. Review Conference of the Parties to the Convention on the Prohibition of the Development, Production and Stockpiling of Bacteriological (Biological) and Toxin Weapons and on their Destruction. BWC/CONF.I/10, Geneva.
5. Goldblat, J. (1996) *Arms Control: Guide to Negotiations and Agreements*. London: Sage.
6. United Nations (1986) *Final Document*. Second Review Conference of the Parties to the Convention on the Prohibition of the Development, Production and Stockpiling of Bacteriological (Biological) and Toxin Weapons and on their Destruction. BWC/CONF.II/13, Geneva.
7. United Nations (1991) *Final Document*. Third Review Conference of the Parties to the Convention on the Prohibition of the Development, Production and Stockpiling of Bacteriological (Biological) and Toxin Weapons and on their Destruction. BWC/CONF.III/23, Geneva.
8. Zilinskas, R. A. (1999) Cuban allegations of biological warfare by the United States: Assessing the evidence. *Critical Reviews in Microbiology*, 25 (3), 173–227.
9. Report of the Ad Hoc Meeting of Scientific and Technical Experts (1990) Annex 3. In E. Geissler (ed.), *Strengthening the Biological Weapons Convention by Confidence-Building Measures*. Stockholm: SIPRI.
10. Geissler, E. (1990) Agreed measures and proposals to strengthen the Convention. In E. Geissler (ed.), *Strengthening the Biological Weapons Convention by Confidence-Building Measures*. Stockholm: SIPRI.

11. Geissler, E. (1990) The first three rounds of information exchanges. In E. Geissler (ed.), *Strengthening the Biological Weapons Convention by Confidence-Building Measures*. Stockholm: SIPRI.
12. Geissler, E. (1992) Further measures to strengthen the Biological Weapons Convention. In O. Thränert (ed.), *The Verification of the Biological Weapons Convention: Problems and Prospects*. Bonn: Friedrich Ebert Stiftung.
13. Hunger, I. (1996) Confidence Building Measures. In G. S. Pearson and M. R. Dando (eds), *Strengthening the Biological Weapons Convention: Key Points for the Fourth Review Conference*. Department of Peace Studies, University of Bradford.
14. Tóth, T., Geissler, E. and Stock, T. (1994) Verification of the BWC. In E. Geissler and J. Woodall (eds), *Control of Dual-Threat Agents: The Vaccines for Peace Programme*. Oxford: Oxford University Press (for SIPRI).
15. United Nations (1993) *Report*. Ad Hoc Group of Government Experts to Identify and Examine Potential Verification Measures from a Scientific and Technical Standpoint. BWC/CONF.III/VEREX/9, Geneva.
16. United Nations (1994) *Final Report*. Special Conference of the States Parties to the Convention on the Prohibition of the Development, Production and Stockpiling of Bacteriological (Biological) and Toxin Weapons and on their Destruction. BWC/SPCONF/I, Geneva.
17. Bartlett, J. T. (1996) 'The arms control challenge: Science and technology dimension'. Paper presented to the NATO Advanced Research Workshop, 'The Technology of Biological Arms Control and Disarmament'. Budapset, 28–30 March.
18. United States (1987) *Soviet Military Power*. Washington DC: US Government Printing Office.
19. PBS Online (1998) *Plague War: Interview with Dr. Christopher Davis*. Available at<http://www.pbs.org/wgbh/pages/frontline/shows/plague/interviews/davis>
20. Federation of American Scientists (2000) *Stepnogorsk Scientific and Technical Institute for Microbiology: 52° 21′ 16N 71° 53′ 13E*. Available at <http://www.Fas.org/mike/guide/russia/facility/cbw/stepnogorsk.htm>
21. United Kingdom (1992) *Verification of the BWC: Possible Directions*. Ad Hoc Group of Government Experts to Identify and Examine Potential Verification Measures from a Scientific and Technical Standpoint. BWC/CONF.III/VEREX/1, 30 March, Geneva: United Nations.
22. France (1992) *Group of Experts on the Verification of the Biological Weapons Convention*. Ad Hoc Group of Government Experts to Identify and Examine Potential Verification Measures from a Scientific and Technical Standpoint. BWC/CONF.III/WP.2, 30 March, Geneva: United Nations.
23. The Netherlands (1992) *Discussion Paper*. Ad Hoc Group of Government Experts to Identify and Examine Potential Verification Measures from a Scientific and Technical Standpoint. BWC/CONF.III/WP.3, 31 March, Geneva: United Nations.
24. Germany (1992) *Options for the Verification of the BWC*. Ad Hoc Group of Government Experts to Identify and Examine Potential Verification Measures from a Scientific and Technical Standpoint. BWC/CONF.III/WP.4, 31 March, Geneva: United Nations.
25. South Africa (1994) *Mandate to Strengthen the Biological and Toxin Weapons Convention*. WP.11 (in reference 16).

26. United Kingdom (1994) *United Kingdom BTWC Practice Compliance Inspection (PCI) Programme. Summary Report.* WP. 2 (in reference 16).
27. Chevrier, M. (2000) Towards a Verification Protocol. In M. R. Dando, G.S. Pearson and T. Toth (eds), *Verification of the Biological and Toxin Weapons Convention.* Dordrecht: Kluwer Academic Publishers.
28. United States (1994) *Statement of U.S. Representative Donald A. Mahley to the Committee of the Whole, September 22, 1994.* WP.16 (in reference 16).

4 Genomics and the new biotechnology

1. Macintyre, B. (2000) Opening the book of life. *The Times,* 27 June, p. 1.
2. Highfield, R. (2000) All human life is here. *The Daily Telegraph,* 27 June, p. 1.
3. Buerkle, T. (2000) Historic moment for humanity's blueprint. *International Herald Tribune,* 27 June, p. 1.
4. Connor, S. (2000) Discoveries bring in age of designer medicines. *The Independent,* 27 June, p. 4.
5. Meselson, M. (2000) Averting the hostile exploitation of biotechnology. *Chemical and Biological Weapons Conventions Bulletin,* 48, 16–19.
6. Pilling, D., Cookson, C. and Griffin, V. (2000) Human blueprint is revealed. *Financial Times,* 27 June, p. 1.
7. Pilling, D. (2000) Stand by for a gene-rush. *Financial Times,* 27 June, p. 15.
8. Lander, E. S. (1996) The new genomics: Global views of biology. *Science,* 274, 536–9.
9. Moses, V. and Moses, S. (1995) *Exploiting Biotechnology.* London: Harwood Academic.
10. Smith, J. E. (1996) *Biotechnology,* 3rd edition. Cambridge: Cambridge University Press.
11. Glazer, A. N. and Nikado, H. (1995) *Microbial Biotechnology: Fundamentals of Applied Microbiology.* New York: W. H. Freeman.
12. McClellan, J. E. and Dorn, H. (1999) *Science and Technology in World History.* Baltimore: Johns Hopkins University Press.
13. Freeman, C. (1995) Technological revolutions: Historical analogies. In M. Fransman, Gerd, J. and Roobeek, A. (eds), *The Biotechnology Revolution.* Oxford: Blackwell.
14. Roobeek, A. J. M. (1995) Biotechnology: a core technology in a new techno-economic paradigm. In M. Fransman et al. (eds), *The Biotechnology Revolution.* Oxford: Blackwell.
15. Sharp, M. (1995) Applications of biotechnology: an overview. In M. Fransman et al. (eds), *The Biotechnology Revolution.* Oxford: Blackwell.
16. Rifkin, J. (1998) *The Biotech Century: The Coming Age of Genetic Commerce.* London: Victor Gollancz.
17. Brown, T. A. (1999) *Genomes.* Oxford: Bios Scientific Publishers.
18. Sanders, C. (2000) Genomic medicine and the future of health care. *Science,* 287, 17 March, 1977–8.
19. Drews, J. (2000) Drug discovery: a historical perspective. *Science,* 287, 17 March, 1960–4.
20. Office of Technology Assessment (1991) *Biotechnology in a Global Economy,* OTA-BA-494. Washington DC: US Government Printing Office, October.
21. Pilling, D. (1999) Survey – Life Sciences: Locals beat back the big boys: India. *Financial Times,* 15 July.

22. Association of the British Pharmaceutical Industry (2000) The Main Functions of the ABPI. Available at <http://www.abpi.org>, 14 September.
23. International Federation of Pharmaceutical Manufacturers Associations (2000) *IFPMA Administration and Objectives*. Available at <http://www.ifpma.org/IFpma2.html>, 14 September.
24. Taylor, T. and Johnson, L. C. (1995) *The Biotechnology Industry of the United States: a Census of Facilities*. Center for International Security, Stanford University.
25. International Dairy Foods Association (1997) *The Voice of the Dairy Foods Industry*. Washington, DC.
26. PhRMA (1997) *Reporters Handbook for the Prescription Drug Industry*. Washington, DC: PhRMA.
27. PhRMA (2000) US is the world leader in drug innovation. *PhRMA Facts*, available at <http://www.phrma.org/facts/phfacts/12_999c.html>, 13 September.
28. Department of Trade and Industry (1996) *Bioguide: Regulations, Information and Support for Biotechnology in the UK*. London: DTI.
29. Pearson, G. S. (1998) *Article X: Pharmaceutical Building Blocks*. Briefing Paper No. 8, University of Bradford. Available at <http://www.brad.ac.uk/acad/sbtwc>.
30. PhRMA (2000) R&D-to-sales ratio for pharmaceutical industry is more than for any other industry. *PhRMA Facts*, available at <http://www.phrma.org/facts/phfacts/12_999c.html>, 13 September.
31. PhRMA (2000) Only 3 out of 10 drugs prove profitable. *PhRMA Facts*, available at <http://www.phrma.org/facts/phfacts/12_999c.html>, 13 September.
32. Halligan, R. M. (1997) What is a trade secret? Trade secrets audits: Part one. Available at <http://www.execpc.com/-mhalligan/tradesec.html>, 21 August.
33. Haseltine, W. (1999) A crisis lurking within: Genes, proteins, and antibodies are the industry's solution. *Financial Times*, 28 October.
34. Pilling, D. (1999) All eyes will be fixed on further consolidation – Pharmaceuticals. *Financial Times*, 29 January.
35. Enriquez, J. (1998) Genomics and the world's economy. *Science*, **281**, 925–6.
36. Thain, M. and Hickman, M. (2000) *The Penguin Dictionary of Biology*, 10th edition. London: Penguin Books.
37. Pearson, G. S. (2000) *The UNSCOM Saga: Chemical and Biological Weapons Non-Proliferation*. London: Macmillan.
38. Working Group on BW Verification (2000) *Presentation to the European Union*. Federation of American Scientists, 20 November, Geneva.

5 The negotiation of the BTWC Protocol

1. United Nations (1994) *Final Report*. Special Conference of the States Parties to the Convention on the Prohibition of the Development, Production and Stockpiling of Bacteriological (Biological) and Toxin Weapons and on their Destruction. BWC/SPCONF/1, Geneva.
2. Dando, M. R. (1999) Strengthening the Biological and Toxin Weapons Convention through negotiation of a Verification Protocol: Will the present opportunity be seized? In C. Spencer (ed.), *Brassey's Defence Yearbook 1999*. London: Brassey's.

3. Dando, M. R. (2000) The negotiation of a verification protocol to the Biological and Toxin Weapons Convention: January 1995–December 1998. *Finnish Yearbook of International Law*, IX, 95–144.

4. Vignard, K. (2000) Biological weapons: From the BWC to biotech. Special Issue of *Disarmament Forum*, 4, 1–57. UNIDIR, Geneva.

5. For information on the Federation of American Scientists' work in regard to the AHG see their website at <http://www.fas.org>.

6. For information on the work of the Bradford Department of Peace Studies in regard to the AHG see their website at <http://www.brad.ac.uk/acad/sbtwc>.

7. Perry Robinson, J. (1998) 'Contribution of the Pugwash movement to the international regime against chemical and biological weapons'. Paper presented to the 10th Workshop of the Pugwash Study Group on the Implementation of the Chemical and Biological Weapons Convention: the BWC Protocol Negotiations: Unresolved Issues. Pugwash Meeting No. 242, 28–9 November, Geneva.

8. See, for example, Meselson, M. (1998) A draft convention to prohibit biological and chemical weapons under international criminal law. *CBW Conventions Bulletin*, 42, December, 1–5.

9. Ad Hoc Group of the States Parties to the Convention on the Prohibition of the Development, Production and Stockpiling of Bacteriological (Biological) and Toxin Weapons and on their Destruction (1995) *Procedural Report: First Session*. BWC/AD HOC GROUP/3, 6 January, Geneva: United Nations.

10. Ad Hoc Group of the States Parties to the Convention on the Prohibition of the Development, Production and Stockpiling of Bacteriological (Biological) and Toxin Weapons and on their Destruction (2000) *Procedural Report: Twenty-First Session*. BWC/AD HOC GROUP/54, 18 December, Geneva: United Nations.

11. Ad Hoc Group of the States Parties to the Convention on the Prohibition of the Development, Production and Stockpiling of Bacteriological (Biological) and Toxin Weapons and on their Destruction (1995) *Procedural Report: Second Session*. BWC/AD HOC GROUP/28, 21 July, Geneva: United Nations.

12. Tóth, T. (1999) Time to wrap up. *CBW Conventions Bulletin*, 46, December, 1–3.

13. Ad Hoc Group of the States Parties to the Convention on the Prohibition of the Development, Production and Stockpiling of Bacteriological (Biological) and Toxin Weapons and on their Destruction (1996) *Procedural Report: Fifth Session*. BWC/AD HOC GROUP/32, 27 September, Geneva: United Nations.

14. Holum, J. D. (1996) *Remarks of the Hon. John D. Holum, Director, United States Arms Control and Disarmament Agency, to the Fourth Review Conference of the Biological Weapons Convention*. 26 November, *Arms Control Text*, Geneva: US Arms Control and Disarmament Agency.

15. Berdennikov, G. (1996) *Statement of Ambassador Grigori Berdennikov, Head of the Russian Delegation at the Plenary Meeting of the Fourth Review Conference of the States Parties to the Convention on the Prohibition of the Development, Production and Stockpiling of Bacteriological (Biological) and Toxin Weapons and on their Destruction*. 26 November, Permanent Mission of the Russian Federation to the Conference on Disarmament, Geneva.

16. Tarmidzi, A. (1996) *Statement by Ambassador Agus Tarmidzi, Head of the Indonesian Delegation at the Plenary Meeting of the Fourth Review Conference of the States Parties to the Convention on the Prohibition of the Development,*

Production and Stockpiling of Bacteriological (Biological) and Toxin Weapons and on their Destruction. 27 November, Permanent Mission of the Republic of Indonesia to the United Nations and Other International Organizations, Geneva.

17. Selebi, J. S. (1996) *Statement by H. E. Mr. J. S. Selebi Permanent Representative of the Republic of South Africa at the Fourth Review Conference of the States Parties to the Convention on the Prohibition of the Development, Production and Stockpiling of Bacteriological (Biological) and Toxin Weapons and on their Destruction.* 26 November, South African Delegation to the Conference on Disarmament, Geneva.

18. South Africa (1997) *Protocol on the Verification of the Convention on the Prohibition of the Development, Production and Stockpiling of Bacteriological (Biological) and Toxin Weapons and on their Destruction.* BWC/AD HOC GROUP/WP.133, 10 March, Geneva: United Nations.

19. Ad Hoc Group of the States Parties to the Convention on the Prohibition of the Development, Production and Stockpiling of Bacteriological (Biological) and Toxin Weapons and on their Destruction (1997) *Procedural Report: Sixth Session.* BWC/AD HOC GROUP/34, 27 March, Geneva: United Nations.

20. Ad Hoc Group of the States Parties to the Convention on the Prohibition of the Development, Production and Stockpiling of Bacteriological (Biological) and Toxin Weapons and on their Destruction (1997) *Procedural Report: Seventh Session.* BWC/AD HOC GROUP/36, 4 August, Geneva: United Nations.

21. Ad Hoc Group of the States Parties to the Convention on the Prohibition of the Development, Production and Stockpiling of Bacteriological (Biological) and Toxin Weapons and on their Destruction (1998) *Procedural Report: Twelfth Session.* BWC/AD HOC GROUP/43, 15 October, Geneva: United Nations.

22. Ad Hoc Group of the States Parties to the Convention on the Prohibition of the Development, Production and Stockpiling of Bacteriological (Biological) and Toxin Weapons and on their Destruction (1998) *Procedural Report: Eleventh Session.* BWC/AD HOC GROUP/41, 16 July, Geneva: United Nations.

23. Pearson, G. S. (1998) Progress at the Ad Hoc Group in Geneva, Quarterly Review No. 4. *CBW Conventions Bulletin*, 41, September, 15–18.

24. Pearson, G. S. (2000) Progress in Geneva: Strengthening the Biological and Toxin Weapons Convention: Quarterly Review No. 13. *CBW Conventions Bulletin*, 50, December, 17–25.

25. Rissanen, J. (2001) BWC update: hurdles cleared, obstacles remaining: The Ad Hoc Group prepares for the final challenge. *Disarmament Diplomacy*, April, 16–26.

26. Pearson, G. S. (1999) Progress in Geneva: Strengthening the Biological and Toxin Weapons Convention: Quarterly Review No. 8. *CBW Conventions Bulletin*, 45, September, 13–17.

27. Pearson, G. S. (1999) Progress in Geneva: Strengthening the Biological and Toxin Weapons Convention: Quarterly Review No. 6. *CBW Conventions Bulletin*, 43, March, 10–15.

28. Pearson, G. S. (1999) Progress in Geneva: Strengthening the Biological and Toxin Weapons Convention: Quarterly Review No. 7. *CBW Conventions Bulletin*, 44, June, 17–21.

29. Pearson, G. S. (1999) Progress in Geneva: Strengthening the Biological and Toxin Weapons Convention: Quarterly Review No. 9. *CBW Conventions Bulletin*, 46, December, 5–12.
30. Pearson, G. S. (2000) Progress in Geneva: Strengthening the Biological and Toxin Weapons Convention: Quarterly Review No. 10. *CBW Conventions Bulletin*, 47, March, 10–14.
31. Pearson, G. S. (2000) Progress in Geneva: Strengthening the Biological and Toxin Weapons Convention: Quarterly Review No. 11. *CBW Conventions Bulletin*, 48, June, 33–8.
32. Pearson, G. S. (2000) Progress in Geneva: Strengthening the Biological and Toxin Weapons Convention: Quarterly Review No. 12. *CBW Conventions Bulletin*, 49, September, 13–24.
33. Mathews, R. J. (2000) Approaching an 'end-game' in the negotiation of the BWC Protocol: Lessons from the Chemical Weapons Convention. *CBW Conventions Bulletin*, 47, March, 1–4.
34. Press Release (2001) *Ad Hoc Group of States Parties to Biological Weapons Convention opens Twenty-Second Session.* Geneva: United Nations, 14 February.
35. Rissanen, J. (2001) *BWC Protocol Bulletin: BWC AHG faced with a major challenge.* E-mail report, 12 February.
36. Pearson, G. S., Sims, N. A., Dando, M. R. and Kenyon, I. R. (2000) *Evaluation Paper 18: The BTWC Protocol: Revised Proposed Complete Text for an Integrated Regime.* Project on Strengthening the Biological and Toxin Weapons Convention, University of Bradford, Bradford, UK.
37. Pearson, G. S. (2000) The Protocol to the Biological Weapons Convention is within reach. *Arms Control Today*, June, 15–20.
38. Pearson, G. S. (2001) *The BTWC Protocol: Implementation of Article III of the Convention: Pragmatic Considerations.* Project on Strengthening the Biological and Toxin Weapons Convention, Briefing Paper No. 33, University of Bradford, Bradford, UK.

6 Compliance measures: Declarations and visits

1. Tucker, J. (1998) Strengthening the Biological Weapons Convention. *Arms Control Today*, January/February, 20–7.
2. Ambassador A. de Mendonça e Moura on behalf of the European Union (2000) *BTWC–EU Statement at the 19th Session of the AHG.* Portugal Delegation to the AHG, 13 March, Geneva.
3. Kenyon, I. (1998) *Non-Compliance Concern Investigations: Initiation Procedures.* Briefing Paper No. 15, Project on Strengthening the Biological and Toxin Weapons Convention, University of Bradford.
4. Dando, M. R. and Pearson, G. S. (2000) Memorandum of Written and Oral Evidence, in Foreign Affairs Committee, Eighth Report, *Weapons of Mass Destruction.* House of Commons, London, 25 July, pp 55–9 and 70–7.
5. Ad Hoc Group of the States Parties to the Convention on the Prohibition of the Development, Production and Stockpiling of Bacteriological (Biological) and Toxin Weapons and on their Destruction (2000) *Procedural Report: Twenty-First Session.* BWC/AD HOC GROUP/54, United Nations, 18 December, Geneva.

6. Pearson, G. S. (2001) *The BTWC Protocol: Improving the Implementation of Article III of the Convention: Pragmatic Considerations.* Briefing Paper No. 33, Project on Strengthening the Biological and Toxin Weapons Convention, University of Bradford.

7. Pearson, G. S. (2000) Progress in Geneva: Strengthening the Biological and Toxin Weapons Convention: Quarterly Review No. 12. *Chemical and Biological Conventions Bulletin,* 49, September, 13–23.

8. Pearson, G. S., Sims, N. A., Dando, M. R. and Kenyon, I. (2000) *The BTWC Protocol: Proposed Complete Text for an Integrated Protocol.* Evaluation Paper No. 19, Project on Strengthening the Biological and Toxin Weapons Convention, University of Bradford.

9. Garrigue, H. (2000) 'The Protocol Provisions for Declarations and for Declaration Follow-Up Procedures'. Paper presented to a NATO Advanced Research Workshop on 'Scientific and Technical Implications of the BTWC Protocol for Civil Industry', 2–5 November, Warsaw.

7 The debate on visits

1. Smithson, A. E. (1999) 'Tall order: Crafting a meaningful Verification Protocol for the Biological Weapons Convention'. Paper delivered at a Symposium on 'Current Problems of Biological Warfare and Disarmament' (S. Wright, Chair), Geneva.

2. Black, S. (1999) 'UNSCOM and the Iraqi biological weapons program: Implications for arms control'. Paper delivered at a Symposium on 'Current Problems of Biological Warfare and Disarmament' (S. Wright, Chair), Geneva.

3. Dando, M. R. and Pearson, G. S. (2000) Memorandum. *Weapons of Mass Destruction.* Eighth Report, Foreign Affairs Committee, House of Commons, 25 July, London.

4. Tucker, J. B. (1998) Verification provisions of the Chemical Weapons Convention and their relevance to the Biological Weapons Convention. In A. Smithson (ed.), *Biological Weapons Proliferation: Reasons for Concern, Courses of Action.* Washington DC: The Henry L. Stimson Center, pp. 77–105.

5. Pearson, G. S. and Dando, M. R. (1999) *The Emerging Protocol: An Integrated, Reliable and Effective Regime.* Briefing Paper No. 25, September. Project on Strengthening the Biological and Toxin Weapons Convention, University of Bradford.

6. Mathews, R. J. (2000) Intention of Article VI: an Australian drafter's perspective. *OPCW Synthesis: Year in Review,* November, 44–7.

7. United Kingdom (1995) *Discussion Paper on Measures.* BWC/AD HOC GROUP/5, 29 June. Geneva: United Nations.

8. Australia (1995) *Declarations as a Component of a Verification Protocol.* BWC/AD HOC GROUP/CRP.1, 10 July. Geneva: United Nations.

9. United Kingdom (1995) *The Role and Objectives of Information Visits.* BWC/AD HOC GROUP/21, 13 July. Geneva: United Nations.

10. Sweden (1995) *Some Possible Elements in a Verification Protocol.* BWC/AD HOC GROUP/24, 10 July. Geneva: United Nations.

11. Sweden (1995) *Short Notice On-Site Information Visits and Inspections as Parts of a Verification Regime for the BTWC.* BWC/AD HOC GROUP/WP.15, 29 November. Geneva: United Nations.

12. Tóth, T. (2000) Prospects for progress: Drafting the Protocol to the BWC. *Arms Control Today*, May, 10–15.
13. Friend of the Chair on Compliance Measures (1995) *Declarations*. BWC/AD HOC GROUP/17, 11 July. Geneva: United Nations.
14. France and Germany (1995) *Declarations in a BWC-Verification Protocol*. BWC/AD HOC GROUP/9, 28 November. Geneva: United Nations.
15. Netherlands (1995) *The Relevance and Effectiveness of (Combinations of) Criteria for Declarations*. BWC/AD HOC GROUP/WP.10, 28 November. Geneva: United Nations.
16. Ireland (1996) *Common Position of the European Union*. BWC/AD HOC GROUP/WP.61, 15 July. Geneva: United Nations.
17. European Union (1996) *EU Discussion Paper on Triggers for Declarations*. BWC/AD HOC GROUP/WP.65, 16 July. Geneva: United Nations.
18. European Union (1996) *European Union Discussion Paper Regarding Short Notice Non-Challenge Visits*. BWC/AD HOC GROUP/WP.67, 16 July. Geneva: United Nations.
19. Pearson, G. S. (1997) *Discriminating Triggers for Mandatory Declarations*. Briefing Paper No. 3, September, Project on Strengthening the Biological and Toxin Weapons Convention, University of Bradford.
20. Pearson, G. S. (1998) *An Optimal Organisation*. Briefing Paper No. 5, January, Project on Strengthening the Biological and Toxin Weapons Convention, University of Bradford.
21. Canada (1996) *Practice Non-Challenge Visit of a Defence Research Establishment*. BWC/AD HOC GROUP/WP.60, 15 July. Geneva: United Nations.
22. Chevrier, M. I. (1998) *The Cost and Structure of a BWC Organization*. Federation of American Scientists, Washington DC, June.
23. Brazil and the UK (1996) *Report of a Joint UK/Brazil Practice Non-Challenge Visit*. BWC/AD HOC GROUP/WP.76, 18 July. Geneva: United Nations.
24. Australia (1996) *Trial Inspection of a Biological Production Facility*. BWC/AD HOC GROUP/WP.77, 18 July. Geneva: United Nations.
25. UK (1998) *Report of a Visit to a Pharmaceutical Research Facility*. BWC/AD HOC GROUP/WP.258, 9 January. Geneva: United Nations.
26. Denmark, Finland, Iceland, Norway and Sweden (1998) *Report of a Trial Random Visit to a Biopharmaceutical Production Facility*. BWC/AD HOC GROUP/WP.298, 21 August. Geneva: United Nations.
27. Austria (1998) *Report on an International Trial Random Visit, Conducted in Austria, August 10–11, 1998*. BWC/AD HOC GROUP/WP.310, 23 September. Geneva: United Nations.
28. Switzerland (1999) *Report on a Trial Inspection Based on a Random Visit to a Vaccine Production Facility*. BWC/AD HOC GROUP/WP.371, 10 June. Geneva: United Nations.
29. Iran (1999) *Report of a National Trial Visit to a Vaccine and Serum Production Facility*. BWC/AD HOC GROUP/WP.345, 14 January. Geneva: United Nations.
30. Pearson, G. S. (2001) *The BTWC Protocol: Improving the Implementation of Article III of the Convention: Practical Considerations*. Briefing Paper No. 33, February, Project on Strengthening the Biological and Toxin Weapons Convention, University of Bradford.
31. Wilson, H. (1999) Strengthening the BWC: Issues for the Ad Hoc Group. *Disarmament Diplomacy*, December, 27–34.

32. Germany (1999) *Follow-Up After Submission of Declarations: Transparency Visits*. BWC/AD HOC GROUP/WP.380, 29 June. Geneva: United Nations.
33. Beck, V. (1999) Preventing biological proliferation: Strengthening the Biological Weapons Convention. In O. Thränert (ed.), *Preventing the Proliferation of Weapons of Mass Destruction: What Role for Arms Control?: a German–American Dialogue*. Bonn: Friedrich-Ebert-Stiftung, pp. 99–106.
34. Germany (1999) *Report on Two Trial Visits Based on a Transparency Visit Concept*. BWC/AD HOC GROUP/WP.398, 24 August. Geneva: United Nations.
35. Spain (2000) *Report on a Trial Transparency Visit to a Biological Defensive Facility*. BWC/AD HOC GROUP/WP.414, 17 March. Geneva: United Nations.
36. Tucker, J. (1998) Strengthening the BWC: Moving toward a Compliance Protocol. *Arms Control Today*, January/February, 20–7.
37. Office of the Press Secretary (1998) *Fact Sheet: The Biological Weapons Convention*. Washington DC: The White House.
38. Rissanen, J. (2000) BWC update: The BWC Protocol negotiation 18th Session: Removing brackets. *Disarmament Diplomacy*, January/February, 21–6.
39. Rissanen, J. (2000) BWC update: Protocol Ad Hoc Group enters deeper into consultations. *Disarmament Diplomacy*, July, 28–32.
40. United States (2000) *U.S. Paper on Friend of the Chair Text on Visits*. Geneva, 2 February.

8 The role of US industry

1. Documentation (2000) BWC Protocol: US testimony. *Disarmament Diplomacy*, September, 37–42.
2. Tucker, J. (1998) Strengthening the BWC: Moving toward a compliance protocol. *Arms Control Today*, January/February, 20–7.
3. Working Group on Biological and Toxin Weapons Verification (1997) *Triggers for Declarations and Inspections/Visits Under a BWC Compliance Regime*. Federation of American Scientists, Washington DC, December.
4. Working Group on Biological and Toxin Weapons Verification (1997) *Rapid Resolution of Questions that Might Arise During Nonchallenge Visits*. Federation of American Scientists, Washington DC, December.
5. Working Group on Biological and Toxin Weapons Verification (1997) *Making Random Non-Challenge Visits Friendly*. Federation of American Scientists, Washington DC, December.
6. Working Group on Biological and Toxin Weapons Verification (1998) *Visits are Crucial*. Federation of American Scientists, Washington DC, September.
7. Working Group on Biological and Toxin Weapons Verification (1998) *Visits: A Unified Concept*. Federation of American Scientists, Washington DC, December.
8. Working Group on Biological and Toxin Weapons Verification (1999) *Views on Visits*. Federation of American Scientists, Washington DC, June.
9. Dando, M. R. (1998) *The Strengthened BTWC Protocol: Implications for the Biotechnology and Pharmaceutical Industry*. Briefing Paper No. 17, Project on Strengthening the Biological and Toxin Weapons Convention, University of Bradford.
10. Carpenter, W. D. and Moodie, M. (undated) *Industry and International Biological Arms Control*. Mimeo, Washington, DC.

11. PhRMA Board (1996) *Statement of Principle on the Biological Weapons Convention*. PhRMA, Washington DC, 16 May.
12. PhRMA (1996) *Reducing the Threat of Biological Weapons: a PhRMA Perspective*. PhRMA, Washington DC, 6 December.
13. Wollett, G. R. (1998) Industry's role, concerns, and interests in the negotiation of a BWC compliance Protocol. In A. Smithson (ed.), *Biological Weapons Proliferation: Reasons for Concern, Courses of Action*. Washington DC: Henry L. Stimson Center, pp. 39–52.
14. Kellman, B., Gualtieri, D. S. and Tanzman, E. A. (1995) Disarmament and disclosure: How arms control verification can proceed without threatening confidential business information. *Harvard International Law Journal*, 36 (1), 72–126.
15. Legal Subgroup of the Working Group on Biological Weapons Verification (1997) *Working Paper on the Protection of Confidential Information in the Proposed Protocol to the Biological Weapons Convention*. Federation of American Scientists, Washington DC, December.
16. Monath, T. P. and Gordon, L. K. (1998) Policy Forum: Strengthening the Biological Weapons Convention. *Science*, 282, 1423.
17. Muth, W. (1999) The role of the pharmaceutical and biotech industries in strengthening the biological disarmament regime. *Politics and the Life Sciences*, March, 92–7.
18. Van Sloten, R. (1999) *Biotechnology and the strengthening of the BTWC*. Paper presented at Pugwash Meeting No. 246, Noordwijk, 15–16 May.
19. Rosenberg, B. H. (1999) Bioterrorism: Mitigation or prevention. *ASA Newsletter*, 99-4, 1–2.
20. Anon (2000) Chronology. *CBW Conventions Bulletin*, 49, 31 May, p. 31.
21. EFPIA (undated) *The Biological and Toxin Weapons Convention: the Position of the European Federation of Pharmaceutical Industries and Associations*. Brussels: EFPIA.
22. European, United States and Japanese Industry (undated) *Joint Position on the Compliance Protocol to the Biological Weapons Convention*. Geneva.
23. PhRMA and EFPIA (undated) *Global Industry Position on Biological Weapons Issues*. Geneva.
24. Anon (2000) Chronology. *CBW Conventions Bulletin*, 50, 13 September, p. 33.
25. Editorial (2000) The CWC and BWC: Yesterday, today, tomorrow. *CBW Conventions Bulletin*, 50, December, 1–2.
26. van Aken, J. (2000) *Pharmaceutical Industry Torpedoes Biowarfare Treaty*. Sunshine Project, March, Hamburg.
27. Barnaby, W. (1999) Forum: Blood on their hands. *New Scientist*, 30 January, p. 45.
28. Pilling, D. (2001) Patents and patients. *Financial Times*, 17 February, p. 6.

9 The chairman's text

1. Pearson, G. S., Dando, M. R. and Sims, N. A. (2001) *The Composite Protocol Text: an Effective Strengthening of the Biological and Toxin Weapons Convention*. Evaluation Paper No. 20, Project on Strengthening the Biological Weapons Convention, University of Bradford.
2. United Nations (2001) *Protocol to the Convention on the Prohibition of the Development, Production and Stockpiling of Bacteriological (Biological) and Toxin*

Weapons and on their Destruction. BWC/AD HOC GROUP/CRP.8 (FUTURE), 30 March, Geneva.

3. United Nations (2001) *Procedural Report of the Ad Hoc Group of the States Parties to the Convention on the Prohibition of the Development, Production and Stockpiling of Bacteriological (Biological) and Toxin Weapons and on their Destruction.* BWC/AD HOC GROUP/55-1, 1 March, Geneva.

4. Garrigue, H. (2001) 'Declarations and declaration follow-up procedures'. Paper presented to NATO ASI No. 977199, 19–29 March, Budapest.

5. Beck, V. (2001) 'Implication of declarations and follow-up procedures for biodefence'. Lecture notes from presentation of a paper at NATO ASI No. 977199, 19–29 March, Budapest.

6. Pearson, G. S. (1997) *Discriminating Triggers For Mandatory Declarations.* Briefing Paper No. 3, Project on Strengthening the Biological Weapons Convention, University of Bradford, September.

7. Dorigo, M. (2001) 'Industrial facilities and the BWC Protocol: Implementation aspects – industrial views'. Paper presented to NATO ASI No. 977199, 19–29 March, Budapest.

8. Ruddock, M. (2001) 'The implications of declarations and follow-up procedures for government'. Paper presented to NATO ASI No. 977199, 19–29 March, Budapest.

9. Walker, J. (2001) 'UK experience from practice visits'. Paper presented to NATO ASI No. 977199, 19–29 March, Budapest.

10. Meier, O. (2001) *Biological Weapons Protocol Proposed: Chairman's Compromise Text Paves the way for Negotiation Endgame.* Press release, VERTIC, 23 April, London.

11. Bustani, J. M. (2000) The Chemical Weapons Convention: model for the future. *OPCW Synthesis,* May, 4–7.

12. Dando, M. R., Pearson, G. S. and Whitby, S. M. (2000) Memorandum: Weapons of Mass Destruction, in *Eighth Report,* Foreign Affairs Committee. House of Commons, London, pp. 55–9.

13. Tóth, T. (2001) 'The Protocol provisions'. Presentation to NATO ASI No. 977199, 19–29 March, Budapest.

10   The United States and the BTWC Protocol

1. Olson, E. (2001) Geneva push on biological arms accord. *International Herald Tribune,* 25 April, p. 4.

2. Editorial (2001) Washington and the BWC Protocol negotiation. *CBW Conventions Bulletin,* 51, March, 1.

3. Tucker, J. B. and Sands, A. (1999) 'Averting failure of the biological weapons non-proliferation regime'. Paper prepared for a strategy session on 'Coping with Nonproliferation Crises'. Monterey Nonproliferation Strategy Group, Washington DC, 3–4 November.

4. Moodie, M. (2000) Fighting the proliferation of biological weapons: Beyond the BWC Protocol. *Disarmament Forum,* 4, 43–51.

5. Pearson, G. S. (2000) The wider public awareness of biological and chemical weapons. *Weapons of Mass Destruction,* Eighth Report, 94–7. Foreign Affairs Committee, London: House of Commons.

6. Kaplan, M. M. (1999) The efforts of WHO and Pugwash to eliminate chemical and biological weapons – a memoir. *Bulletin of the World Health Organization*, 77 (2), 149–55.

7. Rotblat, J. (2000) Essays on science and society: Taking responsibility. *Science*, 289, 4 August, 729.

8. Anon (2000) How the United States negotiates. *Peace Watch*, VI (6), 1–3. Washington, DC: United States Institute of Peace.

9. United States Institute of Peace (2000) *Special Report: Adapting to the New National Security Environment*. Special Report No. 64, December.

10. Thiessen, M. A. and Leonard, M. (2001) When worlds collide. *Foreign Policy*, April, 64–74.

11. Sha Zukong, Ambassador (2000) US missile defence: China's view. *Disarmament Diplomacy*, January/February, 3–6.

12. Walker, W. (2000) Establishing legitimate and effective order in a unipolar world. *Disarmament Diplomacy*, January/February, 11–15.

13. Editorial (2001) Braving the juggernaut. *Disarmament Diplomacy*, March, 2.

14. Andreoni, G. (1999) The disarray of US non-proliferation policy. *Survival*, 41 (4), 42–61.

15. Sweden (2001) *Statement by the Representative of Sweden on Behalf of the European Union*. 23rd Session of the Ad Hoc Group of the States Parties to the BTWC, 23 April, Geneva.

16. de Valle Pereira, Ambassador (2001) *Statement*. 23rd Session of the Ad Hoc Group of the States Parties to the BTWC, 23 April, Geneva.

17. Soutar, I. (2001) *Statement by Ambassador Ian Soutar Permanent Representative of the United Kingdom to the BWC Ad Hoc Group*, 24 April, Geneva.

18. Ember, L. (2001) Biological weapons: U.S. nixes efforts to strengthen bioweapons treaty. *C & EN*, 20 April.

19. Rosenberg, B. (2001) US shadow hovers over the BWC Protocol. *ASA Newsletter*, 18 April, p. 3.

20. Editorial (2001) Bio-apocalypse now. *New Scientist*, 20 April, p. 1.

21. United Nations (2001) *Procedural Report of the Ad Hoc Group of the States Parties to the Convention on the Prohibition of the Development, Production and Stockpiling of Bacteriological (Biological) and Toxin Weapons and on their Destruction*. BWC/AD HOC GROUP/56-1, 18 May, Geneva: United Nations.

22. Sub-Committee on National Security Veterans' Affairs and International Relations (2001) *Hearings on the Biological Weapons Control Treaty* (Representative Christopher Shays), 10 July, Washington, DC. Available at <www.house.gov/reform/us/web_resources/shays_pr_july/_10.htm>.

23. Special Section: The Chairman's Text of the BWC Protocol (2001) *Arms Control Today*, May, 11–29.

24. Smithson, A. (2001) *House of Cards: the Pivotal Importance of a Technically Sound BWC Monitoring Protocol*. Washington DC: The Henry L. Stimson Center, 16 May.

25. Chevrier, M. I. (2001) A necessary compromise. *Arms Control Today*, May, 14–15.

26. Zelicoff, A. P. (2001) An impractical Protocol. *Arms Control Today*, May, 25–7.

27. Chronology (2001) For 20–22 March. *CBW Conventions Bulletin*, 52, June, 49.

28. European Parliament (2001) *Resolution on the Compliance Protocol for the Biological and Toxin Weapons Convention (BTWC)*. European Parliament Plenary Session, 14 June.

29. Baroness Symons (2001) *Written Answer to Lord Judd (HL300) 18/07/01*. House of Lords, 23 July, London.
30. Pearson, G. S., Dando, M. R. and Sims, N. A. (2001) *The US Rejection of the Composite Protocol: a Huge Mistake based on Illogical Assessments*. Evaluation Paper No. 22, Project on Strengthening the Biological Weapons Convention, Bradford University, August.
31. Brown, P. (2001) World deal on climate isolates US. *The Guardian*, 24 July, p. 1.
32. Ember, L. (2001) US search for way to say no. *C&E News*, 16 July, p. 8.
33. Gordon, M. R. (2001) US finds itself at odds with allies over enforcing germ warfare treaty. *International Herald Tribune*, 25 July, p. 4.
34. Ambassador Mahley, D. A. (2001) *Statement*. United States Delegation to the Ad Hoc Group, Geneva, 25 July.
35. United Nations (1994) *Final Report*. Special Conference of the States Parties to the Convention on the Prohibition of the Development, Production and Stockpiling of Bacteriological (Biological) and Toxin Weapons and on their Destruction. BWC/SPCONF/I, Geneva: United Nations.
36. Lacey, E. J. (1994) Tackling the biological weapons threat: The next proliferation challenge. *The Washington Quarterly*, 17 (4), 53–64.
37. Walker, J. (1996) Biological weapons: Attempts to verify. In R. Ranger (ed.), *The Devil's Brew*. Bailrigg Memorandum No. 16, Centre for Defence and International Security Studies, Lancaster University, pp. 36–9.
38. Pearson, G. S., Dando, M. R. and Sims, N. A. (2001) *The Composite Protocol Text: An Effective Strengthening of the Biological and Toxin Weapons Convention*. Evaluation Paper No. 20, Project on Strengthening the Biological Weapons Convention, Bradford University, April.
39. Dando, M. R. (2001) *The New Biological Weapons: Threat, Proliferation and Control*. Boulder: Lynne Rienner.
40. Pearson, G. S. (2001) *New Scientific and Technological Developments of Relevance to the Fifth Review Conference*. Review Conference Paper No. 3, Project on Strengthening the Biological Weapons Convention, Bradford University, July.
41. Rissanen, J. (2001) *BWC Protocol Bulletin*. August, 3, 10, 15, 20. Geneva: UNIDIR.
42. Associated Press (2001) Germ warfare negotiations end. *The New York Times*, 18 August.
43. Sims, N. A. (2001) Four decades of missed opportunities to strengthen the BWC: 2001 too? *Disarmament Diplomacy*, June, 15–21.
44. Cornwill, R. (2001) Now Bush rejects germ warfare treaty. *The Independent*, 26 July, p. 1.
45. Rosenberg, B. H. (2001) Allergic reaction: Washington's response to the BWC Protocol. *Arms Control Today*, July/August, 3–8.
46. Lilija, P., Roffey, R. and Westerdahl, K. S. (1999) *Disarmament or Retention: Is the Soviet Biological Weapons Programme Continuing in Russia?* FOA-R-99-01366-865-SE. Division of NBC Defence, FOA, Sweden.
47. Rimmington, A. (1999) Fragmentation and proliferation? The fate of the Soviet Union's offensive biological weapons programme. *Contemporary Security Policy*, 20 (1), 86–110.
48. Chronology (2001) For 10 April. *CBW Conventions Bulletin*, 52, June, 54.
49. Grabow, Lt. Col. C. L. C. (1991) *Implications and Effects of Advanced Biological and Biological/Chemical Weapons at the Operational Planning Level*. AD-A240 460. Naval War College, Newport, RI, 21 June.

50. Geissler, E. and van Courtland Moon, J. E. (1999) *Biological and Toxin Weapons: Research, Development and Use from the Middle Ages to 1945.* SIPRI Chemical and Biological Warfare Series, No. 18. Stockholm: SIPRI.
51. Gertoff, R. (2000) Polyakov's run. *Bulletin of the Atomic Scientists,* 56 (5), 37–40.
52. Asker, J. R. (2001) Washington outlook: Threat assessment. *Aviation Week and Space Technology,* 30 July, p. 3.
53. Chief Medical Officer (2000) *Deliberate Release of Biological and Chemical Agents: Guidance to Help Plan the Health Service Response.* London: Department of Health, March.
54. Pearson, G. S., Dando, M. R. and Sims, N. A. (2001) *The Composite Protocol Text: An Evaluation of the Costs and Benefits to States Parties.* Evaluation Paper No. 21, Project on Strengthening the Biological Weapons Convention, Bradford University, July.

11 Epilogue

1. Miller, J. et al. (2001) On secretly fighting germ warfare: US tests limits of a 1972 treaty. *New York Times,* 4 September, p. 1.
2. Loeb, V, (2001) US seeks duplicate of Russian anthrax: Microbe to be used to check vaccine. *Washington Post,* 5 September, p. 16.
3. Miller, J. (2001) When is a bomb not a bomb? Germ experts confront US. *New York Times,* 5 September, p. 1.
4. Begley, S. (2001) Unmasking bioterror, pp. 23–32 in *Newsweek,* Special Issue on Biological and Chemical Terror: How Scared Should You Be?, 8 October.
5. Korb, L. and Tiersky, A. (2001) The end of unilateralism: Arms control after September 11. *Arms Control Today,* October, 3–7.
6. United States Mission to the United Nations (2001) *Press Release: Statement by Avis Bohlen,* 10 October, New York.
7. Rissanen, J. (2001) Regrets and uncertainty over Protocol at First Committee. *BWC Protocol Bulletin,* 25 October, New York.
8. White House (2001) *Statement by the President: Strengthening the International Regime against Biological Weapons,* 1 November, Washington D.C.
9. Aldhous, P. (2001) Biologists urged to address risk of data aiding bioweapons design. *Nature,* **414,** 15 November, 237–8.
10. Editorial (2001) The end of innocence? *Nature,* **414,** 15 November, 236.
11. Pearson, G. S., Dando, M. R. and Sims, N. A. (2001) *Key Points for the Fifth Review Conference.* Project on Strengthening the Biological Weapons Convention, University of Bradford.
12. United States Mission to the United Nations (2001) *Statement of Honorable John R. Bolton to the Fifth Review Conference of the Biological Weapons Convention,* 19 November, Geneva.
13. Rissanen, J. (2001) *BWC Review Conference Bulletin,* 30 November, Geneva.
14. VERTIC (2001) *Bioweapons Conference Fails: US Successfully Sabotages Attempts to Strengthen Biological Weapons Ban.* Press release, Verification, Research, Training and Information Centre, London.
15. Sims, N. A. (2001) *The Evolution of Biological Disarmament.* Oxford: Oxford University Press (for SIPRI).
16. World Health Organization (2001) *Public Health Responses to Biological and Chemical Weapons.* Geneva: World Health Organization.

Index

abrins 105
Ad Hoc Group (AHG) of BTWC
    xiii, 41, 48, 52, 53, 54, 61, 75–98,
    99, 115, 116, 123, 130, 136, 137,
    140, 141, 146, 166, 170, 171, 172,
    174, 184
    Chairman, Tibor Tóth 48, 49, 78,
        80, 82, 84, 86, 87, 90, 91, 92,
        93, 94, 116, 119, 128, 139, 140,
        152, 155, 156, 159, 164, 165,
        166, 172, 174, 175, 178
    European
        Group 78, 97, 129
        Parliament 174
        Union 100, 101, 102, 121, 133,
            134, 137, 170, 171
    Facilitators 78, 91
    Friends of the Chair (FOCs) 78,
        80, 87, 88, 90, 91, 92, 120
    mandate 59, 75, 78, 80, 82, 83, 84,
        99, 145, 167, 175, 177, 178, 179
    meetings/sessions 75, 78, 80, 82,
        84, 86, 87, 88, 90, 91, 92, 93,
        100, 116, 120, 121, 125, 128,
        129, 130, 131
    negotiations 77, 87, 116
    non-aligned movement 78, 96, 97,
        120, 130
    Portugal 100, 101
    practice visits/investigations 92,
        123, 124, 125, 126, 127, 129,
        136
    procedural
        reports 75, 78, 80, 91, 92, 172,
            178; annex/es 78, 80, 84,
            86, 91; July–August 2000
            session 91; Sessions II–VI
            80; 6th session 84; 11th
            session 87; 12th session
            86, 87; 22nd session 140;
            23rd session 172, 178; 24th
            session 174, 178, 179
    rules 78

Russia 97
South Africa 93, 94, 97
Ukraine 97
United States 97, 99
and VEREX 116, 136
Western Group 78, 97, 128, 130,
    131, 137
working methods 92
working papers 80, 86, 90, 177
Australia 116, 123, 125, 129
Austria 123, 127
Brazil 123, 124
Canada 122
Denmark 122
Finland 122
France 120
Germany 120, 123, 128, 129
Iceland 122
Iran 123, 127
Ireland 121
Italy 122
Japan 123
Netherlands 120, 121, 122
Non-Aligned Movement 130
Nordic countries 123
Norway 122
South Africa 89, 130
Spain 129
Sweden 118, 119, 122
Switzerland 123, 127
United Kingdom 89, 116, 117,
    119, 122, 123, 124, 130
United States 130, 131
aerobiology/aerosol
    dissemination 120
anthrax 1, 16, 46, 56, 181, 182
antibiotics 20, 67
arms control 5, 13, 24, 170, 183
    agreements 73, 74, 118, 123, 167,
        178
    biological 9, 13, 75, 77, 112, 113,
        126
    chemical 9, 40, 77, 113

arms control – *continued*
  conventional 113
  landmines 77
  nuclear 77, 113
  small arms 77
Arms Control and Disarmament
    Agency (ACDA) USA xii, 22, 83
Australia
  and AHG 116, 123, 125, 129
  and CWC inspections 25
  Group export control system 27
Austria
  and AHG 123
  BTWC Protocol practice visit 127

Bacillus anthracis 56
bacterium/a 56, 64
  toxins 16
bacteriological agents 54, 56, 105
  warfare 3
  weapons 3, 44
biodefence 100, 108, 120, 123, 128,
    153, 167, 175, 178
biological
  agents 15, 16, 17, 48, 54, 55, 59,
      98, 102, 105, 145, 152,
      153, 181
    animal pathogens 105, 114, 144
    destruction 102
    dual-use nature 117
    human pathogens 105, 114, 144
    peaceful use 6
    plant pathogens 105, 144
    protozoan 105, 144
    hostile purposes 48, 57, 97, 105,
        148
    zoonotic pathogens 105, 144
  laboratories 73
  production facilities 73
    civil 74
Biological and Toxin Weapons
    Convention (BTWC) 2, 5, 6, 8,
    15, 41, 42, 43, 44, 46, 47, 48, 49,
    50, 52, 53, 54, 56, 57, 58, 96, 99,
    100, 102, 109, 111, 113, 114, 116,
    120, 122, 123, 130, 132, 134, 138,
    139, 142, 143, 148, 149, 171, 174,
    175, 176, 177, 178, 179, 180, 181,
    184

Ad Hoc Group (AHG) xiii, 41, 48,
    52, 53, 54, 61, 91, 93, 94, 99,
    Ch. 5, 115, 116, 121, 123, 136,
    137, 140, 141, 146, 152, 161,
    163, 166, 167, 174, 179
Article
  I 6, 48, 53, 97, 105, 143, 144,
      145, 162, 181
  II 102
  III 102, 172
  IV 8, 163
  V 18, 9, 15, 41, 42, 43, 48, 161,
      163
  VI 8, 9, 41, 42, 43
  VIII 8
  X 53
  XI 42
botulinal toxins 29, 105
commercial
  confidentiality 60, 125
  proprietary information (CPI)
      53, 71, 123, 124, 125, 126,
      127, 134, 136, 137
compliance 9, 41, 50, 58, 60, 116
  measures 11, 53, 54, 99, 117,
      159, 161, 165, 183
  regime 19, 54, 57, 114, 163
Confidence-Building Measures
    (CBMs) xiii, 41, 44, 45, 46, 47,
    48, 107, 134, 136, 149, 163
Depositary States xii, 43, 49
disease outbreak/reporting 45, 100
draft 12
  UK xii, 6, 9
entry into force 41, 90
General Purpose Criterion 9, 34,
    54, 97, 100, 105, 144
hostile purposes 97, 129, 148
inspection visits 14, 59
  on-site 50, 54, 56, 60, 175
  trial 50, 60, 123
international measures 9, 10, 12,
    132, 175
national
  authorities 92
  biological defense R&D 47, 120,
      123
  biological offense R&D 120
  measures 9, 10, 12, 17

Biological and Toxin Weapons
  Convention (BTWC) – *continued*
  national – *continued*
    security information 123
    negotiation 5, 6, 9, 14, 16, 24, 43
      Canadian working paper 10
      UK position 9
    non-compliance 10, 50, 58, 60,
      111, 113
      investigation of 12
    and President Nixon xii
    organization (OPBW) 123
    prohibitions 6
    regime 41, 114
    Review Conferences 15, 41
      Final Declarations 42, 44
      First 6, 8, 42
      Second xiii, 42, 44
      Third xiii, 43–4, 46, 48, 49,
        99, 181
      Fourth 47, 54, 80, 82, 84, 121,
        171, 184
      Fifth 82, 83, 139, 172, 174, 178,
        179, 181–4
      Sixth 179
    scope 48
    Special Conference xiii, 41, 52, 54,
      59, 60, 75, 82, 93, 121
    strengthening 13, 15, 67, 70, 72,
      82, 112
    trial inspections 50, 60
    vaccines 47, 100, 108, 120
    VEREX xiii, 17, 41, 47, 48, 49, 50,
      54, 57, 58, 116, 118, 136, 145,
      175
      meetings 50, 51, 52
      negotiations 80, 116
      on-site measures 124
      report 53, 54, 69, 116, 175
      working papers 57, 58, 59, 60
    verification xiii, 9, 13, 15, 41, 42,
      45, 49, 50, 54, 61, 74, 129, 138,
      142
      functions of xiv, 14, 15
      legally binding instrument 53,
        54, 82, 84
      measures 9, 11, 13, 14, 47, 48,
        49, 50, 51, 52, 53, 58, 116,
        121

    regime 13, 14, 19, 54, 58, 59,
      60, 83, 118, 123
    violations 10, 13, 14, 15, 19, 49,
      50, 129, 175
      militarily significant 56, 61
  BTWC verification Protocol 12, 15,
    22, 27, 41, 54, 58, 59, 80, 83, 88,
    90, 91, 93, 94, 96, 99, 100, 101,
    102, 105, 106, 107, 108, 110, 111,
    113, 114, 117, 119, 121, 122, 126,
    127, 128, 131, 137, 138, 139, 140,
    143, 144, 149, 150, 156, 161, 163,
    166, 167, 168, 171, 172, 173, 174,
    175, 176, 177, 179, 180, 183
    Ad Hoc Group xiii, 41, 48, 52, 53,
      54, 91, 93, 94, 99, 115, 116,
      123, 136, 137, 140, 141, 146,
      166, 170, 171, 172, 174
    aerobiology/aerosol
      dissemination 120
    annexes 88
    annual declarations 59,
      100
    appendices 88
    articles 88
    assistance 90
    biodefence 100, 108, 120, 123, 128
    Chairman's composite text 139,
      140, 143, 144, 145, 148, 151,
      152, 153, 154, 157, 161, 162,
      163, 165, 166, 170, 171, 174,
      175, 176, 177, 179
      Annex A 143, 145, 149
      Article 1 142, 143
      Article 2 142, 143, 144, 146,
        153, 155
      Article 3 144: annual and
        current transparency
        threshold levels 144, 145;
        lists of agents and toxins
        144, 153; list of equipment
        144, 145
      Article 4 146, 150, 151: annual
        declarations 147, 150;
        declarations 148, 150, 151,
        152, 156, 159, 160; initial
        declarations 147, 148;
        submission of declarations
        147, 150

BTWC verification Protocol – *continued*
Chairman's composite text –
continued
Article 5 156
Article 6 156, 157, 159, 160:
clarification requests 160;
declaration clarification
procedures 156, 159;
Director-General 159, 160;
randomly-selected
transparency visits 155,
156, 157, 158, 159; Technical
Secretariat 156, 158, 163;
voluntary assistance visits
156, 157, 159; voluntary
clarification visits 160, 161
Article 8 157, 159, 160, 161
Article 9: facility investigations
145, 162; field investigations
162
Article 16 160
biocontrol agent 155
biodefence 143, 144, 146, 149,
150, 153
Conference of States Parties 156,
161
declaration format 145, 146,
147, 148: triggers 144, 145,
146, 147, 148, 151, 152, 153,
154, 155
executive council 150, 157, 160,
161, 162
high biological containment
(BL3) 152, 153
maximum biological
containment (BL4) 151
offensive biological weapons
programmes 148
plant inoculant 155
plant pathogen containment 152
production facilities 153
Preamble 142
vaccine production 152
challenge investigations 12, 102,
117, 135, 136, 161, 163, 172,
176, 177
clarification
procedures 100, 101, 102, 119,
136, 138, 163

visits 101, 119, 120
compliance measures 90, 94, Ch.
6, 114, 117, 118, 120, 128, 130,
163, 176
consultations 100, 119
Co-operation Committee 163, 164
declarations 12, 58, 59, 74, 92, 96,
98, Ch. 6, 116, 117, 118, 128,
134, 136, 138, 148, 163, 172,
176
follow-up procedures 96, 100,
106, 109, 111, 163, 164, 172,
176
regime 100, 102
definitions 90, 172
draft 80, 90
entry into force 59
executive council 97
implementation measures 100,
111
information exchange 59, 118
legal issues 90, 172
listed agents (and toxins) 100,
103, 105, 106, 108, 122
mandate 123
maximum biological
containment (BL4/P4) 45, 96,
100, 103, 107, 108, 120
national legislation 18, 90, 163,
180
negotiations xiii, 59, 60, 61,
Ch. 5, 99, 100, 116, 130, 134,
139, 166, 169, 172
non-governmental
organizations 77, 123
non-compliance issues 12, 57,
111
organization (OPBW) 90, 91, 93,
106, 121, 123
Protocol 1st Review Conference
155, 157
ratification 59
regime 52, 54, 58, 59/60, 61, 83,
118, 163, 164, 165
rolling text 80, 83, 84, 85, 86, 87,
88, 89, 90, 91, 93, 94, 104, 116,
128, 140, 142, 143, 144, 145,
146, 147, 150, 153, 155, 171,
173

BTWC verification Protocol – *continued*
  rolling text – *continued*
    agents   102, 105, 106: animal
      105, 144; human   105, 144;
      plant   105, 144; toxins
      105, 144; zoonotic   105, 144
    Annexes A   84, 85, 87, 90, 104,
      105, 144
    Appendices   85, 104, 105
    Article I   84, 94
    Article III   84, 89, 90, 94, 102,
      103, 104, 107, 109, 110, 111
    Article VII   85, 90, 94
    Article XIII   84
    Article IX   85
    Articles XI–XXIII (administrative)
      84
    biodefence: facilities   94, 96,
      100, 107, 108, 120, 123;
      programmes   103, 120;
      BL4   107
    clarification   102, 108, 109, 110,
      111, 119: procedures   89, 94,
      100, 101
    Conference of States Parties   109,
      112, 144
    consultations   100, 102, 109,
      110, 111, 119
    co-operation   94, 102, 109, 110,
      111
    declarations   Ch. 6, 116, 117,
      119, 123, 124, 125, 127, 131:
      activities   105, 110, 111,
      119; annual   100, 102, 103,
      107, 123; clarification   110,
      111, 112, 119; consultative
      meetings   111, 112; criteria
      101, 102, 105, 106; facility
      105, 107, 108, 110, 111, 114,
      119, 123, 128, 129; follow up
      96, 100, 106, 109, 111;
      format   105, 120; initial
      102; national   108; transfers
      105; triggers   94, 107, 108,
      120, 121, 122
    Director-General   111, 112, 144
    entry into force   103
    equipment   102
    export control regimes   94

  green-light procedure   94, 97,
    134, 135, 162
  high-containment
    laboratories/facilities   45,
    120
  investigations   92, 101, 102, 109:
    alleged use   117;
    challenge   101, 117;
    initiation   97
  listed agents (and toxins)   100,
    102, 105, 106, 108, 120, 122
  maximum containment
    facilities   45, 96, 100, 103,
    107, 108, 120
  organization   106, 121, 123, 129:
    Executive Council   112
  red-light procedure   94, 97, 134,
    162
  regime   97
  Technical Secretariat   106, 107,
    108, 109, 110, 111, 129
  thresholds   94, 102, 143
  toxins   100, 102, 105, 106
  transfers   94, 96, 102
  vaccine production   100, 103,
    108, 120, 124, 125, 129, 152
  visits   98, Ch. 6, 117, 118, 119,
    122, 134, 136: challenge,
    practice   124; clarification
    97, 100, 101, 112, 119, 120,
    121, 136; confidence-
    building   110; follow up
    100, 106; qualitative/
    quantitative approach   117;
    randomly-selected   89, 94,
    96, 100, 107, 109, 110, 127,
    128, 130, 131, 136, 137;
    regime   100, 108, 119, 120;
    routine (non-challenge)
    114, 115, 119, 121, 123, 136,
    137, 138: practice   123, 124,
    125, 126, 127, 129; schedule
    109; scope   107; transparency
    96, 107, 110, 121, 126, 128,
    129, 130, 131, 136
  voluntary assistance   89, 108,
    109
technical co-operation   90, 92
threshold quantities   98, 145

BTWC verification Protocol – *continued*
  transfers 92
  vaccine production 100, 103, 108,
    120, 124, 125, 129, 152
  facilities 108, 120, 136, 153
biological warfare 3, 48, 55, 73, 139,
  178, 179
  agents 2, 3, 7, 15, 16, 55, 56, 57,
    138, 148
  disarmament 9
  Soviet system 20, 57
  trillion dose criterion 55
    fermentation capacity 56
  viruses 3, 56, 105
biological weapons (BW) xii, xiii, 2,
  4, 6, 10, 15, 20, 24, 26, 44, 47,
  49, 55, 59, 72, 83, 97, 105, 117,
  142, 143, 144, 149, 162, 164, 167,
  172, 176, 180
  agents 6, 15, 17, 45, 48, 55, 56, 57,
    97, 106, 114, 117, 144, 152, 153
  aerosol attack 17
  anti-animal 2, 3, 17
  anti-personnel 17
  anti-plant 2, 3, 17
  delivery 48, 56, 57
  development 17, 48
  microbial 45, 48, 105
  militarily significant quantity
    14, 15, 17, 54, 55, 61, 132
  production 14, 17, 48, 57
  proliferation 20, 56, 134, 168,
    179: militarily significant
    57, 132, 151, 165
  research 17
  sabotage 17
  terrorist use 17, 55: toxins 45,
    48, 57, 105, 142, 143, 144,
    152
  trillion dose criterion 55:
    fermentation capacity 56
  vectors 105, 144, 152
  viral 56, 105
  weaponization 57
anthrax 1, 16, 56
botulinum/botulinal toxins 2, 16,
  29, 36, 105
international legal restrictions 2
and Iraq xiii, 47, 72, 73

offensive, proliferation of xiii, 21,
  22, 33, 56, 57
offensive programmes xii, 1, 59,
  74, 113, 132, 165, 166, 179
  France 2
  Iran 22
  Iraq 2, 22, 113
  Japan 2
  leakage from 17
  militarily significant 57, 58,
    59
  South Africa 2, 74
  Soviet Union xii, 2, 13, 20, 57
  United Kingdom 2
  United States 2, 5
production facility/ies 13, 18, 57,
  74
proliferation 22, 56, 57, 179
viruses 3, 56
weaponization 17, 48, 57
as WMD 4
biology 1, 62, 63, 66, 67, 77
biopharmaceuticals 127
Biopreparat – *see* Soviet
  Union/Russian Federation
bioreactor vessel 72, 153
biotechnology 67
  for chemical production 32
  dual-use nature 19, 20, 21, 22, 57,
    59, 73, 74, 101
  facilities 72, 74, 125, 145, 147,
    150, 153, 155, 157, 158, 159,
    160
  and genetic engineering 68, 153
  industry 63, 64, 69, 92, 117, 132,
    137, 153, 155, 172
  misuse xiii, 57, 61, 73, 74
  modern revolution xiii, 32, 177,
    180
  new – *see* Chapter 4
  old 63
  Soviet organization 20
botulinum/botulinal toxins 2, 16,
  29, 36, 105
  and BWC 29
  and CWC 29
Brazil
  and AHG 123, 124, 171
Bristol-Myers Squibb 71

Brussels
  Conference 2
  Declaration 1874 2
  Treaty 1948 4
Bush, President George 25, 26
  President George W. 166, 170,
    171, 179
BZ 28, 29, 30

Canada
  and AHG 122
  and BTWC negotiation 10
  and BTWC trial inspections/visits
    50, 123
CFE (Conventional Forces in Europe)
    Treaty
  routine inspections 117
chemical(s)
  dual-use 114, 164
  industrial 28
  misuse 115
  toxic 27, 31, 35, 36
    CWC definition 34
chemical industry 28, 30, 40, 67,
    68–9
  civil 22, 27, 31, 32
  and CWC negotiations 32–3, 63,
    133
  dual-use nature 27, 30, 31, 33, 37,
    40
  misuse of facilities 37, 114, 115
  modern 28
    civil production 27
  multipurpose plant 31, 40, 115
  verification under CWC 30, 32
  worldwide 23, 63, 71
chemical warfare 3, 27, 55
  agents 37
  novel 35
chemical weapons (CW) 4, 15, 24,
    25, 26, 27, 28, 34, 36, 37, 44,
    134, 180
  agents 28, 29, 114
    anti-animal 114
    anti-human 114
    destruction 102, 114, 164
    harassing 28
    lethal 28, 29
    means of distribution 28

  non-lethal: BZ (psychochemical)
    28, 29, 30
  potential 29
  production processes 29
  arms control 27
  ban 24, 25, 27
  binary 29
  definition 27, 28, 35
  destruction of stockpiles and
    production facilities 27, 33,
    114, 164
  development 26, 28
  illegal/illicit production 27, 33,
    114
  international legal restrictions 2, 3
  lethality 15
  link to biological weapons 2, 6, 24
  precursor chemicals 28, 34, 36
  use
    in Iran/Iraq war 25
    in Yemen by Egypt 26
  verification 10, 27
  as WMD 4
  World War I 3
Chemical Weapons Convention
    (CWC) 22, 23, 24, 25, 27, 28,
      36, 40, 50, 56, 60, 101, 102, 114,
      116, 120, 123, 133, 134, 139, 156,
      163, 164, 177, 178
  Annex on Chemicals 36, 37, 39,
    40
    Schedule I 37, 114, 115, 134:
      ricin 36, 97; saxitoxin 36,
      97
    Schedule II 37, 115
    Schedule III 37, 114, 115
  Article II 34
  Article VI 33, 36, 37
  Article IX 37
  and botulinal toxins 29
  challenge inspections 33, 36, 37,
    56, 114
    practice 36
  and chemical industry 33
  and Chemical Manufacturers
    Association (CMA) USA 33
  compliance 115, 116
  Confidence-Building Measures
    (CBMs) 115

Chemical Weapons Convention
(CWC) – *continued*
and confidential/commercial
proprietary information
(CPI) 39
control regime 40, 115
declarations 114, 115, 156
definition of toxic chemical
34–5
destruction requirement 101, 114,
164
detection of militarily
significant violations 24, 33
Director-General 163
discrete organic chemical (DOC)
inspection 115
draft 25
entry into force 26, 27
facility agreements 115
General Purpose Criterion 34, 35,
36, 115
illicit production 114, 115
implementation 36, 40
inspectorate 40
OPCW 115, 164
mandatory declarations 36
chemicals 37
facilities 37, 39, 40, 114
national
authorities 36
measures 115
negotiations 24, 26, 27, 35, 36, 63,
92, 115
non-challenge inspections 109
non-compliance 36, 114
on-site inspections 25
and OPCW 27, 36, 37, 39, 40,
115, 123
ratification 33
red-light procedure 97, 134
routine inspections 36, 37, 39, 40,
114, 115, 117, 119
negotiated facility agreement 39
system 39, 40
US 40
scheduled chemicals 115
trial inspections 36, 50
verification 23, 24, 25, 26, 27, 30,
32, 33, 34, 36, 40, 60

challenge inspections/
investigations 36, 37, 134
mandatory declarations 36, 37,
114
regime 114, 115, 116
routine inspections 36, 37, 39,
40, 114, 115, 119
China 167, 170, 171
Director-General, Department of
Disarmament and Arms
Control 169
chlorine 28
cholera 1
Cold War 23, 26, 44
Comprehensive Test Ban Treaty
(CTBT) 90, 164, 170
Conference of the Committee on
Disarmament (CCD) 17
Conference on Disarmament (CD) 36
Confidence-Building Measures
(CBMs) iii
BTWC xiii, 41, 44, 45, 46, 47, 48,
107
confidential/commercial
proprietary information (CPI)
39, 53, 71, 123, 124, 125, 126,
127, 134, 136, 137
CS gas 28
Cuba 15, 43

Denmark
and AHG 122
Department of Peace Studies,
Bradford 77
Depositary States/Governments – *see*
BTWC
deoxyribonucleic acid (DNA) 145,
152
human sequence/blueprint 63
recombinant 65
disarmament 5, 9, 24, 83
drum driers 73

Egypt
CW use 26
Eli Lilly 70
En-Mod Convention 42
Europe
and biotechnology 68, 137

Europe – *continued*
  Federation of Pharmaceutical
    Industries and Associations
    (EFPIA)　137, 138
  export control(s)　96, 167, 175
    regimes　100
Federation of American Scientists
    (FAS)　74
  and biological arms control　77,
    123, 134, 137
fermentation　69, 72
  units　67
fermenters　56, 73, 74, 127, 145,
    154
  slurry　73
Finland
  and AHG　122
First World War　4, 28, 29
  biological warfare　1, 2
  chemical warfare　3
France
  and AHG　120
  and BW　2
  and BTWC draft　12
  BTWC national measures　12
  and VEREX　58
  and verification　12
Friends of the Chair (Ad Hoc Group,
    BTWC)　78, 80, 87, 88, 90, 91,
    92

General Purpose Criterion　7
  BTWC　7, 34, 54
  CWC　34, 35, 36
genetic
  code, human　62
    civil applications　62
  engineering　1, 64, 68
    commercial application　64
  manipulation　120
Geneva
  Ad Hoc Group meetings　48, 74,
    130, 140, 167, 168, 169, 170,
    173, 174, 178
  Conference on Disarmament
    (CD)　36
  Conference 1925　3
  CWC negotiation　115
  IFPMA　68

Protocol 1925　3, 4, 6, 8, 11, 12,
    45, 138, 149
UNIDIR　77
genome/s　64, 66
  Human Genome Project　63
  human sequence　63, 65
  link with information
    technology　67
genomics – *see* Chapter　4
  advances in　1
  medicine　66
  revolution　xiii, 61
Germany
  and AHG　120, 123, 128, 129
  Bonn (Kyoto Protocol)　174
  and CW/BW　4
  and VEREX　59
glanders　1
Glaxo　71
  Smith Kline　63
  Wellcome　63
Gulf War　xiii, 25, 47, 72

Hague, the
  conferences　2
  Regulations　2
Harvard/Sussex Program on CB
    Armament and Arms
    Limitation　77
herbicides　5, 26
high-containment laboratories/
    facilities (BL3)　45, 120,
    152
Human Genome Project　63
Hungary
  and verification　10

Iceland
  and AHG　122
incubators　73
India
  patent laws　68
  pharmaceutical industry　68
Indonesia
  and AHG　83
information technology
  link with genomes　67
  revolution in　66

insulin 64
Intermediate Nuclear Forces
    Treaty (INF)
    routine inspections 117
International Atomic Energy
    Authority (IAEA) 120
International Dairy Foods Association
    (IDFA) 70
Iran 167, 171
    and AHG 123
    biotechnology industry 22
    BTWC Protocol Practice visit 127
    BW programme 22
    pharmaceutical industry 22
    war with Iraq 25
Iraq
    biological production
        capability 73
    and BW xiii, 47, 72, 178
        monitoring 73
    and chemical weapons 72, 115
    dual-use capability 113
    Gulf War 1991 72
    micro-organism stocks 73
    multipurpose plants 115
    offensive BW programme 2, 22,
        113
    use of pesticide 115
    and UNSCOM 113
    war with Iran 25
    and WMD 72, 73
Ireland
    and AHG 121
Italy
    and AHG 122
    pharmaceutical industry 68
    and verification 10

Japan
    and AHG 123, 128
    Bioindustry Association 137
    and BW 2
    and BW use in China 4, 149
    and biotechnology 68
    and CWC inspections 25
    Kyoto Protocol 170, 171, 174
    and verification 10, 12, 14

League of Nations 3

malaria 1
maximum containment
    laboratory/ies (see also
    high-containment laboratories)
    Biosafety Level 4 (BL4/P4) 45,
        96, 100, 103, 107, 108, 120,
        151
Merck 70, 71
microbiology 67
    dual-use nature 117
    military programmes/
        facilities 120, 122
    modern 63
    pesticides 69
    production 122
micro-organisms 1, 63, 105, 153,
    154, 155
    genetically engineered 72
    Iraqi stocks 73
milling machines 73
Mongolia
    and verification 10
Morocco
    and verification 10
mustard gas 28, 30
    sulphur 29, 30

Netherlands, the 9
    and AHG 120, 121, 122
    bid as BTWC Protocol seat 91
    BTWC trial inspections 50
    and VEREX 59
nerve
    agents 30
        relation to commercial
            pesticides 30
        sarin (GB) 16, 28, 29,
            30
        soman (GD) 28, 30
        tabun (GA) 28, 29
        VX 28, 30
    gases 26, 30
Newcastle disease
    virus 105
Nixon, Richard xii, 5
non-governmental organizations
    (NGOs) 77, 90, 123
Nordic countries
    and AHG 123

North Atlantic Treaty Organization
(NATO)
Advanced Research Workshop
(ARW) 54
Studies Institute 148
Norway
and AHG 122
BTWC Protocol trial visit 127
nuclear weapons 4, 26, 77, 113
lethality 15

Organization for the Prohibition of
Chemical Weapons (OPCW) 27,
36, 37, 39, 40
Executive Council 36

pathogens 72
animal 105
human 105
plant 105
zoonotic 105
pesticides
commercial 30
microbial 69
Pfizer 70, 71
pharmaceutical industry 30, 32, 68,
71, 117, 132, 172
American 69
Association of the British
Pharmaceutical Industry
(ABPI) 68
commercial confidentiality 71
European Federation of
Pharmaceutical Industries and
Associations (EFPIA) 137, 138
International Federation of
Pharmaceutical Manufacturers
Associations (IFPMA) 68
Japanese Bioindustry Association
137
patent protection 71
Pharmaceutical Research and
Manufacturers of America
(PhRMA) 70, 71, 134, 135,
136, 137, 138, 172
R&D 70, 71
UK 126
worldwide 67

phosgene 28
plague 1
poison weapons 26
Poland
and verification 10
Portugal
and AHG 100, 101
Protozoa
pathogens 105
psychochemical 30
Pugwash Movement 168
CBW study group 77

Q-fever 50

revolutions
biology 66, 177
industrial 67
information technology 66
scientific 65, 66
ricin 36, 105
Rinderpest
virus 105
riot control agents 26, 28
Russian Federation 21, 167, 170,
179
and AHG negotiations 83, 89
Biopreparat sites 21
Duma and CWC 40
Trilateral Process 21

Sanger Centre, Cambridge 62
sarin (GB) 16, 28, 29, 30
saxitoxin 36
Second World War xii, 2, 4, 26, 29
single-cell proteins 73
smallpox 1
Smith Kline Beecham 63
soman (GD) 28, 30
South Africa 172
and BTWC 60, 61
Protocol negotiations 75, 84, 89,
93, 94, 130
IFPMA 1998 Assembly,
Cape Town 68
offensive BW programme 2, 74
and Special Conference
(BTWC) 59

Soviet Union
  and arms race 5
  biological warfare system 20
    Fifteenth Directorate, army 20
    Main Directorate Biopreparat 20
  biopesticides 20
  Biopreparat 20, 21
    Berdsk site fermenters 21
  as BTWC Depositary State xii
  and CWC 25
  Ministry of Defense 57
  Ministry of Medical and
    Microbiological Industries 20
  and nuclear weapons 6
  and offensive BW programme xii,
    2, 13, 20, 57, 178, 179
  Sverdlovsk anthrax outbreak 46
  vaccines 20
  and verification 10, 13, 23
Spain
  and AHG 129
spray driers 73
Standard Industrial Classification
  (SIC) 69
staphylococcal enterotoxin 105
Stockholm
  Conference (1986) 44
  International Peace Research
    Institute (SIPRI) 2, 14, 15, 17,
      23, 26, 27
sulphur mustard 29, 30
Sweden 6
  and AHG 122
  and CBW 26
  non-compliance concerns in BTWC
    11, 42
  and BTWC verification 10, 15,
    118, 119
Switzerland
  and AHG 123
  BTWC Protocol practice visit 127
  bid for BTWC Protocol seat 91
  and BTWC Q-fever study 50

tabun (GA) 28, 29
tear gas 5
terrorism
  biological 17, 180
Thrips palmi 43

Tóth, Ambassador Tibor, Hungary
  Chairman, Ad Hoc Group 48, 49,
    78, 80, 82, 84, 86, 87, 90, 91,
    92, 93, 94, 116, 119, 128, 139,
    140, 152, 155, 156, 159, 164,
    165, 166, 172, 174, 175, 178
  Chairman, VEREX 50, 51, 52
toxins 54, 59, 69, 72, 102, 105, 142,
    144, 148
  agents 16, 45, 48
  bacterial 16, 105
  botulinal/botulinum 2, 16, 29, 36,
    105
  and BTWC Protocol 100
  chemical 16
  gene 72, 152
  hostile purposes 57
  from micro-organisms 2, 45
  myco- 105
  phyco- 105
  phyto- 105
    abrins 105
  ricin 36, 105
  saxitoxin 36
  staphylococcal enterotoxins 105
  zoo- 105
  weapons xii, 6, 44, 45, 48
United Kingdom
  and Ad Hoc Group 89, 116, 117,
    119, 122, 123, 124, 130, 174
  Association of the British
    Pharmaceutical Industry
    (ABPI) 68
  and BTWC xii, 6, 60, 61; draft
    BW convention of 1969 xii
  as Depositary State xii, 171
  and trial inspections 50
  and Protocol negotiations 75,
    89
  and BW 2
  British Army Medical Corps 1
  and CD 36
  and CWC inspections 25, 164,
    165
  Department of Peace Studies,
    University of Bradford 77
  draft CBW convention of 1933 4
  Foreign Office 176
  Government 174

United Kingdom – *continued*
  Porton Down 55
  practice visits
    challenge 124
    non-challenge 124
  Trilateral Process 21
  and VEREX 58, 60
  and verification 9, 10
United Nations
  Charter 8, 43
  Commission for Conventional
    Armaments 4
  First Committee 179, 182
  General Assembly xii, 26
    and BTWC xii, 9, 12, 43, 44
  Institute for Disarmament Research
    (UNIDIR) 77
  Secretary General 10, 44, 163
  Security Council 8, 10, 11, 42
    Resolution 620 of 1988 44
    Resolution 687 of 1991 72
    Resolution 715 of 1991 72
    UNSCOM (Iraq) 72
United States of America
  and Ad Hoc Group (BTWC) 54,
    75, 97, 99, 128, 129, 130, 131,
    134, 136, 137, 151, 154, 167,
    168, 169, 170, 171, 174, 176,
    177, 180
  Albright, Madeleine, Secretary of
    State 136
  Armed Forces Medical Intelligence
    Center 18
  Arms Control and Disarmament
    Agency (ACDA) xii, 22, 83, 182
  and arms race 6
  Army manuals 2
  and biodefence 120, 128, 153,
    167, 175, 178, 181
  and BTWC 60, 167
    as Depositary State xii
    Protocol 61, 130, 132, 167, 172,
      173
    Special Conference 60
    strengthening 69
  and BW 2
  and biotechnology 67, 68, 69
  Bush, George and CWC 25, 26,
    166

Bush, George W.
  Administration 166, 170, 171,
    179, 182
Central Intelligence Agency
  (CIA) 19, 181
and chemical arms control 27,
  156
chemical industry 71
  imports/exports 32
Chemical Manufacturers
  Association (CMA) and
  CWC 33, 133
and chemical weapons
  destruction 26
and CWC 25, 60
  trial inspection exercises 36
Congress
  Hearings xiii, 134, 138, 172, 179
  Office of Technology Assessment
    (OTA) 15, 17, 29, 30, 67
Cuban BTWC violation
  charge 15, 43
Daly, William, Secretary of
  Commerce 136
drug development 70
Federation of American Scientists
  (FAS) 74, 134, 137
Food and Drug Administration
  125
Fort Detrick xii
Institute of Peace (USIP) 168
internal BW legislation 17
Laird, Melvin, US Defense
  Secretary 5
MacEachin, Douglas, Deputy CIA
  Director 19
Mahley, Ambassador Donald and
  BTWC AHG 54, 132, 174,
  177
National Missile Defence 169
  Security Council 173
Nixon, Richard
  and BTWC xii, 166
  and Vietnam 5
offensive BW programme 2, 5, 6,
  166
Office of Technology Assessment
  (OTA) 15, 17, 29, 30, 67
Pentagon 130

United States of America – *continued*
  pharmaceutical
    companies 71, 137
    industry 69, 71, 72, 134, 137,
      139, 166, 167
  Pharmaceutical Research and
    Manufacturers of America
    (PhRMA) 70, 71, 134, 135,
      136, 137, 138, 172
  Pine Bluff xii
  Public Service Broadcasting 57
  Reagan, Ronald 60
  Secretary
    of Commerce 130
    of Defense 130
    of State 130
  Senate
    and BTWC xii
    and CWC 40
  and Soviet offensive BW
    programme 57
  Trilateral Process 21
  unilateralism 168, 178
  use of herbicides and riot
    control agents in Vietnam 26
  and verification xiv, 13, 14, 23,
    49, 60, 61, 132, 173, 176
  weaponization of
    BW agents: anti-animal 2;
      anti-plant 2; botulinal
      toxins 29
    CW agents: BZ 29
  and WMD 4, 17
  White House 130
  working papers
    for CCD 16
    for VEREX 16
UNSCOM
  in Iraq 72, 113
USSR – *see* Soviet Union

vaccines 20
  and BTWC 47, 129
  production 73, 100, 103, 152
    facilities 108, 120, 124, 125,
      136, 153

VEREX xiii, 16, 41, 47, 48, 49, 50,
  54, 57, 58, 118, 136, 145, 175
  and declarations 116
  meetings 50, 51, 52
  on-site measures 124
  negotiations 80, 116
  reports 53, 54, 69, 116, 175
  working papers 57, 58, 59, 60
verification xiii, xiv, 5, 9, 10, 12, 13,
  14, 15, 23, 25, 54, 132, 173, 175,
  176, 177
  adequacy of xiv, 24, 61, 132
  effective xiv, 24, 61, 132, 145
  and BTWC 41, 45, 48, 49, 50, 51,
    58, 59, 61, 116, 129, 142
  and CWC 23, 24, 25, 26, 27, 30,
    32, 33, 34, 36, 40, 60
  detection of militarily
    significant violations 24, 33,
    54, 58, 61
Vietnam
  anti-war protest 5
  use of CBW 5
  US use of herbicides and riot
    control agents 26
viruses 1
  as BW agents 3, 56, 105
  Newcastle disease 105
  Rinderpest 105
VX 28

weapons of mass destruction (WMD)
  4, 18, 29, 44
  Iraq 72, 73
Western European Union 4
World Health Organization
  (WHO) 46, 184
  Laboratory Biosafety Manual 45
World Trade Organization (WTO) 68
World War I 1, 2, 3, 4, 28, 29
World War II xii, 2, 4, 26, 29

Yemen
  Egyptian CW use 26
Yugoslavia
  and BTWC verification 10, 15

3 5282 00541 3623

Printed in the United States
1265500001B/154-291